When No One Else Would Fly

Colonel C. J. Tippett, USAFR, Ret.
&
Corinne Tippett

The Westchester Press

Also by Corinne Tippett

Just A Couple of Chickens

WHEN NO ONE ELSE WOULD FLY

Images from Colonel C. J. Tippett's archive & public domain
Chavante Indian Images by Jean Mazon
Cover and book design by Corinne Tippett

Published by The Westchester Press
Portland, Oregon
www.thewestchesterpress.com

Library of Congress Control Number: 2013934741

ISBN 978-0-9843611-1-3

For Dad and Sue

With writings from

Cloyce J. Tippett
Louise H. Tippett
Mary Jane McBarnet
Louise Lines Hossack
Harry Hossack

When No One Else Would Fly
The Life of Colonel Cloyce Joseph Tippett

This copy was produced through a Print-On-Demand supplier.
If the printing is flawed, please contact us through
www.TheWestchesterPress.com.

Table of Contents

Colonel Cloyce Joseph Tippett USAFR, Ret.
1913 - 1993

Introduction

Cloyce Joseph Tippett, known to everyone as Tip, was enraptured with flight from the first time he saw an airplane. It was in the summer of 1929 and he was sixteen years old.

American aviation was poised to influence world events, and Tip would be in the cockpit when it happened. He would achieve the American Dream at a pivotal time of world history.

Tip grew up in a working class family during the Great Depression. He studied aeronautical engineering because he had to understand airplanes in order to fly. He joined the army because it would give him access to planes and he could be paid to fly.

In the last decade of his life, Tip wrote a memoir and handed it to his son, Michael Tippett. Michael handed it to his daughter, Corinne Tippett, along with half a truckload of archived documents from Tip's storage space.

When Corinne realized the extent and significance of the things her grandfather had done, she knew that she held a piece of American history. It was a story that comes from those rare times when an overwhelming passion drives a person to do extraordinary things with their life.

The story is told through Tip's own first person account, framed by Corinne's narration. It begins with Tip's memoir.

It is His Story.

Chapter One

1929

The Jenny in Port Clinton, Ohio

I spent summer vacations at the family cottage on Lake Erie, near Port Clinton, Ohio, with one or two friends. I was sixteen years old and we would fish, and swim, and visit Put-In Bay and other islands in my stepfather's small Chris-Craft speedboat. It was the summer of 1929 that I watched a barnstorming WWI vintage Curtiss Jenny take passengers from a small field near Port Clinton.

The pilot was decked out in high-laced boots, leather jacket, jodhpur pants, helmet, and goggles. First impressions being what they are, I decided at that moment what my future look would be. His name was George, and it was a matter of a few minutes before I was his helper. He needed five gallons of gasoline for his OX-5 engine and I was only too willing to furnish the gas from the local filling station at a cost of about seventy-five cents. For the gas and two hours of work washing the ship after he finished flying, I was given a ride of about ten minutes.

I became his permanent sidekick, flying around to the various small towns in that area, landing in open pastures and selling rides for one to ten dollars. The ten-dollar ride included a loop, which was a spellbinding thing to watch in the old Jenny. By

summer's end, I had worked for, and purchased, enough flying time
to solo the Jenny, but George was reluctant to let me fly for fear of
destroying his machine. He permitted me to land and take off, do
eights in the air, and sideslips into short fields. He said I did well, for
someone with six hours of flight time.

Late one evening, after twenty minutes of take-offs and
landings, George stepped out of the plane and told me to take it
around solo. I doubt there is any excitement more electric than
that one brief moment when you open the throttle to take off on
your first solo flight. Then George was offered a job flying between
Chicago and Cleveland. The airline was called Century Air Lines
and operated tri-motored Stinson aircraft. As George was to live in
Cleveland, he had no further use for the Jenny, which by this time
was showing her age. He offered the plane to me for $700. As I did
not have $700, it became obvious that in order to secure this little
beauty, I would have to barter.

After much devious thought, the obvious became reality
and I traded my stepfather's Chris-Craft speedboat for the Jenny.
My stepfather and mother were visiting Florida at the time. I felt
that advising them of their good fortune and my big business deal
might cloud their vacation, so I kept mum about the whole thing.
As the day for their return drew nearer, the glamour and glitter of
my trade began to dim. The farmer who owned the field where I
kept the ship advised me that he was about to turn out his cows. He
said that I had better remove the plane or his cows would probably
eat the fabric off it. Life was now taking some serious turns that
I had not, hither to, dealt with. Serious and complicated decisions
had to be made and stories concocted to offset the crisis that
suddenly became apparent. Buying a replacement boat was out of
the question. Offering my weather-beaten Jenny to my stepfather
was even more ridiculous. I decided to wait and see what happened
when I told my stepfather of the deal.

When my stepfather learned that he was in the airplane

business, his first words were indecipherable. I explained that I was carried away and persuaded to do the deal when I was in a state of mental vacuity. He agreed with that statement and explained that he hated airplanes and stayed inside when one was flying over, convinced that it might fall on him. When the tirade subsided a bit, the first words I could understand were "Sell it." I was supposed sell the airplane and give him the money, but the sale never happened. The plane was stored in a barn for the winter and I went on to my senior year in high school.

Tip with an aircraft that is probably a Focke-Wulf FW 44J, not the Curtiss JN4, although at this time in his life, he already possessed his own Jenny.

Tip survived his early flight training and the return of his stepfather, and went on to pursue aviation through every avenue he could find. From the time he soloed in the Jenny, he knew that aviation was to be his life. By 1929, flight was no longer an unattainable dream. Individuals with access to a plane who were willing to ignore the engine noise, exhaust stink, and tight confines of the cockpit could fly wherever they chose at a moments notice; answerable only to the weather, their own piloting skills, and the demands of the aircraft.

The Curtiss JN-4 (Jenny) in flight in 1918 with the US Army Signal Corps. Courtesy of Laura Scudder and George Johnson, released to public domain.

The trade of the plane for the Chris-Craft speedboat was not entirely fair, even if the speedboat was several years old. $700 in 1929 was equivalent to about $9000 today and the aging Jenny wasn't really worth that much. Tip couldn't have known that commercially-operating Curtiss Jenny aircraft were on the verge of being grounded on the basis of flight safety. It was an airplane and Tip treasured it.

Aviation was enjoying a time of incomparable freedom from government restrictions. The skies were open and opportunity had landed in Tip's hometown. There were no licensing requirements to be a pilot and no formal registration process for the plane. Not coincidentally, civil aviation crashes reached their highest fatality rate in US history in 1929. As a result of this, regulation would grow and Tip would become one of the people instrumental in the effort to standardize and increase the safety of general aviation. But that lay in the future. For now, Tip needed only time, gasoline, and the next open field to pursue his flight ambitions.

The Curtiss JN4, known as the Jenny, had been produced in quantity for use in WWI as a training plane. So many had been released to the public market as surplus that it was the most commonly used plane for barnstorming and flight instruction. The Jenny was a biplane, with dual cockpits, built of wood and fabric. The OX-5 engine that powered it was also used primarily because it was so readily available and affordable, not because it was the best engine for the purpose. Whatever engineering flaws the OX-5 had, it earned an enthusiastic following. It was well known and replacement parts were both readily available and affordable. Pilots who knew how could repair it in the field. The OX-5 was reliable enough, but pilots had to expect it to quit in flight. The JN4 was so stable and light that engine failure did not necessarily mean a crash landing. In the early days of aviation, a person's ability to fly was gauged by their combination of aircraft handling and mechanical skill. The OX-5 engine was within economic reach of the public, and the JN4 was available in larger numbers than anything else, so that was the plane many people, including Charles Lindbergh and Amelia Earhart, first flew.

The lessons from George got Tip started, but he was on his own to learn the rest of it by trial and error in the Jenny. Wooden half-hoops on the outer undersurface of the JN4 lower wings provided protection during landing, as the Jenny - or the novice pilot - had a tendency to put a wing down at an inopportune time. The OX-5 engine could spit oil and unburned gasoline, which would sometimes ignite the flammable coating given to the fabric covering to make the aircraft weatherproof. But the Jennies flew and pilots like Tip learned. When government contracts for carrying the US Mail by air became available, the JN4 became the most frequently used aircraft in the new airmail industry.

The end of summer brought the beginning of an important year for Tip, and for the rest of the country. Returning to school in September, he had to balance flying time with classes, sports, extracurricular clubs, and working in his stepfather's store. Less than a month later, on Black Tuesday, October 29, 1929, the stock market crash marked the beginning of the Great Depression.

There was no aspect of American society that escaped the hardships. In 1929, public enthusiasm for aviation was huge. Tip had no reason to think that this economic event would require him to change his aviation career plans, but it would. Charles Lindbergh had completed his solo trans-Atlantic flight two years earlier, on May 21, 1927, and was well established as an American celebrity. Other celebrity pilots were finding their way to cockpits and media headlines.

President Herbert Hoover took office just in time to struggle with the unprecedented economic depression. Tip described his last year of high school as a happy time, and it was only later that he recognized the impact the world economy had on his post-school decisions.

Tip was born Charles Cloyce Tippett in Bowling Green, Ohio on February 14, 1913, one year after the Titanic sank and a year before the First World War began. Tip's mother, Verna Blanche Krofft, was twenty years old and a homemaker when Tip, her only child, was born. His father, Charles C. Tippett, was twenty-four and a machinist. Charles was tall, lean, and handsome, and Tip inherited his father's good looks. From his mother, he got his good-natured expression and generous spirit, charming everyone he met just as Verna adopted and nurtured every living thing that crossed her path.

Aviation would always be ten years older than Tip. The Wright Brothers first flight at Kitty Hawk, 540 miles away in North Carolina, was in 1903. The most famous aviators of Tip's era also had a ten-year lead on him. Charles Lindbergh was eleven years old when Tip was born. Lindbergh was only fifty-seven miles away in Detroit, Michigan. Amelia Earhart was sixteen years old, and growing up in Atchison, Kansas. French aviator and author Antoine de Saint-Exupery was thirteen years old and much farther away in Lyon, France. Many of the planes that Tip would fly were already being made and flown with more exuberance than prudence. The first pilot to fly a loop-the-loop did it in 1913, and the first parachutist jumped for sport in that year as well.

Verna and Charles had been married for five years before Tip was born. Both Verna and Charles were born and raised, along with many brothers and sisters, in the Bowling Green area. They were surrounded by farmland but were not of farming families. In the early days of their marriage, they found work as field hands. Their parents had worked skilled trades, or any job they could find. Charles followed his own father's example of working as a machinist in the factories that surrounded Bowling Green.

By the time Tip was seven, in 1920, Verna had unsuccessfully filed for divorce more than once. When Charles filed for divorce, the petition was granted and he returned to his own mother's house to live. Verna, with Tip, moved to Fostoria, Ohio, and opened a boarding house. One of the paying guests was a man who was himself going through a divorce. Verna had found a new life partner.

My father and mother divorced and both remarried. My father moved to Luckey, Ohio, where he was employed at a large lime company. My stepfather, Adolf Eyth, was a very nice man who owned and operated the only confectionery store in Fostoria. It was a typical soda fountain of that time, with wire chairs and glass-topped tables. Chocolates and sweets of all kinds filled a showcase and five flavors of ice cream rounded off the goodies. Making friends in Fostoria with a confectionery store to come home to after school was most rewarding.

I attended a Catholic Jesuit school, St. Wendelin, whose teachers were Notre Dame nuns and Jesuit priests. Oddly enough, none of my family were Catholic. I became a convert at the age of ten. Living in a Catholic neighborhood, all my friends were Catholic and marched off to have their catechism lessons on Saturday afternoons leaving me with no one to shoot at with my BB gun. Consequently, I started to go with them. Needless to say, the priest

was astounded when he learned that my parents were unaware that I
was attending Catholic classes preparing for proper baptism. Father
John O'Connor called on my parents and explained the situation to
them. They didn't object to my choice of worship and, as a matter
of fact, were pleased with my decision.

St. Wendelin high school students were attending classes
in a small house across from the parish church. Total student body
added up to about 148 students, ranging from freshmen to seniors.
Classes were disciplined and our teachers were not only superbly
prepared for their assignments, but also expected us to be. It
was unthinkable to come to class unprepared or with homework
unfinished. Participation was the key. In Latin class, we spoke Latin.
In French class, the minute the door closed, we were linguistically in
Paris.

For such a small school, we excelled in sports. Our football
team consisted of no more than thirty or forty candidates at any
one time. Our first team was mostly second and third year students.
Of a total of eight seniors in our graduating class, five were on the
team. Our coaching staff consisted of Mr. Cy Scharf, a graduate of
Notre Dame and an engineer at the local factory. He was unpaid.
His assistant was Father John E. Duffy, a Jesuit priest who played
football at the University of Detroit, a big tough fellow to whom
perfection was incidental. I will be forever grateful for the values
that he instilled in me whether in the classroom or at football
practice. Mind you, some of the values were pounded into me,
especially during scrimmage. Father Duffy later won the Purple
Heart medal in Bataan.

Football in those days, and especially at our school, was
a bit different than is played now. Once the game was on there
was little or no substitution, mainly because we had none. My
position on the team was playing tackle. At that time I was six feet
tall and weighed about 155 pounds, a formidable sight decked out
in shoulder pads and gear. Unfortunately this did not prevent the

opposing team players from treating us in a most un-sportsmanlike fashion. Most of the schools we played, such as the local public high school in Fostoria, had a student body a hundred times the size of St. Wendelin and football teams that outweighed us. They had more football players at practice than we had in our entire student body.

The Fostoria High vs. St. Wendelin game was the "Army-Navy" high school football game in Fostoria. Blood flowed freely and a broken nose or two was not unusual. Prior to the opening kick off, our team would huddle with Father Duffy and say a few Hail Mary's, which was meant to bolster our determination to uphold the integrity and honor of St. Wendelin, but in most cases was sincere enough to give us a winning score. I was the team kicker and my kickoffs were generally over the goal posts, averaging fifty to sixty yards. I might have had a career in pro-football had I not been a generation or two ahead of my time.

Tip's father, Charles Tippett is on the left, and stepfather, Adolf Eyth, is on the far right. Verna is on the left, and Alice is on the right. Tip is in the foreground.

On June 24, 1923, Tip was baptized and given the name
Cloyce Joseph Tippett. He would use this as his legal name for the
rest of his life, dropping the name "Charles". Tip's attention was
focused on his activities at St. Wendelin and on flying, and his home
life was stable and happy. The breakup of his parents' marriage
was, to this only child, a source of additional family rather than a
deprivation. Tip had a good relationship with his stepfather, and
kept in touch with his father and new stepmother, Alice. Charles
had moved out of his own mother's house after he met and married
Alice Hebler.

At St. Wendelin, Tip participated in every club and sport the
small school offered. When he started attending, classes were held in
a small, ivy-covered two-story frame building with long tall windows.
By the time he graduated in 1930, the school had plans drawn for
a new high school that would rival Ivy-League establishments for
size and grandeur. St. Wendelin was a co-educational school. The
girls had names popular in the 1920s, like Mildred, Betty, Emma, and
Florence. They wore their hair cut short, bobbed to the jaw line, and
fashionable sailor collars. Boys wore their hair severely short on the
sides and back, only long on the top. Tip's curly hair was a constant
challenge to this style and he made good use of hair oil and comb.
Cloyce was an unusual name among classmates called Albert, Francis,
Thomas and James. He picked up the nickname "Tip" at this time
and kept it for the rest of his life.

In the time between his birth in 1913, and his graduation
in 1930, aviation was making fast progress, fueled by war and
competition. In 1923, while ten-year-old Tip was finalizing his
religious training at St. Wendelin High School, President Warren
Harding died unexpectedly of a stroke in San Francisco and
was succeeded by Calvin Coolidge. In Germany, Hitler made an
unsuccessful grab for power and was sentenced to a five-year
prison term which he would spend writing his book "Mein Kampf."
In the United States, the Attorney General ruled that it was legal

for women to wear trousers anywhere they wanted. Tip's mother promptly posed for a photograph in pants, then went back to her wardrobe of skirts and dresses.

In 1924, as Tip continued grade school, twenty-one-year-old Charles Lindbergh was buying his first airplane, a WWI Curtiss Jenny, from a barnstormer in Georgia. Lindbergh had taken his first flight when he was twenty years old. Amelia Earhart had made her first flight at age twenty-three, four years earlier, also in the cockpit of a barnstormer. World War I, which had ended in 1918, had provided the first opportunity for air combat and the aces of Britain, France, and America proved that the advantages aviation offered were not just observational. Early aircraft had been part of war planning in the same capacity as hot-air balloons or lighter-than-air dirigibles. They were useful as observation platforms, although airplanes could move around better. The numbers and range of aircraft of the time limited their impact, but the victories gave military strategists much to think about in the decades before World War II.

Tip was fourteen when Charles Lindbergh made his non-stop solo New York to Paris flight in 1927. The first trans-Atlantic crossing had been completed in 1919, by a US Navy NC-4 flying boat, which made several stops along the way and carried a full crew. It was a milestone for early aviation, and marked the beginning of international airmail service, but it didn't capture the imagination of the world like Lindbergh's flight. Nonstop flights were more significant to the public, as they proved the ranges of aircraft and the endurance of pilots. Making the flight solo carried a special distinction, as it does today. Even if the average person didn't know specifically what it took to accomplish a record-setting flight, they did know that such a thing was harder and required more courage to do alone.

In 1929, his last year of St. Wendelin, Tip began to spend extra time studying mathematics. He was helped by Father Duffy, who saw the need for Tip to be proficient in math in order to further his aviation and engineering dreams. When most young people were still trying to decide what to do or beginning to follow in the family business, Tip had already found his focus and was determined to fly.

While living in Fostoria, the Eyth family was joined by Tip's cousin, Paul Krofft, who was five years younger than Tip. He was Verna's nephew and came to live with them after his own parents died. Paul was raised like a brother to Tip, and they stayed in touch as Tip left high school and left home. Tip graduated from high school in 1930, finishing with a good academic record and happy memories. He had been the leading man in the school play, excelled in basketball, tennis, and football, and had many extra curricular adventures to his name. And he owned a Jenny.

My stepfather opened a restaurant in Port Clinton, Ohio, called the Lake House. The specialty was Lake Erie pickerel and steaks. The restaurant was an instant success and the family moved to Port Clinton upon my graduation from St. Wendelin. I took a permanent job at the restaurant as night-shift chef and manager while waiting to hear from the University of Detroit. My position at the restaurant was uncomplicated by the presence of other employees. Business after ten o'clock at night was slow, to say the least. Winter temperatures in Port Clinton bordered on frozen solid, or just plain very cold. These temperatures dissuaded a great number of potential customers and I could not blame them.

An interesting phenomenon was developing in Port Clinton, Toledo, and the Cleveland area during this time. Prohibition was in effect and Canada was only eight miles away, across Lake Erie. Several businessmen had begun importing beer and whisky illegally through Port Clinton. They used very fast boats, some airplanes, and occasionally large barges when the coast guard was employed elsewhere. Truckloads of beer and liquor were funneled through Port Clinton with nary a policeman in sight. This intrigued me and I questioned one of our three policemen about this situation. I was told that it was best not to speak of such instances again, and that I was probably imagining it.

At about eleven o'clock one night, when I was on duty at the counter, several large trucks with tarp-covered loads parked in front of the restaurant. It was snowing and very cold. Alone in the restaurant, I was standing in the doorway looking out at the procession. One burly fellow got out of the lead truck and walked up to me and asked if we were open for business. When I said yes, he motioned toward the trucks and twelve customers walked in. This was the most business we'd had at one time all winter.

One of the men was well dressed in an overcoat, hat, and scarf. He seemed to be the leader and asked what they could be served. I told them either fish or steak, and they all chose steak, fried potatoes, and coffee. As I was alone, I suggested one of the customers serve the coffee, which they wanted right away, while I started the steak and potatoes. Within a few minutes, a half dozen of my customers were back of the counter setting up bread and butter plates and sorting out silverware. The whole episode turned into a rather pleasant buffet. I was referred to as "Kid."

"Hey kid, where's the catsup?"

"Hey kid, fix me another steak."

By two a.m., everyone seemed pleasantly served and ready to leave. I had noticed several of the men were armed with shoulder-holstered 45 automatics. This observation increased the service quality considerably. The bill was astronomical; twenty steak dinners at $2.95 each ($38 in today's currency), no charge for bread or coffee. The gentleman who paid the bill gave me a five-dollar tip ($63 today). After being used to ten-cent tips, this night took care of my monetary needs for some time. I later learned that the gentleman's name was Bugs Moran.

Bugs Moran, also known as George Clarence Moran, was

thirty-nine years old at the time of this encounter. The winter of 1930 was less than a year after Moran's escape from the Chicago St. Valentine's Day massacre of February 14, 1929, in which seven of his close associates were gunned down in a mob hit ordered by Moran's enemy, Al Capone.

Although Moran kept control of his gang after the massacre, he was seeking other territories to expand his influence. He was heavily involved in bootlegging and Port Clinton was only 244 miles from Chicago. At the time of this profitable evening for Tip, Bugs Moran was Number Six on the Chicago Crime Commission's Public Enemy list. Al Capone was Number One.

Tip's challenge, now that he had graduated from high school, was to pursue a formal college education without letting go of his passion and determination to fly. While his family was warm and supportive, they were not wealthy and could offer no financial help with higher education. Tip would have to work his way through college and support himself at the same time. The Great Depression was a year old and President Herbert Hoover, inaugurated only ten months before the stock market crash, was trying to solve the economic collapse with public works projects and new tax tariffs, while the media continued to refer to it as a recession.

My stepfather and I decided that I should go to Detroit in the summer and try to enroll in some summer courses to begin my college education. In the meantime, I was to visit my father's sister in Toledo who was married to an auto mechanic and garage owner. I was to stay for a while and then travel on to Detroit. I had saved almost six hundred dollars ($7,759 today) for my travel expenses and my entry fee to the university, a fortune!

Aunt Daisy had married Mr. Laberdee two years before and I had never met him. He was a muscular, pleasant fellow, always oil-stained. As I had nothing to do at the house, Aunt Daisy allowed me to go to the garage with Mr. Laberdee for the day. We drove to the garage in Mr. Laberdee's souped-up Studebaker. I was beginning to feel comfortable with my new Uncle. The garage was a low, dirty building completely surrounded by derelict cars and boats of all descriptions, as well as bits and pieces of automobile engines. Inside, the garage was dark and stacked with more engines in various states of repair and assembly. What caught my eye immediately was an OX-5 airplane engine, the very engine that I had been flying around with in my Jenny. This one was a relatively new Curtiss OX-5, still in its original crate.

My continued prowling uncovered several radial airplane engines and one or two in-line engines being readied for installation in home-built aircraft. I was pleased to learn that Mr. Laberdee was an experienced airplane engine mechanic doing all sorts of odd jobs for airmen in the Toledo area. My week-long stay extended into a month, two months, and finally the decision not to enroll at the University of Detroit. Through Mr. Laberdee, I met several "airmen" who were building their own aircraft to be powered with four-cylinder Henderson motorcycle engines. These ships were being built from kit plans and the work being done mostly in their garages. When my friends learned that I was a pilot (thirty hours in a Jenny!) I became most popular. One of the Heath Parasol home-builts was about ready to fly and they had no pilot.

Mr. Laberdee proudly arranged for me to make the test flight of the aircraft over the weekend. It was not difficult to find a flat, open field around Toledo in those days. The little airplane was trailered to a relatively smooth potato field and prepared for flight. This consisted of trying to start the engine, which showed every indication of being uninterested in the business of flying. After we replaced the spark plugs for the second or third time, the engine finally started and ran smoothly for several minutes. I took advantage of this by taxiing the little plane the length of the field and back again. All seemed well as I headed into the wind, checked the mag (only one) and opened the throttle. The home-built plane was more agile than the lumbering old Jenny and responsive to the controls. It was quite stable for the short time we were airborne.

After I cleared a wire fence at the end of the potato field, the Henderson started backfiring and losing RPMs. A quick glance at the few instruments on the panel indicated a loss in oil pressure and a rise in oil temperature. As there was another potato field ahead, the plane and I made a unanimous decision to land. The engine quit about the time the landing was made, and no damage was suffered to the pilot or aircraft. This feat of derring-do made me a full-fledged member of the aviation buffs and hangers-on at the garage.

A few days later, I was invited to fly a Waco powered with a Wright Whirlwind engine by one of Mr. Laberdee's customers. The aircraft was hangared at the Toledo airport. I had, up to that time, avoided airports, as the Jenny was seldom airborne long enough to get to an airport, and neither of us was licensed, which was now a requirement. The invitation to fly a Waco Taperwing at that time was like meeting a present-day stranger at a cocktail party and being invited to fly his Lear jet. It would only be a twenty to twenty-five minute flight, but the hitch was that, on the return flight from an open field in Canada, the Waco would carry eleven cases of scotch in the front cockpit.

The proposition was that I would make three trips a week, for which I would be paid thirty-five dollars per trip ($496 today). Enough of my Jesuit background came to the fore and I sadly turned down the offer. I would have gladly flown the Waco for free if the threat of ending up in the slammer wasn't lurking at the edges of the deal. As a matter of fact, the pilot who did accept the job was picked up after a couple of trips. The Waco was confiscated and the pilot sent to prison for a year.

It is easy to see how private aviation would be attractive

to ambitious bootleggers in the border states between the US and Canada. Efforts to legally ban alcohol in Canada had been ongoing but unsuccessful, and the movement of spirits across the border was well established by this time. While airplanes could not move as much liquor as boats navigating the Great Lakes, it must have been a temptation for many owners looking for ways to fund their expensive private aviation interests.

Building Heath Parasol plane kits was an affordable hobby for aviation enthusiasts able to consider such a project during the Great Depression. The open-cockpit, single-pilot monoplanes were considered easy to fly, and could be assembled using tools a carpenter would have on hand. They required no special engineering skills for completion. Of the several hundred Heath Parasol kits successfully built and flown in the United States during this time period, a significant number of them were aimed at the Canadian border from neighboring northern states. Prohibition would continue for three more years before being repealed in 1933. It hadn't made a significant impact on American consumption habits, but it had a tremendous effect on organized crime.

Tip's time with Mr. Laberdee and the kit builders was the kind of mechanical education he could not get in school. This opportunity to learn about the engines by working on them came to Tip through his father's family. Hands-on machining and engine knowledge was the only kind of family business tradition that Tip had. His father and grandfather were both machinists and line mechanics in the machine-based factories or small manufacturing of their day. The richness of these skills and access were as much a boost to Tip's flight career as a college education would have been. Any pilot who had to rely on someone else for the mechanics and maintenance of his aircraft was severely limited in his career. Knowing the engine as well as the aircraft was the hallmark of a true airman.

Pilots everywhere were testing the limits of distance

and endurance with a series of record-setting flights that were extensively covered in newspapers and newsreels in 1930. The United States Army Air Service, using four planes and numerous crews, had accomplished the first flight around the world in 1924. It took them almost six months and not all of the original four planes finished the journey. The round-the-world *speed* record was set five years later by a zeppelin, floating on course for twenty-one days. Transoceanic or continental flight by zeppelin was competing for business with rail systems by offering a faster, more comfortable passage. The hydrogen-filled lighter-than-air craft were being built and flown regularly and were an affordable alternative to fixed-wing aircraft. The spire of the Empire State Building, finished in 1931, had been intended as a mooring tower for dirigible traffic.

First-in-flight records were significant, but speed records captured as much attention. As soon as the distance and speed records were set, the challenge went out to accomplish the same journey non-stop. This was a technological challenge, pushing the aircraft in fuel efficiency, higher altitudes, and better designs. Even better than non-stop was solo; the prize in terms of public acclaim. A record set solo demonstrated aviation proficiency beyond a doubt, as well as navigational expertise, stamina, and courage.

The aircraft of 1930 were still mostly biplanes, although single-wing and multi-engine experimental craft were making regular flights. Tip kept no clippings or mementos of the pilot superstars of his day, but he did keep images of all the planes. Photos of the famous planes were traded around and highly prized, and featured in Tip's photo albums more frequently than family members.

While aviation was making record progress, the entire country was suffering acutely and nothing the government did seemed to have any effect. Public reaction against President Hoover's attempts to improve the economy swept President Franklin Delano Roosevelt into office, and his 1932 election was followed by the 1933 implementation of his New Deal policies. One challenge of the New Deal was how to get public funds to private sector banks and businesses in a responsible and well-directed way. The money needed to come to the people in the form of jobs, which would in turn stimulate the economy to self-sufficiency and growth. The Reconstruction Finance Corporation (RFC) was a governmental organization formed in 1930 under President Hoover. The intent was to make loans through this independent organization to banks and businesses for projects that would accomplish stable economic growth. The RFC was soon to figure significantly in Tip's life.

Up until now, Tip had relied on his ability to work in exchange for his aviation education and access, but he was fast approaching the end of what he could learn in this way.

One morning, Mr. Laberdee suggested I should sharpen my skills by enrolling in an aeronautical university. There was a good one he had heard about in Fort Wayne, Indiana, called the Midwestern Aeronautics University. Correspondence was exchanged and I was accepted for classes starting in September, 1930. My mother and stepfather drove me to Fort Wayne from Port Clinton. Tuition was paid, a small double room was assigned, farewells were said, and the first stage of my professional learning was under way. My roommate was named Bob and was from Olean, New York. He would later become a test pilot for Piper Aircraft. Bob was an ingenious lad and by the end of the first week had gotten us part-time jobs at the biggest hotel in town, aptly named the Fort Wayne Hotel.

When we were assigned our jobs at the hotel, I thought the chef was pulling my leg. I was assigned the job of feeding corn meal to the live oysters every evening. Bob's work in the stock room took care of our food situation at home. With crackers, French pâtè, smoked oysters, sardines and almost anything else he could carry out in his pocket, we were fed well by the hotel, which allowed us to save a large portion of our meager budget.

To alleviate our transportation problem, we purchased a used four-cylinder Henderson motorcycle with a sidecar attachment. This provided us with adequate wheels to drive to Port Clinton during our time off. We would occasionally stop at the YMCA and swim or exercise. As they were holding Golden Glove matches in a few weeks, I decided to enter and see how I would fare. Boxing was one of my favorite sports and I was quite good at it, having had boxing lessons since the age of eight. The eliminations at the YMCA were quite easy and I made it on the boxing team. Two of us won our matches in Fort Wayne and were named for the finals in Chicago.

I won't dwell too long on the Chicago adventure. Ernest Hemingway seconded the out-of-town boxers. He was in my corner for the first two bouts that I won. I drew a tie on the third and was boxing for the Golden Gloves Welterweight Championship in my next match. I had watched my opponent fight two fights that night, winning both by knock out. I figured that I could easily outbox him and besides, he looked tired.

The first round, Hemingway advised that I keep doing what I was doing, which was keeping as far away from my opponent as possible, with an occasional feeble jab to keep him off balance. But I thought I saw my chance to be a real hero. I got set and threw a tremendous right-hand punch. I mentally calculated that it would finish him and I would win the championship with my first knock out. My right-hand punch was about as lethal as a Virgin Mary. As a matter of fact, as a boxer and a jabber, I never considered using my right hand as a lethal weapon, nor did my trainers encourage me to. I remember hearing the referee count six while I was sitting on the canvas seeing all kinds of beautifully-colored lights. It was the first time I had ever been really tagged in boxing. With the help of the ring ropes, I managed to stand at the count of nine. For those few seconds I was completely helpless. My arms felt like string and my legs like rubber bands. The referee stopped the fight and

awarded a TKO to my opponent. Thirty seconds later, I felt that
nothing had happened. I also felt that I could quite possibly be
in the wrong line of work and decided that my boxing career was
finished. Hemingway was furious that I disregarded his instructions
and lectured me for ten minutes afterwards. I would meet "Papa"
Hemingway again later on, much to our mutual surprise.

Following the Chicago experience, we were once again
back to work at both school and the hotel. One evening, the chef
called me from my hideaway with the oysters and handed me a
white jacket with instructions to deliver a room service tray to one
of the hotel suites. This was no problem as I had handled food trays
before. I went up to the room and tapped on the door, coming face
to face with a breath-catching beauty. She had on a dressing gown
and was reading from a book or script as she motioned the tray
to be set up along side the sofa. She looked familiar to me as she
thanked me and smiled, giving me a fifty-cent tip and signing the
room service slip. Her name was Ann Sothern and she was in a play
at the Fort Wayne Theater. We saw the play twice.

Tip remained enrolled at Midwestern University until late
1933. The boxing championship in Chicago took place in 1931.
Ernest Hemingway was thirty-two years old and after a life spent
mostly roaming or in Cuba, he was establishing his first American
family home in Key West. He was in Kansas City, Missouri with
his wife, Pauline, for the birth of his third child, Gregory. He
was attracted back to his hometown of Chicago for this boxing
championship. Hemingway was an enthusiastic boxer and often
seconded matches, coached young boxers, or acted as referee. His
impatience with Tip's performance was entirely in character, and
the dressing-down Tip received was possibly legendary. At the time,
Hemingway had just published his novel "A Farewell to Arms" and
was working on his non-fiction book on bullfighting called "Death in
the Afternoon," which would be published in 1932.

Ann Sothern had already appeared in several motion pictures by the time Tip brought her room service in Fort Wayne. These were bit parts, but she was less than two years away from starring roles and a film career that would cover decades. She was in her early twenties at this time and a stunning beauty.

Aviation passion was high across all social classes in the United States in 1932. Charles and Anne Morrow Lindbergh were being subjected to a kind of public celebrity status the world had never seen before. In the five years since his record solo flight across the Atlantic, Lindbergh had continued to attract attention, regardless of his intentions. In February of 1932, he and Anne suffered the loss of their infant son in a botched kidnapping attempt, which was triggered by their fame and publicly-known fortune.

Pilots and aircraft designers were as famous as movie stars. On May 20th, 1932, at the age of thirty-five, Amelia Earhart completed her solo trans-Atlantic flight, capturing the longest solo flight record for a woman. This was not only a flight victory for women; it was also another significant accomplishment for non-stop distance flying across the oceans that separated the continents of the northern hemisphere. Fixed-wing aircraft captured public imagination, and history has focused on the planes of this era. But at the time, lighter-than-air travel was yet to prove intolerably dangerous, and dirigibles held many of the flight records. The competition between the two aircraft technologies swung to airplanes in June of 1931 when Wiley Post took the round-the-world speed record away from the Graf Zeppelin with his Lockheed Vega. What had taken the dirigible twenty-one days, Post accomplished in eight-and-a-half days. He became an aviation celebrity.

The lights of the stage were a welcome diversion for Tip and his friends. In 1933, he was twenty years old and feeling it was time to make a decision. Jobs were paying less and tuition was costing more. Scarcity in the depression was coupled with inflation, and narrowed career options more than in times of plenty. Tip was impatient to move forward with his aviation career. He drove himself to excel in school and in the cockpit to accomplish his goal.

In June of 1933, he earned his first pilot's license through his own effort and expense, while still attending classes. Despite the fact that he'd already been flying for four years, Tip was proud and relieved to be able to brandish Pilot's License #32475 whenever needed. He could now consider airports among his possible landing sites.

The learning process at the school was in full flight. Drawing boards, engine maintenance, aircraft maintenance, rules and regulations, tests, and an unending series of programs was slowly molding us into usable technicians. The flight courses were a welcome relief to the sometime boredom of the classroom and shop work. I had been giving serious thought to applying for entry into West Point or Annapolis or the Army Air Corps training center at Randolph and Kelly Fields during my final couple of months at Midwestern University. A serious depression was upon us and I learned to my dismay that two years of college would not meet the requirements for entry into the Army Air Corps flying school. I felt that taking the complex exams for entrance to West Point or Annapolis would not only consume a tremendous amount of time, if I was able to successfully pass them, but also that I would be in an academy for four more years with another year for flight training, which would make me almost too old for any Captaincy. I would have been twenty-four years old at graduation.

My stepfather was very helpful when he learned of my dilemma. He had a good friend who was a colonel in the quartermaster corps stationed at nearby Camp Perry, Ohio. In 1933, a full colonel in the army ranked just a tad lower than the Pope in the Vatican. Colonel McGrath agreed to look into the situation and report back in a few days. One week later, he called to invite us to his office at Camp Perry where he explained that my situation could be resolved if I would enlist in the Army Air Corps for a three-year period. The colonel would arrange for me to be sent to Schofield Barracks in Hawaii for the term of my enlistment, and I would immediately enroll in the military-sponsored West Point prep school there. At the end of the year, I would be in line to be accepted for Air Corps training at West Point or Annapolis. This program seemed too good to be true and my only question was "When do we leave?"

The colonel advised that he had arranged for me to be inducted at the nearest army recruiting office, which was in Harrisburg, Pennsylvania. My mother had the program all planned. We would drive to Harrisburg, have a nice lunch, talk to the recruiting officer and then decide what to do. The recruiting office was on the second floor of a small dingy building in downtown Harrisburg. I was one of fifteen or twenty waiting for an interview on October 23, 1933. When I was called, my mother walked into the captain's office with me. I noticed that all the other men were steered into a small outer office when their names were called, not into the captain's office. The captain seemed a pleasant fellow and said he had received a letter from Colonel McGrath about me and congratulated me on my choice of service.

"Raise your right hand and repeat after me," he said. Following this one-minute ritual, he shook hands with me and said the fearful words that meant a turning point in a career.

"You're in the army now!"

Chapter Three

1933 to 1935

In The Army, New York and Hawaii

Mother was expecting me to ride back to Port Clinton with her, letting the captain know when I would like to report for duty. Instead, the captain advised that I would be leaving for New York that night. I was told to report back in his office in two hours. With promises ringing in her ears that I would write once a week and that I would be careful flying those army airplanes, Mother went back to Port Clinton alone. When I returned to the captain's office, I was not quite prepared for the sudden change in the captain's character since the swearing-in ceremony. As I remember, the captain said, "Tippett! You're in charge of twenty-six enlisted men that you will deliver to Fort Slocum in New York! Your instructions are contained in this envelope. The sergeant will give you funds for food on the train. Dismissed!"

I had never been on a train, nor had I ever been in New York City. My twenty-six charges were about as rough-looking a bunch as I had seen. Mostly from Pennsylvania, they were from eighteen to twenty years old. I picked two of the biggest and toughest-looking of the group and made them my assistants, telling them to keep the lot under control or they would go straight to the guardhouse when we arrived at Fort Slocum. My orders were quite clear as to how we would arrive at Fort Slocum, train changes, schedule, and much to my relief the enlisted men were quite subdued (thanks to my two goons). There was very little conversation amongst them.

Arriving at Fort Slocum, we were met by Sergeant Pascoto at the gate and marched to a barracks about two miles further in. A moderate rain was falling which soaked the entire group. At the barracks we were told to strip and shower, after which we were assigned bunks and told reveille would be at 5:30 a.m. with chow call at 6:00 a.m. Lights out now!

The US Air Force did not yet exist in 1933, so military aviation was under the control of the army. It would be another fourteen years, two years after the end of World War II, before the air force became a separate service. Despite the air battles of WWI, flying was considered primarily as a means to gather information in support of ground troops rather than an active offensive element. The US Army Air Corps had been created in 1926 and boasted more than 1,500 aircraft by 1933, but before Tip could get to them, he had to complete the regular army regime of basic training and hard work, despite the influence of Colonel McGrath.

When Tip reached the army facility at Fort Slocum, located on a barren island in the Long Island Sound, he went through the standard thorough army medical evaluation. He was vaccinated against small pox and typhoid, weighed, and measured. The barracks that would now be his quarters resembled a commercial chicken house. New York State was the farthest from home Tip had ever been.

Tip's classic army photograph shows a young man in a dress uniform that seems too large. His characteristic curly hair is close-cropped and he is almost unrecognizable.

The first three weeks at Fort Slocum were a nightmare. It was endless kitchen patrol, marching, cigarette-butt detail, and more close-order drills. I had begun to wonder if I would ever see an airplane again. Correspondence from home was maintained and of course, I had to say that the Army Air Corps was great, and flying training was about to commence. A letter from one of my good friends from Port Clinton, Ralph "Rats" Burholt, inquired if I thought he could get into the Air Corps with me. What a great idea! Get Burholt in the Air Corps and he could suffer the humiliation, homesickness, and indignities that I had been going through.

Ralph had two years of college at Michigan State and

was a top athlete. I immediately suggested he go to Harrisburg, Pennsylvania and enlist as I did. In the meantime, I called my stepfather and alerted him to speak to the colonel about Burholt and to get him assigned to Fort Slocum.

I felt a bit guilty about my glowing reports of army life in the letters I had written to my friends. I did exaggerate a bit about the great times, but why should I be the only enlisted man from Port Clinton at Fort Slocum in the Army Air Corps? Burholt's arrival would make two and with my seniority at the post, I could turn over my latrine duty to him.

Burholt arrived and survived his basic training. Our relationship was a bit strained for a couple of weeks, but eventually all was forgiven. I was now company clerk and authorized to issue three-day passes, upon approval of the sergeant of course, so Burholt and I roamed the streets of New York on weekends and received a liberal education from our accompanying sergeant as to the machinations of a big city.

Rumors had been rampant about our assignment overseas. One minute we were going to the Philippines, the next to Hawaii. Finally our orders came through and we were to embark on the USS Republic sailing from New York, through the Panama Canal, to San Francisco and then to Hawaii. Call it preferential treatment or luck, but Burholt and I were assigned to the officer's deck on the Republic and put in charge of the physical education program. We held daily classes and worked with the children aboard. We were quite comfortable on the trip. The Republic was an aging WWI troop transport and had a cruising speed of about ten knots. The trip to Panama took days and we were given shore leave for the two days we were there. Shopping and Gorgona rum punches took up most of our time, along with some sightseeing. We found Panama pleasant but not exciting and were ready to leave when the Republic sailed.

The trip to San Francisco was smooth, although slow. We

had five days leave in port and spent the entire time touring the city, which we found fascinating. A shortage of funds restricted our activities somewhat, but we did manage to crash a few nightclubs and dance palaces. At the end of our leave, we reluctantly boarded the Republic and set sail for Honolulu. Up to now, military life was not only bearable but also quite pleasant. This was all to change shortly.

During these first months of Tip's life away from home, he began a tradition of correspondence with his mother that he would maintain for the rest of her life. Tip sent a telegram from the ship's radio room:

"To Mrs. A J Eyth, Dearest Family. Boarded ship at 2 AM. Sailing at 8 AM. Rats is on board also. As yet am not seasick. Am in squad room A 1st company. Will write you as often as possible. Tell the gang I said hello. Love = Cloyce."

The USS Republic was originally built as a non-military passenger liner in Belfast, Ireland for a German shipping company. It had been stranded in New York City at the outbreak of WWI and remained inactive in New York for three years until the United States joined the war and promptly confiscated it for use as a troop transport. First named the USS President Grant, it transported troops across the Atlantic for the duration of WWI, and then was laid up again. Around 1922, it was renamed the Republic and given an overhaul and rebuild, readying it for army service on the New York to Hawaii route, which it would make repeatedly until the end of WWII.

The sea route to Hawaii from New York in 1933 required Tip and Burholt to steam down the entire eastern coast, then down Central America to the Panama Canal. Once through the canal, they headed north past Mexico and Southern California to San Francisco, then west to Hawaii. Transcontinental air passage was not an army option due to the volume and weight of goods and personnel that had to travel the route. What seems an extraordinarily long way by sea was a routine voyage for the time. Most shipping or travel that started on the east coast had used this route since the Canal had opened twenty years earlier, in 1914.

Tip distinguished himself with his service aboard the USS Republic, which he boarded just after his twenty-first birthday, on February 16, 1934. The children he mentions would have been military families, transferring from mainland service to duty in Hawaii.

While Tip was on assignment aboard the Republic, Wiley Post took off on his successful attempt at the first round the world *solo* flight record. Post had already set the round-the-world speed record with his navigator, Harold Gatty, but was unhappy that the accomplishment did not rank high enough to move him where he wanted to go in his career. So he outfitted his Lockheed Vega, the Winnie Mae, with navigation technology that was still experimental at the time and on July 22, 1933, he did the flight alone. The Vega was the same type of plane that Amelia Earhart had flown in her record flight. It was a rugged and reliable design, but it was also a single-engine aircraft, which added to the risks faced when attempting the record flights.

If the aviation accomplishment party could have been held five months later in the year, the public could have celebrated with beer, wine, and hard liquor. On December 5, 1933 the twenty-first amendment to the Constitution repealed the eighteenth amendment and Prohibition passed into history. The Great Depression still held the United States, and most of the developed nations of Europe, in the grip of punishing poverty and stagnation. Devastating drought in what were supposed to be food-producing states of America's Midwest produced giant dust storms and the Great Black Blizzard of 1933 reached all the way from Oklahoma to New York City.

Events in Europe were leading to world war, but this was still to be visible only from the perspective of history. German politics were a local German issue, although Britain and France kept a nervous eye on developments there. While Tip steamed toward the Pacific, Adolf Hitler took a leadership role in Germany's Nazi party and passed legislation that gave him legal dictatorial power. German-born Albert Einstein saw these political developments with clear vision and serious concern. He emigrated from Germany to the United States that same year and continued his work in theoretical physics, but from then on for the benefit of United States.

At the time of Tip's approach to Hawaii, the island chain was still a territory. Hawaii would gain statehood in 1959, and Tip's correspondence from this time was marked with T.H., for "Territory of Hawai'i." Honolulu, the USS Republic's destination, was the largest city in the islands, and the army base on the island of Oahu included entire families as well as single servicemen.

Upon arrival in Honolulu, we were bussed to Schofield Barracks, a sprawling military encampment of ten thousand men about twenty miles from Honolulu. The true reality of peacetime depression army life struck home quickly. The military, in those days, had been made up of men from every way of life and profession. Gambling was big business, and semi-professionals made thousands of dollars monthly at the big poker games after payday. About a week after payday, these guys would have all the loot, then play against each other for tremendous stakes. Naturally this situation fomented loan sharking between paydays and 50 to 100% interest was not unusual. A certain amount of violence was inevitable. Burholt and I stayed clear of the gambling group and concentrated on working toward any assignment that would keep us off latrine duty.

Adjoining Schofield Barracks was Wheeler Field, an Army

Air Corps base to which Burholt and I were assigned following boot
camp. It was a small base housing a Boeing P-12 pursuit group and
a few Tommy Morse recon planes. The assignment at Wheeler Field
was more to our liking; smaller groups, decent quarters, fair chow,
and airplanes! We soon learned that the main, and most important,
base on the island was Ford Island, which had Luke Field. The main
maintenance base for all the air squadrons was on Ford Island along
with the 72nd Bombardment Squadron and three more squadrons
of P-12s and Tommy Morse's.

   After three months at Wheeler Field, Burholt and I were
transferred to the headquarters squadron at Luke Field. I was
assigned a position as field draftsman, a job that consisted of sitting
in front of a giant drafting board waiting for something to draft.
It was just as well that there was no drawing activity as I was not a
draftsman to begin with. The officers at Luke Field were a friendly
lot, all second lieutenants with one or two first lieutenants and a
captain who, in that era, was one step below Saint Peter. As I had
ample time, looking for something to draft, I spent a lot of time on
the flight line. Two of the second lieutenants were University of
Detroit graduates who had gone straight into the Air Corps, and
were sympathetic with my story about not enrolling there. They
flew the two-seater Morse scouts and would alternately schedule
me to fly with them. The ship had dual controls and I was able to
keep current in my flying, as well as garnering time in heavier, more
powerful aircraft.

   Schofield Barracks and Wheeler Field, in addition to Ford
Island and Luke Field, were part of a group of installations that
shared a common mission; to protect the main military asset of the
island of Oahu. This was Pearl Harbor.

   Tip's effort and ambition to fly under the auspices of the
Army Air Corps had landed him right at the heart of a future
wartime disaster, but he was there in 1934; nearly eight years

early. By the time the Japanese made their devastating attack on Pearl Harbor on December 7, 1941, Tip would be in Birmingham, Alabama. He would hear of the attack with the rest of the country, and listen carefully for specifics on the event, which had happened in a region he knew well.

Tip had achieved his goal to fly. Now it was up to him to capture as much experience and education as he could, both through formal instruction and by using his natural charisma to encourage others to teach him. In addition to his duties as draftsman, Tip had enrolled in night classes at the University of Hawaii and was picking up additional math, geometry, and navigation skills. His personal photo album was filled with the history of Wheeler Field and the record-setting flights that took place there six years before his arrival. He made little mention of the celebrity pilots who flew the aircraft, but he carefully recorded the names of the planes.

Wheeler Field, built in 1922, was already making historical aviation headlines. Seven years before, in 1927, while Tip was still a freshman at St Wendelin, and soon after Lindbergh's trans-Atlantic success, James D. Dole, a Hawaiian pineapple producer, organized a well-publicized race from Oakland, California, to Honolulu, Hawaii. The first-in-flight record from the continental US to Hawaii had already been set that year by both military and civilian pilots, but Dole continued with the promotion. With a first prize of twenty-five thousand dollars, (about $290,000 today) and second prize of ten thousand dollars, the race drew media attention and a startling variety of aircraft. But it turned into a disaster.

Out of the eight planes that officially started the race on August 16, 1927, only four were still flying two hours after the starting gun, and just two completed the passage. Copilots Art Goebel and William V. Davis Jr. victoriously landed Woolaroc, a single-engine monoplane Travel Air 5000, and were awarded the prize. Second place went to Aloha, piloted by Martin Jensen.

The death toll of participants in the "Dole Derby" was shocking and cast a pall over the entire effort. It happened because the world was caught up in a frenzy of aviation firsts that pushed safety aside. The limits of aircraft and pilot were being mapped the hard way, and many people were willing to try what had never been accomplished. But they underestimated the difficulty of the journey. When no more planes landed after Woolaroc and Aloha, James Dole quickly offered another ten thousand dollars for the rescue of the missing crews. Several other organizations offered even more money for retrieval, or even information, on the vanished planes, but they were never found. One last contestant, Dallas Spirit, had trouble at take-off but was given another chance to enter the race. The pilots chose to search for the missing aircraft instead. Loaded with more fuel and instrumentation than Lindbergh had carried in his flight across the Atlantic, Dallas Spirit kept in close communication using onboard telegraph, but they, too, went down and were never seen again.

The Dole Race became known as the greatest aerial disaster of the time, but it was also a reflection of the aviation capabilities of 1927. Blind flying and instrument flying were both critical skills in open ocean crossings, and pilot certification standards did not require the training. It was becoming clear that the level of proficiency required to pass certification as an aircraft pilot was not sufficient for every kind of flying which a pilot might encounter. It was also becoming clear that those aviators who did successfully complete record flights, especially solo, were not just lucky - they were supremely skilled and attentive.

The Army Air Corps was aware of the difficulty of trans-oceanic navigation. It was the motivation behind the Air Corps sponsored first-in-flight trans-Pacific record set by Lieutenants Maitland and Hegenberger just two months before the Dole Race. The Army Air Corps was illustrating the need for navigation beacons to be placed throughout the islands of the Pacific Ocean by showing both the difficulty of flying without them, and their use once in place. Lieutenant Hegenberger specialized in navigational instruments and had been preparing for the flight for more than a year. Maitland was an experienced pilot and instructor, as well as a racer. Their experience and preparation, as well as their navigation method, were the keys to their success.

The Dole Air Race had generated considerable discussion regarding aviation safety and Tip watched while he trained and studied. In the same way that Tip had carefully acquired mechanical engineering knowledge, he also expended effort on "extra" piloting skills. Tip's personal style may have appeared easy and relaxed regarding the tasks he had to complete, but he was never casual about flying or the care and preparation of the instruments and aircraft.

Public enthusiasm for experimental flights waned after the Dole Air Race, and later fliers trying to raise funds for other first-flight adventures found it hard work. The historical significance of the flight records being set on Hawaii airstrips was well celebrated by Hawaiians. Tip had several photographs of the tri-motor Fokker monoplane, Bird of Paradise, that his fellow Army Air Corps Lieutenants Maitland and Hegenberger landed in that 1927 first trans-Pacific flight. He had images of Woolaroc, winner of the Dole Air Race. He also had a picture of Southern Cross, flown by Kingsford Smith and crew in May, 1928, on the first trans-Atlantic crossing from the United States to Australia - with a stop in Hawaii along the way.

On January 11, 1935, Tip successfully completed a course titled "Military Law - the Law of Military Offenses," as well as "Military Sanitation and First Aid," at his post on Luke Field. Less than ten miles away on the same day, Amelia Earhart took off from Wheeler Field in her Lockheed Vega on her successful attempt to make the first solo trans-Pacific crossing. Tip was twenty-two and just starting his aviation career. Earhart was thirty-eight and only two years away from her disappearance on another flight record attempt. Tip had no picture of the Vega in his album and made no mention of Earhart, but he would have been aware of the well-publicized event that competed for attention on exam day. Tip was now a regular at all of the airfields throughout the island. He took his Transport Pilot's license and a brand-new Pilot's Book down to the Honolulu First Judicial Court and swore an affidavit that his tally of 69.55 hours of solo flying time was true and correct. His book was duly witnessed and notarized, ready for new flight log information.

The notary public who served Tip on that day in 1935 was Ethan S. Kiehm. To Tip, Mr. Kiehm was a functionary of the courthouse who was available to get Tip's paperwork properly registered, but the man was more than a notary public. Ethan Sungkoo Kiehm was the child of Korean immigrants to Hawaii and is considered the first American-born Korean in Hawaii. Ten years after signing Tip's pilot's book, Mr. Kiehm would become aide to the first president of the Republic of Korea, Syngman Rhee. He would ride out the Korean War at Rhee's side before returning to Hawaii and an American military life. But in the meantime, Mr. Kiehm stamped Tip's book and Tip went looking for opportunities to fly.

On weekends, I made arrangements with a commercial operator at the airport to fly passengers in a Kinner Bird biplane on sightseeing flights around the island of Oahu. This was a very equitable arrangement for both of us, as I was building up flying time and he was getting passenger fares with no pilot costs. Another enlisted pilot at Luke Field was B. J. Parker, a sergeant who also did commercial flying in his off time. Parker used an OX-5 powered Waco and we traded planes occasionally for passenger work.

One weekend, we decided that we could expand our client base if we flew to the islands of Molokai and Maui, and spent the day flying around there. We decided to use the Kinner Bird on this foray. The flight to Molokai was over water, about thirty miles.

We figured we were taking a calculated risk flying over such a long stretch of open ocean, but the straits were full of fishing boats and if we had any trouble we could ditch alongside one of these boats.

The flight to Molokai was uneventful and we flew passengers all day and into late afternoon. It was just getting dark when we took off to return to Honolulu. It was a particularly dark night and we had neither navigation lights nor cockpit lights. After flying about twenty minutes, we did not see the lights of Honolulu, which should have been directly ahead of us, and we realized that something was definitely wrong with our heading. Parker and I were talking back and forth over a throttled engine, trying to determine what went wrong when we saw a small light off to our right. We turned and flew over it, recognizing it as a fishing boat working commercially out of Honolulu. We then saw another similar light just beyond the first light and figured that the heading back to Honolulu was the reverse of the heading of the fishing boats. Fortunately, we were right, and shortly the lights of Honolulu were visible and we were able to locate our airport and land safely. I mentally filed the Molokai flight experience into the "I'd better not do that again" category, to be called upon whenever a similar circumstance presented.

Life at Luke Field was settling in a most enjoyable routine. I flew almost daily in the big twin-engine biplane bombers called "Keystones." Pilot and copilot sat in an open cockpit and a third man at a rear observation window was amidships, further towards the tail of the aircraft. When the bomb bay doors were open, the rear observer had to spread-eagle on the fuselage frame to walk to the rear of the aircraft. Once a crewmember walked into the open space and fell out of the aircraft. Fortunately, he had his parachute on, although we usually didn't use them for these regular flights, and no one knew he was missing until we landed. As luck would have it, we were over land when he fell and he was returned to Luke Field uninjured, but embarrassed.

Peacetime flying consisted of an early morning two-hour patrol around the island. Unless assigned special duty for the day, one could be on the beach at Waikiki by early afternoon. Meeting the Matson Line passenger ships twice a week was also a rewarding pastime. New tourists were in abundance and the more attractive ones were sought out and pursued. Easy access to the Royal Hawaiian and Moanna Hotel ballrooms furnished entertainment and dancing at little or no cost since most of our new friends stayed at one of those hotels or the other.

One item that enhanced our financial situation in Hawaii was a small diamond ring that my mother had given to me in case the government ran out of money. About a week before payday, Burholt and I would usually come up short. This seemed to coincide with dates to go dancing. The local pawnshop would go no higher than fifteen dollars for a loan on the ring, but this would carry us over until payday. Our pay at that time was twenty-one dollars a month and the ring was pawned monthly until one day it disappeared. We never found out who grabbed it, but it served us well.

One beautiful Sunday morning, I had persuaded a friend of mine that a trip around Oahu was unforgettable. Mr. Tuttle was the vice president of a local bank and the uncle of a girl I was dating, and eventually married. He was an aviation enthusiast but had never experienced his fascination from the inside of a plane. We departed the airport at around five-thirty a.m. The weather was perfect; light fluffy clouds at three thousand feet and a light wind. We had flown about an hour and were on the windward side of the island when something attracted my attention.

It was strange, because I knew that there was something wrong, but for a second or two could not pinpoint the trouble. It was more of a feeling I had rather than an immediate problem with the ship. Seconds later, I started losing RPMs and it dawned on me that the number one cylinder on the Kinner engine had broken

loose from the casing and was jumping up and down at each stroke
of the firing rotation, causing the motion I was noticing as I looked
over the nose of the aircraft. I knew there was an emergency field
at Waimanalo, where they had a gunnery range for the P-12s, and
immediately headed toward it.

As so often happens in this type of emergency, although
you know where the field should be, you cannot locate it. Finally,
I had to shut off the engine, and we were gliding. We had about
two thousand feet of altitude and plenty of time to find the field,
which thankfully proved to be directly under us. As I lined up on the
grass strip runway, I could see that two of the P-12s were parked
at the other end, making my planned landing on the proper strip
impossible. I had no choice but to sideslip alongside the runway and
land in the taller grass and sand. Once again, fortune smiled and the
landing was without incident. We were sent back to Honolulu in an
army truck. The engine was repaired the next day and the ship was
flown back to Honolulu.

Tip's grassy landing was both skillful and fortunate, especially
considering that once the tail of the Fairchild KR 21 biplane was
down, the pilot could no longer see over the nose and would have
to take his chances with potholes or obstacles ahead of him. The
hair-raising ride and safe landing made news in two of the local
papers and Tip gathered public acclaim for it that he didn't really
want, but accepted graciously. His pilot's log on October 28, 1935,
reads only "Waimanalo - forced landing - Tuttle" and an hour of flight
time.

Open cockpit flying in Hawaii in 1935 was exquisite. There
were fewer aircraft in the skies than today and almost no rules other
than common sense and courtesy. Pilots had to keep an eye out
for each other and birds, but the great attraction was freedom of
movement and the literal birds-eye view. Biplanes were slower than
future closed-cabin models, as well as noisy, smelly, and cramped, but

there was a closer connection to the actual flight for the passenger and pilot. Tip was free to soar, swoop, loop, and roll around all of the sights of Hawaii's cliffs and beaches. He took his passengers the long way from Honolulu to Kahuku, flying over Diamond Head, over Waimanalo Beach, by blowholes, and back home over Waikiki Beach. The volcano Mauna Loa was active in 1935, threatening the village of Hilo, and was a spectacular sight from the air. The coast of Oahu was studded with airfields, and Tip spot-landed on them all. He came in for a landing, touched the airfield, then powered up and took off again. Or he landed and parked for a breakfast picnic.

His passengers could see sharks and whales through the clear blue-green waters offshore. They flew past the waterfalls, palm trees, and canopy forests that ring the main island. Tip could choose any altitude he wished, although he knew that a higher altitude was as much a safety reserve as constantly keeping an eye out for an emergency-landing site. Altitude gave him time to deal with a mechanical failure, as he had proven with the Fairchild. Tip's arrangement with the commercial operator was an outstanding success. He was a reliable and charismatic pilot, the perfect tour guide, and was willing to fly almost every day. Pilot vernacular of the day named the engine first when referring to the aircraft. For the pilots, an aircraft consisted of two separate entities; the engine and the plane. The engine merited most of Tip's attention in his flight log. His pilot logbook from this time is packed with some of the most iconic aircraft of his day.

Many of the dual-cockpit biplanes that Tip was flying had been designed as training planes, but they were perfect for carrying passengers on paying rides. The first aircraft engine manufacturers had focused on large planes and big engines, but Depression-era economics brought that expensive manufacturing down. Smaller, lighter aircraft required smaller engines, and several companies took the financial risk to turn out lower horsepower, air-cooled engines in enough quantity to make the price affordable to a civilian market that was falling in love with aviation, but still struggling to make ends meet. These engines were not always the best, or the most reliable, but they were available and they worked well enough. In civilian aircraft, being able to anticipate the behavior of a cranky or unpredictable engine and fly in ways which compensated was the key to a successful journey.

The Kinner Bird BK that Tip flew was manufactured by Brunner-Winkle, and powered by a Kinner engine. It was a three-seater, allowing Tip to take two passengers at a time. The Kinner Lincoln PT-K was designed for sport flying and was particularly well suited for loops. Tip flew a Great Lakes 2T-1 fitted with a Menasco engine, which gave the already stable plane a welcome power boost. The closed cabin and side-by-side seating of the single-wing Aero Taylor Cub gave Tip a nice option for days when rain threatened but didn't close the airport. For sunny days, the fabric-covered Warner Fleet 1 put Tip back in the fresh air and familiar configuration of a biplane. Tip recorded his meticulous checks of the biplanes rigging that kept them tuned and tight.

The Menasco powered Ryan STA was a gleaming favorite of the small commercial fleet which Tip had access to. The dual cockpits were on top of this all-metal monoplane, and the single wing was underneath the forward controls. The passenger, in the rear, had an unobstructed view overhead and underneath, free from the obstruction of the upper wing in a biplane. Known for both grace and speed, the Ryan STA was a pleasure to fly, and Tip took full advantage of its aerobatic capabilities, recording rolls, spins, and loops in his log book during a September 1935 Ryan flight.

With Tip's professional training in the Keystone bombers, he entered the world of big dual-engine multi-passenger planes. The Keystone was not a World War I surplus aircraft like so many of the planes available to the Army Air Corp. It was of contemporary manufacture, although still configured as a biplane, and used throughout the Pacific for bombing missions. Applying his Keystone experience to his civilian flying, Tip was able to fly the Stinson SM-1DA, known as the Detroiter, which was also a modern plane for the time. It had a single high-overhead wing with a fully enclosed cabin that could seat six.

The military Thomas Morse Scouts that Tip was having the opportunity to fly for the Army Air Corps were the classic aircraft of the 1930s film industry. These planes appeared in almost every war epic of the era, often getting painted between scenes to represent the other side of the aerial dogfight. The two-seat configuration was an adaptation from their original single-cockpit fighting configuration for their use as training planes. The smaller, more tightly built biplane was a different flying experience compared to the Curtiss Jenny, which had been designed by some of the same architects of the Thomas Morse. Faster, more maneuverable, and intended for combat, the Thomas Morse Scout was teaching Tip the invisible landscape of the air.

Between training flights in the Keystone Bombers and passenger flights throughout the Hawaiian Islands, Tip was earning experience he would have been hard pressed to gather any other way. He had joined the army so that he could both fly and earn a living, and his plan was working.

The outrigger canoe club in Honolulu was our hangout during the day when we were off duty. Many colorful characters were in residence at that time, including Lansdowne Finnegan, who was a professional wrestler in a time when wrestling was turning flamboyant. Finnegan was posing as an Irishman of questionable royalty, but was a good guy and we had many interesting times together. Unfortunately, he wasn't around when I needed him.

A navy seaman named Russ White and I were in the Waikiki area one Saturday night and as we were passing the outrigger club heard music in the upstairs pavilion. We decided to investigate.

Tip shares a beer in Honolulu in 1935 with friends.
Prohibition had been repealed only a year earlier, near the time
Tip turned 21, and so raising a beer legally was still a novelty.

It appeared to be a normal outrigger club dance with the exception that most of the groups were "Kanakas," a name we used for Hawaiian hangers-on at the beach, mostly gangs. We decided that it was no place for us and as we walked around the pavilion, we passed a group of three or four toughs. I caught shoulders with one and said my pardon, but I hadn't taken two steps before he grabbed me from behind, swung me around and used some very unflattering language referring to our ethnic background and that of our parents. He also said that we were afraid to fight and that he would be waiting for me at the bottom of the stairs leading out to the beach.

The stairway leading down was covered and the exit was about one half block from the main street. It was a very dark area. As about half the male group had disappeared down the stairwell

following my challenger, I said to Russ that it appeared we were
going to be worked over by the gang. I suggested that he follow
me down the stairs and that I would bust the first guy I saw, then
run like hell towards the street. Our battle plan was flawed, for at
the bottom of the steps I could make out someone's outline only
dimly. I took a roundhouse swing at him and connected, which was
a stupid thing to do as it cost me precious time. I remember getting
banged around a bit and woke up under a shower at the Club with a
couple of MPs standing over me and a Honolulu policeman shining
his light in my face.

   I had apparently been slugged by a beer bottle. Russ said
that he punched the guy that got me with the beer bottle and then
ran like hell for the lighted street, according to our plan. He went
for help and returned with a couple of navy shore-patrol types
hoping to grab some of the gang, which had disappeared. I learned
later that the shore patrol rounded up fifteen or twenty sailors
roaming around the area and tracked down some of the gang from
the Club and did a number on them. Feelings were running very
high at that time in Honolulu. Gangs of thugs were attacking both
soldiers and sailors far too frequently. At one time during this era,
we were authorized to carry side arms when going into Honolulu.

   Tip kept excellent files filled with paperwork from his time
in the army. Along with copies of active duty orders was a series of
physical exam check sheets. Each sheet after his stay in Hawaii noted
that he wore a dental bridge, which later came as a huge surprise
to his family. This Saturday-night fight had cost him his front teeth,
something he never afterwards let on. Tip went back to accumulating
hours in the cockpit and his regular army routine.

   In flight hangars throughout the aircraft manufacturing
industry, rocket testing was gaining attention. Engineers hoped
that rocket engines would eventually replace propeller power on
aircraft. Aviation was making incredible leaps. Biplanes were still the

fundamental training planes, and the most commonly held private planes, but with advances came setbacks. Wiley Post, the aviator who had captured the first round-the-world-solo flight record, and his passenger, tremendously popular celebrity Will Rogers, died in Alaska on August 15, 1935. Post was flying a modified aircraft he had built himself, and Rogers was collecting material for his syndicated humor column. Will Rogers had been an energetic advocate for the advancement of aviation throughout his career. He was much mourned by the American public.

In 1935, behind closed gates, the Holocaust began in Germany. Whispers of what was going on in some of the Jewish labor camps made it to foreign ears, but were considered exaggerations or rumors. The United States Congress passed the Neutrality Act into law, ensuring that the US would not become involved in the increasing instability in Europe. The start of World War II for America was six years in the future and the country was still suffering an economy that kept everyone focused on essentials. Two of America's top pilots toured German aviation facilities and both came back with recommendations for neutrality. Charles Lindbergh reported on Germany's superior flight technology and construction with admiration as well as warning. Eddie Rickenbacker, head of Eastern Airlines and a World War I flight ace, described systems and organizational structure that were set up for conquest. Rickenbacker felt that Germany's system, especially regarding aviation, so far outstripped American military aviation that the only prudent path was for the US to stay out of the conflict. When he returned from Europe, Rickenbacker was called to Washington D.C. for consultation on ways in which the civil aviation movement might support future military flight preparations.

Tip was having civilian complications of his own by this time. He had met, and began dating, Louise Frances Hossack. She was a year younger than Tip and had been born in Venice, California. Tip and Louise had been enjoying the hotel dances, walks on Waikiki, and

beach picnics for three months when Louise learned that her family
was soon scheduled to move back to California. Louise's father,
Harry Hossack, and her uncle, Howard Tuttle, both worked for the
Reconstruction Finance Corporation, the government-sponsored
company formed to help combat the depression by stimulating
business activity. Howard had taken the flight with Tip that resulted
in the recent emergency landing, and the whole extended family
was as fond of him as was Louise. Tip was powerless to prevent her
departure, and conflicted over his own prospects.

Burholt received his appointment to flight school and
sailed off to San Francisco to report to a squadron at Crissy Field
in the Presidio. But my application had different results. I had
been advised that my application to take the flight tests and the
written examinations had been approved for a second lieutenant's
commission in the Army Air Corps. But the tests were to be given
at the Oakland, California air reserve base at the Oakland airport.
I was in a catch-22 situation. I couldn't go to Oakland because I
was still enlisted in the regular army, and I couldn't take the tests
required for the Army Air Corps commission without going to
Oakland.

I mentioned my dilemma one night at dinner with my
girlfriend, Louise Hossack, and her family. Her parents came up
with the suggestion that I purchase my way out of my enlistment
using a new rule in effect at the time. This rule applied only for a
short time in the military, and I do not know to this day why the
ruling existed or for what purpose. Captain and Mrs. Alfred Larsen,
who were friends of the Hossack family, financed the plan and I
applied for a purchase release and was approved. Two hundred and
fifty dollars later, I received an Honorable Purchase Discharge and
left immediately for Oakland, California to take my commission
exams.

On December 21, 1935, Tip was discharged from the army with an excellent character reference. He was twenty-two and had spent two years and two months in the army, ranked as a private. He had his Transport Pilot License with three classes, 1A, 2S, and 3S; 211 hours of private flight time; a significant amount of Army Air Corps flight time; and had his engine mechanic rating. His honorable discharge certificate cites "Purchase; Section III, A. R. 615-360," a short-lived and very welcome section in the army regulations governing honorable discharges. The buy-out clause was tucked in between the mental and physical disability discharge. In today's dollars, the $250 discharge purchase would have been $3800, a significant sum for a young man at the time, and attractive to the depression-era cash-strapped peacetime army. Tip's ability to purchase an honorable discharge from the army was an extraordinary opportunity for him, and was the beginning of a career path guided by Harry Hossack's advice and influence. Hossack was primarily a banker, but he had connections with people and government offices far beyond those of a regular government employee.

Louise's family and friends may have had an interest in seeing Tip pursue his non-military career more fully. The couple was dating frequently, and while Tip only briefly mentions it in his own account, Louise was a significant feature in his off-duty life. The Hossacks were headed for California, and now Tip was able to go there as well. For Tip, the target was the flying commission, but for the Hossacks, the target was Tip.

Honorable Discharge
from
The Army of the United States

TO ALL WHOM IT MAY CONCERN:

This is to Certify, That* _Clayton J. Tippett_
† _6913912, Private, Air Corps, Unassigned;_
THE ARMY OF THE UNITED STATES, as a TESTIMONIAL OF HONEST
AND FAITHFUL SERVICE, is hereby HONORABLY DISCHARGED from the
military service of the UNITED STATES by reason of ‡ _Purchase;_
Section III A.R. 615-360.

Said _Clayton J. Tippett_ was born
in _Bellvue, Ohio_, in the State of _Ohio_.
When enlisted he was _20_ years of age and by occupation a _Painter_.
He had _Brown_ eyes, _Brown_ hair, _Fair_ complexion, and
was _6_ feet _2_ inches in height.

Given under my hand at _Fort McDowell, Calif._ this
_21st_ day of _December_, one thousand nine hundred and _Thirty-five_.

Earle L. Hubbard

Major, Cavalry,
Commanding.

See AR 345-478.
* Insert name; as, "John J. Doe."
† Insert Army serial number, grade, company, regiment, and arm or service; as "1620302"; "Corporal, Company A, 1st Infantry"; "Sergeant, Quartermaster Corps."
‡ If discharged prior to expiration of service, give number, date, and source of order or full description of authority therefor.
W. D., A. G. O. Form No. 55
May 1, 1923

Tip solved his army catch-22 of transitioning from the regular army to the Army Air Corps by buying an honorable discharge with Harry Hossack's help. Tip's goal was to study aviation at Randolph and Kelly Fields, but he had to get there by any means he could arrange.

Chapter Four

1935 to 1937

Introducing Louise and Oakland, California

Life is full of little surprises and my arrival in San Francisco in December 1935, to report to the Oakland Army Air Corps reserve base, was a big one. I was told that the series of exams I would be given would require at least three months of study and that it would not be necessary for me to remain in the area. I could do the courses by correspondence with the exception of the flight test, which could be completed in about three days.

I had no choice but to try to find a job in the area. I flew a few passenger trips for local fixed-base operators and did some checkout instruction, but I could find no permanent flying job. Louise's family had moved back to San Francisco at about the same time that I arrived in Oakland. Harry Hossack, father of Louise, was a highly respected banker, graduate of Harvard University, and sought after by Washington politicians because of his astuteness in economics, among other things. Mr. Hossack knew of my plight and offered me their guesthouse to use while I was trying to locate a job. He was a gruff grumpy sort, whose bark (very loud) was much worse than his bite. We would play Chinese checkers and pinochle by the hour in the evenings, and I would generally win, much to his chagrin. What it boiled down to was that my system of cheating was better than his.

Although Tip had no permanent piloting job, he did have numerous flight opportunities, with and without passengers. By January 5, 1936, Tip was flying Fleet 7 and Fleet 2 biplanes with the Kinner engines that he knew well. He flew Louise over San Francisco Bay in an open-cockpit Warner Waco RNF. Louise might have preferred a flight in the two-seat closed-cabin monoplane Rearwin Sportster that Tip often flew out of Oakland, but perhaps it was not available that day.

Oakland is directly across the bay from San Francisco and was often clear when the big city was fog bound. On sunny days, Tip could fly over the bay and give his passengers exquisite views of San Francisco's skyline. In early 1936, many of the tall buildings that are associated with San Francisco today had not yet been built. But Telegraph Hill's Coit Tower stood visible for miles if the fog allowed, as well as the Russ Building and the Pacific Telephone Building, now known as the PacBell Tower. Tip could land passengers at Crissy Field, right on the edge of the bay and in full view of the incomplete Golden Gate Bridge. From there, it was a short walk over to the Palace of Fine Arts for a picnic. Both the Bay Bridge and the Golden Gate Bridge were under construction. The Bay Bridge would be finished first, using financing arranged by Harry Hossack's Reconstruction Finance Corporation, on time and under budget. The distinctive towers of the Golden Gate Bridge were up, supporting short stubs of unfinished road that lead only to the turbulent waters of the gate.

Just offshore from Fisherman's Wharf was the island prison of Alcatraz. In Tip's time, it was an active federal penitentiary. Al Capone was in residence as Tip flew over, as was George "Machine Gun" Kelly. Nearby Treasure Island was being created to house the Golden Gate Exposition. An inaugural party was planned for the opening of the bridges.

A flying tour of the San Francisco Bay gave sparkling views of ocean liners coming in through the gate, headed for small crowds waiting at the jetties. One crisp January morning, Tip flew a passenger over the Oakland speedway, catching the race from the air. Other days, he went all the way out to Sacramento. Despite the delay that Tip was experiencing while studying for entrance to the Army Air Corps, he was still able to pursue his flying and his courtship of Louise. He was having a series of small successes in a time when success was rare. Still years from the end of the suffering caused by a depressed economy and severe drought, the entire country was focused on meeting basic needs. In March 1936, while Tip was still waiting to be called for testing, the iconic photograph of the Great Depression was taken only 250 miles away from Oakland. Known as "Migrant Mother," the photograph of Florence Owens Thompson and her children was captured by Dorothea Lange in Nipomo, California. The woman's lined and dusty face, her expression, and the faces of her children came to represent the sense of hopelessness that a huge number of people were feeling in America and throughout Europe.

One of Mr. Hossack's good friends and clients was a mining engineer, George Fuller. Mr. Fuller was in charge of a very large dredging operation in the Yuba River, Grass Valley area of Northern California. One evening during dinner, he mentioned that if I would be interested in working with the dredge, he could offer me a job. The job was panning gold in various parts of the Yuba River to determine the "colors" or gold content in the area. Having had no previous experience in gold panning, I was reluctant at first to consider leaving the city to go into the boondocks of the mining country. My new boss convinced me that he could teach me the technique of gold panning in a week. He also hinted that there was an airport at Marysville, only a few miles down the road where I could probably make arrangements to fly occasionally.

The following week I was picked up by my new boss and driven to Smartsville, California, where I was deposited in front of an old, weather-beaten white house and told that it was my living quarters. The old couple living there welcomed me with open arms. My room rent and board was thirty dollars a month ($470 today). It's difficult, looking back, to give an accurate description of my room, the facilities, and the area in general. My bed was a rickety wooden thing of questionable vintage. The mattress was straw with an occasional stem popping through the cloth. On a clear night, I could lie in bed and look straight up at the stars through a hole in the roof that was "going to be fixed tomorrow."

I had a wash basin in my room, but all toilet facilities were out in back of the house about thirty yards away. One electric bulb and candles provided light. I noticed a curious phenomenon whenever anyone went to the outhouse. The entire chicken flock would come running after them and gather around the back of the toilet, where apparently they feasted on feces. One meal a week, usually Sunday, consisted of roast chicken and I always managed to avoid that meal.

Smartsville consisted of a country store where one could hang out in the evenings and listen to some of the local lore from the older citizens. I had purchased a Model A Ford Coupe for $75 ($1150 today), and I was told that if I had a flat tire, never to run my hand around the inside of the casing to find a nail as there were many rattlesnakes on the road and their fangs could penetrate the tire casing. If you scratched your hand on the fang, you would get the full effect of the snake venom. As soon as I could establish credit, I bought a new set of tires.

Occasional jaunts were made to a larger village just up the road called Rough and Ready. It had most recently lost its last operating gold mine and was practically abandoned, with the exception of the lifelong inhabitants who had previously retired.

The entire region was friendly and in a very short time I began to enjoy the "outback". I established contact at the Marysville airport with a local operator and made arrangements to rent one of his planes over the weekends to fly passengers in the Grass Valley area. The airport had a small grass strip on top of a hill near the town, which was adequate for the Challenger Robin I was flying. Sometimes we would be three aircraft flying off the field, which necessitated our setting up our own traffic control system. We each decided on courses and in what quadrant we would fly as well as our approach to the field. Hazy weather and dust thrown up from take-offs made visibility somewhat restricted at times.

In the meantime, my friend Burholt could not pass the physical exam for appointment to Randolph and Kelly Fields and the Army Air Corps flying school. He failed the "Schneider Index" portion of the exam. This test dates back to World War I and measures the heart's response to stresses. It should have been eliminated from modern tests long ago. In any event, Burholt was reassigned to the enlisted Army Air Corps and transferred to Crissy Field and an observation squadron flying Curtiss Hawks.

At Crissy Field, Burholt had become friendly with several of the pilots who would fly him to the Marysville airport, where I would meet him. He would alert me to his arrival at Marysville by flying over my rooming house and dropping a note tied to a rock advising me of their landing time. On one occasion, the rock went through the roof and landed on my bed. I think he was lucky and hit the hole in the roof that was already there. We would spend the weekend touring the area and generally end up on Saturday night in Marysville at one of the dance palaces, such as they were. He would be picked up on Sunday afternoon or Monday morning to be returned to Crissy Field.

The town of Marysville, California, had been named eighty-six years earlier to honor Mary Murphy, the wife of the area's

main landowner. Mary was a survivor of the 1846 Donner Party
expedition, when her trip by covered wagon across the Sierra
Nevada mountain range was disastrously delayed by snow. The
town was bordered by both the Yuba and Feather Rivers, which
flow west out of the Sierra Nevada. Tip's work with the 1936 gold
mining operation used hydraulics to strip the gold-bearing rock and
sediment from the hillsides and flush it into sieves. When he flew
the collection of aircraft available to him at the Marysville strip, he
could take in the breadth of California's Central Valley to the south,
with views of the farming and wide dry pastures, all the way to the
sudden mountains of the east. Sacramento was not far by air and Tip
had enough fares to fill his spare time.

     Tip's passenger plane service had taken a step up with the
closed-cabin Curtiss Challenger Robin and Taylor Cub monoplanes,
even as his standard of living had suffered a setback. Burholt, flying
a Curtiss Hawk out of Crissy Field, was back in a biplane and still
subject to the views and fresh air of the Hawk's open cockpit.
Burholt's failure to progress to Randolph and Kelly Fields was a blow
to his hopes for a serious flight career, as that program was the
portal to higher flight education both on the ground and in the air.
The Schneider Index was a series of cardiovascular and circulatory
tests performed during both activity and rest. It was a stress test,
supposed to determine the fitness of a man to withstand the forces
his body would encounter at altitude and against the g-forces in
turns, dives, and loops. Although Ralph Burholt failed the Schneider
Index, he lived into his eighties and flew for decades.

     Tip was determined to gain access to those flight
opportunities and he had envisioned doing it with Burholt. Although
Tip does not mention it, he had already completed the required
study to sit for the Army Air Corps exams in Oakland. He had
applied for the exam and was on a waiting list. He diligently
continued his appeals to report for testing, but had no idea when he
would be called. While he was waiting, he was not considered part of

the army at all, since he had purchased an honorable discharge. This left him free to pursue his own plans, but also left him without any income or supporting benefits. He was twenty-three and at a loss about what to do next.

Tip, at twenty-three, was now able to fly paying passengers at any airport, and in any single-engine aircraft. He had achieved a way to fly regularly, but now he needed to find his way to making it a career.

After three months in the gold mining business, I called it quits. My aviation career seemed to be floundering and I felt that I could certainly find something somewhere in the aviation field. The one weekend I spent in San Francisco with the Hossacks, I discussed my feelings with Mr. Hossack. He agreed that there was very little future in the gold panning business. As a matter of fact, he wasn't too enthusiastic about my future in the aviation business either.

Aviation per se was in the doldrums. Pilot jobs were few and far between in the San Francisco area. However, things were picking up in Los Angeles. Douglas Aircraft was building the DC-3 and the airlines were buying them. Once again, Mr. Hossack came to the rescue with his good friend, Sheriff Eugene Biscailuz, a potent political lawman who had been sheriff for years. Sheriff Biscailuz was a very good friend of Mr. Donald Douglas, President of Douglas Aircraft in Santa Monica, and at Mr. Hossack's suggestion, wrote a letter of recommendation to Mr. Douglas for me. I presented the letter to Mr. Douglas's secretary in early November 1936, and was sent to the office of the vice president of Engineering. I was told to start work the next day on the three o'clock shift as a junior project engineer.

Tip was born with charismatic networking skills, but Harry Hossack's local connections were powerfully helpful. Harry had a handsome and charming younger brother, Laurence, who worked in the personnel department of the Los Angeles Sheriff's office. Laurence had married a lady officer and was in the process of divorce, after which he would marry another. Laurence worked under Sheriff Eugene W. Biscailuz, who was a towering figure in 1930's Southern California, and had connections to rich celebrities and business leaders. Biscailuz is credited with forming the present day system for California's Highway Patrol. Under his leadership, the Los Angeles County Sheriff Department became the largest in the country. Biscailuz was a strong personality, proud of his Basque and Hispanic origins. He had connections in the classic old style, and Tip benefited greatly from his influential introductions. Sheriff Biscailuz wrote to H. H. Wetzel, the vice president of Douglas Aircraft on June 9, 1936.

"Dear Mr. Wetzel,

This will serve to introduce C. J. Trippett, *(a misspelling by the Sheriff)* a nephew of Capt. L. J. Hossack who is in charge of personnel of this Department. Mr. Trippett was recently honorably discharged from the Army Air Corps. Capt. Hossack feels that with the experience acquired, his youth, etc., he will develop into a valuable man for your plant. Anything that you can do for the boy will be appreciated by me personally.

Yours very Truly,

E. W. Biscailuz, Sheriff."

Douglas Aircraft's DC-3 was the plane that changed civil passenger aviation, and was a great leap forward in both speed and range capability. It was well built and well designed, and quickly gained an enthusiastic fan base that persists today. The DC-3 first flew on December 17, 1935, out of Clover Field in Santa Monica, which was the same airport that Tip was using less than a year later as he flew passengers in his free time away from the Douglas factory. The DC-3's distinctively sleek, all-metal style was unique for the time. Boeing had been the first to manufacture an all-metal skin and separated single wings, but lost the market share to Douglas due to business decisions and design differences. Aviation experimentation had covered every design configuration possible in the thirty-two years since the Wright Brothers first flight. The DC-3 had twin engines built into the wings, one on each side instead of one across the bottom or top of the plane, and the fuselage was clad in polished aluminum. Biplane design, and the idea of using wood and fabric for construction, were left behind forever. Future commercial aviation craft would look more like the DC-3 than any aircraft that came before it.

Initially, the commercial airlines of 1936 were tentative with their orders for DC-3s. The economy was still depressed and competition was high for passenger fares, routes, and mail contracts

that supported many of the airline businesses. The first DC-3s were
equipped with sleeping berths and in-flight kitchens, but the major
airline managers wanted more seating capacity instead. Prior to the
DC-3, coast-to-coast airline travel involved a series of short plane
flights followed by hours on a train. With the DC-3, passengers
would board the beautiful craft and arrive at their destination after
only fifteen hours and three refueling stops. Air travel in the US was
about to become popular.

Douglas Aircraft was flooded with orders as the DC-3
began to replace the train as the most common way to travel across
the continent. It would be a staple in the development of the air
fleet during WWII. It would eventually be used for every conceivable
military air function due to its reliability and capacity. The factory
was hard pressed to keep up with demand. Once again, Tip was
flying almost every day either with paying passengers, students, or
solo. In Santa Monica, he rotated through a similar fleet of planes to
the ones he flew in Hawaii and Oakland. He now added the Kinner
Meteor to his fleet of experience. The full name of the Meteor was
the General-Western P2S and it had an open two-seat cockpit
with a single wing high overhead. As a flight experience, it was a
combination of the monoplane wing configuration with the tandem
biplane seating. Only six of these planes were made, manufactured
locally in Santa Monica.

My title at Douglas Aircraft, Junior Project Engineer,
confused me somewhat until I learned that my primary
responsibility was keeping track of the wings they were removing
from American Airline DC-3's that were being flown in for leading
edge repair (the leading edge of the wing kept popping open). One
amusing incident I recall, but not amusing to the company and the
quality-control people, was a lost DC-3 wing. I came on my shift
at three o'clock and had a red pencil note on my desk to search the
plant for the wing off one of the American Airlines ships. Property

had checked it in and Repair and Engineering had signed for it, but no one could locate it. After an hour or so of tracing the paper work with no success, I decided to start from the beginning. I went out to the area where the planes were parked when they were flown in and sure enough, there sat ship #12 with one wing still attached.

Incidences such as this won me a five-cent increase in wages to fifty-five cents an hour ($8.44 today), and a supervisory position building wings for the O-46 observation plane being built by Douglas for the Army Air Corps. I was doing a great deal of flying. My job at Douglas allowed me time from the early morning until three in the afternoon to instruct students and fly commercial passengers. In the meantime, Burholt had completed his enlistment period and came to work at Douglas also. We shared an apartment in Santa Monica and managed to work the same shifts. I found the work at the Douglas factory most interesting and fascinating. The factory was quite small in comparison with present day corporations and the work more personal.

Santa Monica had wide views of the Pacific Ocean, and the approach to Clover Field took Tip out over surf and white beaches. The mild, easy weather of Southern California offered clear flying days more often than fog. Tip had the coastline of Los Angeles, the cliffs of Malibu, and the low mountains of the Angeles National Forest to entertain his passengers. The hours of flight time continued to build his skills, although he was not immune to the occasional ground loop, as he recorded on August 16, 1936 in a Kinner Fleet. A ground loop is an unintentional and sometimes violent swing to the right or left during take-off or landing, often catching a wingtip on the ground.

Tip's yearly salary at Douglas was $1,250 ($18,500 today), and he was supplementing it with additional flying and instruction for the Huchendorf Flying Service out of Clover Field, earning another $1,500 ($22,200 today). By now, he had 245 hours of flight time, and he also had an aviation job, even though it was not a pilot position.

May 20, 1937

Douglas Aircraft Company letterhead from Tip's archive.

I was still trying to find a flying job and augment my qualifications. I completed an instrument course in Primary Instrument Flying. The airlines at that time were flying a mixture of VFR (visual flight rules) and primary instruments. The radio ranges in use at that time taxed the skills of the pilots who were trying to land under instrument conditions in heavy weather. Many of the older pilots relied on their "seat of the pants" skills rather than instruments.

Once again, Sheriff Biscailuz gave me a letter of recommendation. I presented it to the president of Western Air Express, an interstate airline flying into Nevada and locally in California. Mr. Alvin P. Adams was, at twenty-six, the youngest president of any airline in the US. We later became great friends, spending time at his Colorado ranch and my (future) South American abode. Adams called in his chief pilot and instructed him to set up a flight test for me in a Boeing 247D the next morning as they could use another co-pilot.

That night, I re-read my instrument exam questions in anticipation of an oral exam from the chief pilot. I wasn't worried about the flying. My self-esteem probably exceeded my ability, but the thought of failure never entered my mind. The next morning, the headline in the morning paper finished my anticipated career with Western Air Express. Flying into Salt Lake City in a heavy snowstorm, the chief pilot crashed into the Wasatch Mountains, destroying the aircraft and all the passengers and crew. The airline had lost one third of its fleet and they did not need another co-pilot.

On December 15, 1936, in Salt Lake City, Utah, the Western Airlines pilots suffered static on their critical radio rangefinders during ice fog conditions. This was exactly the kind of problem that had caught Tip's attention in his studies for his instrument qualifications, and made him a believer in instrument ratings. The pilots crashed into Lone Peak, south of Salt Lake City. Later analysis of the crash site revealed that they missed clearing the top of the mountains by only twenty feet, but they were over thirty-five miles off course in the zero-visibility weather. The pilots had tried to rely on instrument readings once they lost visibility, but the technology failed them. There was no backup system they could switch to and no help available from the airport.

A month later, in January, 1937, Tip was awarded his Transport Pilot license. By then, he had recorded more than 326 hours in his pilot log. This license made even more commercial flight options available to him, and he had a heavy instruction and passenger schedule. He was flying every day and working steadily for Douglas Aircraft and the flying service. Tip now added a Lambert Monocoupe to his flight experience. This was a fast, single-wing plane with a two-place cabin. By now, Tip had flown so many closed-cabin aircraft that the protective novelty of not being exposed to the elements was routine. The Warner Rearwin and Continental Cub planes were similarly comfortable in comparison to the now less frequently flown biplanes. Aviation was making progress in both comfort and speed as well. As the Douglas DC-3 made coast-to-coast flight routinely available to middle class passengers, Howard Hughes proved that an even faster crossing was possible when he set a Los Angeles to New York City speed record of just over seven hours in an aircraft he designed himself.

Hughes was one of the wealthiest people in the world, and

well known for both his aviation contributions and his filmaking. He
was eccentric and influential. Once he acquired Trans World Airlines
(TWA), he took it to national commercial domination through
mergers and management.

Events were beginning to move faster in Tip's personal life as
well as in commercial aviation.

Mr. Hossack and his daughter Louise had invited Burholt
and me to spend the weekend in San Francisco. We started out
Friday, late afternoon, in my 1932 Model B Ford convertible. We
had with us our pet alligator, which we had named "Herman," a
gift from a friend in Florida. Herman lived in our bathtub and ate
raw hamburger when he felt like it. He would take the hamburger
out of our hands if we were quick, which we were, because he
did not differentiate between fingers and hamburger. The further
we progressed into the mountainous area, the worse the weather
became. We finally stopped in a mountain village for some coffee
and to dry out a bit (the convertible was not waterproof) but we
were asked to leave when we put Herman on the counter and asked
for some hamburger for him. Apparently, the owner had never
seen a live alligator before. After this experience, we agreed to leave
Herman at home next time.

The weekend in San Francisco was a great success. Louise
Hossack agreed that we had been dating long enough to become
engaged. Her father and mother approved, Burholt approved, so
we became engaged. I had no ring, as I hadn't expected to become
engaged when we started out. For some reason that I cannot recall,
we decided to marry in May in Santa Monica, California. Burholt
was to be the best man. The gravity of the forthcoming wedding
put both Burholt and me into shock. I was very happy to be getting
married, but with no permanent job on the horizon the decision, as
I drove back to Santa Monica, seemed now to be premature.

The single-minded intensity that Tip showed in pursuit of his aviation career contrasted significantly with his good-natured but unfocused approach to his romantic life. Tip left home in Santa Monica on a road trip to see his long-distance girlfriend, and came home firmly engaged.

Louise was not unfocused. She was direct, strong-minded, and knew that Tip was her man. Harry Hossack was also a goal-driven personality and between the two of them, Tip's year of indecision was brought to an end.

Louise Frances Hossack, 1914 - 1994, was born in Los Angeles, California. Her father had called her "Bobs" because of her babyhood habit of bobbing her head in agreement to everything that was said to her.

Louise, at the time of her engagement to Tip in 1936, was twenty-two and modestly glamorous. She wore her hair in a jaw length cut that complimented her graceful neck. Louise was tall and could look Tip in the eyes with a tilt of her head. They made an attractive couple, lean and lanky, intelligent, and quick in conversation.

Harry Hossack and Louise Lines, Louise's mother, were both on record as being age thirty-five when Louise was born. The baby was a happy surprise and would be their only child. Daughter Louise later noted that her mother had adjusted her age somewhat when she married Harry, so although Louise Lines was not yet forty when she had the baby, she was close to it. Young Louise grew up in a household that prized literature, education, good behavior, and family ties. Mother Louise was from Pennsylvania and bore baby Louise after most of the family had moved to Venice, California, to live together in a three-house compound created by the family matriarch, Louisa Hitcheler Lines. As each of the Lines four children married or divorced, they came back to the compound for refuge. When Tip's Louise was born, her parents lived in the family compound and raised her with the other cherished only child in the family, cousin Mary Jane. The children were like sisters.

"My mother was a great person," Louise once said, "All sorts of people confided in her and asked for her advice and comfort. I think the easiest way to portray her is to say that everyone called her by her nickname, Love. My father, on the other hand, was the scourge of the neighborhood. He was autocratic and irascible and I never dared bring any friends home to play during the hours he might be around. He had a splendid brain, high moral principles, and a charm that surfaced every now and then along with his sense of humor. It took me about twenty-two years to learn to love him as he was."

Harry Hossack's family came to Los Angeles from Nebraska. He was somewhat estranged from his own father. It was the Lines side that defined the family, and Louise would go back to them at times when Tip was flying uncomfortable aircraft in inaccessible places. Love's sister, Jean, had married a man named Howard Tuttle. Harry Hossack formed a close friendship with his brother in law, Howard, and the two began to work together, a career move that would take them to Hawaii, where all of them would later meet Tip.

Louise was not the only one caught by Tip's good-natured charm. In later letters, Harry would refer to Tip as his "adopted son." Harry would dedicate himself to guiding Tip's future through the aviation world by using influence and advice. Harry's hand was behind many of Tip's career developments and opportunities, but wedding planning was women's work. The entire wedding was in the hands of a long line of Louises.

On Saturday, May 22, 1937, Tip took an early morning solo flight in a Taylor Cub. His only note in his pilot log was "Local Clover Field" with a flight time of one hour. Later that day, after the sun went down, Cloyce Joseph Tippett married Louise Frances Hossack at Saint Monica's Church, in Santa Monica, California. The ceremony was held in the Catholic tradition, following Tip's wishes. The reception followed the church wedding, back at the Venice home compound with Louise's aunt, Mary Lines, playing hostess. Louise honored her Hawaiian connection by wearing a lei and a wrist bouquet of gardenias with her white organza dress. Louise's best friend, Joy Rutherford, was her maid of honor and Tip's steadfast companion, Ralph Burholt, was best man. Louise's mother wrote an account of the wedding week to her sister in Hawaii.

"Dear Jean,

Just ain't no use for me to try and tell you all about the doings here. You would put it down as the ravings of a doting crazy mother, but as long as I live, I can see that kid of mine as she entered the church. So happy, so radiant, and so beautiful! Had pictures taken which if they are good at all will tell the story better than I can. Everything moved along smoothly and on time, about 50 at the church and 27 at Mother's. Had supper served by a caterer from Santa Monica. Awful good eats. Of course, a bride's cake with all the trimmings. Mary and I worked three days on the house. Dirty? Just foul and being eatin' by moths, actually never saw such destruction. It's been years since it's been cleaned, just made me sick. I think Mother got some pleasure out of it all. She is so confused mentally that nothing really reaches her. Had to be told over and over again what we were doing. She did get in her lick when the kids were in to see her just before going in the church. They left that night for Ohio, a happier couple couldn't be found on earth.

   Affectionately,
   Love"

Cloyce Joseph Tippett on his wedding day, with his best man, Ralph Burholt.

Love was in her sixties when Louise married, and Louisa, the family matriarch, was in her eighties. As young Louise departed with her new husband, the California branch of the family lost their last energetic youngster.

No definite honeymoon plans had been made as I had a couple of flying jobs to complete. My mother insisted we come to Port Clinton and see them and visit in that area. It seemed like a good idea and as Burholt was from Port Clinton, he decided to come with us on the honeymoon. We boarded a bus and headed for Port Clinton and Lake Erie. The trip on the bus with my best man in tow turned out to be rather riotous.

Louise was a woman of distinct opinions and a willingness to adventure – within limits. She was a talented artist who left too few accounts of her life in her own words. Her perspective of these times adds a dimension to Tip's account that is seldom harmonic, but always bluntly practical. She told very little of her engagement to Tip and never wrote her own memoir, but had one firm piece of advice for her granddaughters upon their coming of age.

"Never," Gran said firmly, "*ever* allow your husband's best friend to come along on the honeymoon!"

SAN FRANCISCO 1936

This photograph of Louise was taken a year before her wedding, on the streets of San Francisco, her favorite city.

Chapter Five

1937 to 1938

To Ohio and Back, Then on to Texas

Tip's first three months of married life played out against another nationwide plunge into recession as President Roosevelt sought to balance the budget by cutting government spending. Aviation commanded headlines just two weeks before Tip and Louise's wedding in 1937 when the Hindenburg tried to dock in Lakehurst, New Jersey. While newsreel cameras were rolling, the hydrogen-filled zeppelin burst into flames and crashed to the ground, killing thirty-five of the ninety-seven people on board. The Hindenburg disaster was not the worst crash in zeppelin industry, but it was the most famous and is blamed for ending the lighter-than-air commercial industry. Commercial airplane travel across the Atlantic would not begin for another two years. After the film of the Hindenburg disaster played in every theater worldwide, trans-Atlantic passengers opted for ships rather than board a zeppelin.

Amelia Earhart was firmly established in aviation with her solo flights and previous record-breaking efforts. On the May 1937, weekend of Tip's wedding, Earhart had resumed her round-the-world flight attempt after repairing damage she had sustained in an aborted takeoff in Honolulu. She and her navigator, Fred Noonan, weren't injured in the minor crash, but the landing gear of the plane was damaged. As Tip and Louise honeymooned in Ohio with Tip's mother, Earhart flew farther toward the South Pacific. On the first of July 1937, a week after Tip and Louise wed, she left Papua New Guinea for Howland Island on the most challenging leg of her journey, and disappeared.

The most uplifting advances in aviation science took place behind the scenes in 1937. Monoplanes and multi-engine designs, all embodied in the DC-3, were beginning to propagate beyond experimental models. Jet engine technology was moving off the drafting board and into the hangar bay as both England and Germany made successful advances that year.

Worldwide, conflict was building. Spain was embroiled in civil war and Nazi Germany was committing human rights violations which would lead to future atrocities. Japan invaded the Chinese mainland and declared war. The United States held to the Neutrality Act in the face of growing conflict and chaos between many powerful nations.

At Tip's mother's house in Ohio, Tip and Louise were reading these headlines from a place of relative comfort. Tip had a modest income providing the kind of flight lessons he had planned while back in California.

We stayed with my mother just outside Port Clinton, in a modest, five-bedroom house with an acre or two of landscape. One would think that spending your honeymoon at your parent's home would be the end of the marriage right then. Not at all. My mother was a most incredible person! The old cliché "never met a person I didn't like" was invented for my mother. Neither human nor animals were enemies. She was the female Pied Piper of all she surveyed. At that time, in or around the house, there was one monkey, seven Chihuahuas, three Mynah birds (all could talk), five noisy parrots, two Coon Hounds, and breeding cages just behind the house that held at least two hundred parakeets. Any stray cat or dog, and sometimes person, could find a haven with my mother.

Mother lived in a happy little world of her own. Her aim in life was to make everyone happy; animals and people alike, and she was very good at it. Time passed very quickly in Port Clinton. I was doing some local passenger flying and flight instruction, mostly out of the Toledo airport. Louise kept busy with my mother and the animals when I was with old friends and relatives in the area. Burholt had returned to Los Angeles to work for Douglas Aircraft.

Civil passenger air service was a business in the Great Depression that simply refused to fold. Each small business that set up shop at an airport somehow found enough customers to keep the aircraft flying. Tip was no longer trading flight time for aircraft access; he was now a fully paid pilot. Every time he moved, he went directly to the local airport and signed up with the local passenger flight service. Many of the airplanes were the same as those he had flown in Honolulu, Oakland, Santa Monica, and Marysville. In Toledo, Ohio, he encountered some that were only to be found in the late 1930s. The Aeronca C3 was commonly referred to as "The Flying Bathtub" for the unique placement and positioning of the pilot's seat. It was one of the lightest planes in the air, built like a glider, and supposed to be almost impossible to crash. If the engine quit mid-flight, which it frequently did, the C3 would glide to a landing provided the pilot could find a tree-free site. The pilot sat so low in the cabin that his view of the landing field was the best of any aircraft before or since. The Aeronca C3's snub-nosed front end and single overhead wing were totally distinctive.

Tip flew the Szekely Curtiss-Wright Jr. in August of 1937 out of Sandusky, Ohio. His log shows flights to and from Cleveland three days in a row but makes no particular mention of the extraordinary design of the aircraft. The plane had an open cockpit with the tandem seating and fresh air benefits of a biplane but with a single overhead wing. It was, like the Aeronca C3, light and glider-like, but the propeller of the single engine was in the middle of the plane. Instead of being positioned at the nose, the blade was on the back of the overhead wing, behind the pilot and passenger, and set up in a pusher configuration. This must have created differences in the way the aircraft handled in flight, but it was the tendency of people to walk into the spinning blade that caused the final demise of the design.

By this time in his aviation career, Tip had flown dozens of different aircraft designs. His willingness to pilot anything that could fly would reap enormous benefits in the future, but for now all he wanted was to advance his plan to fly at Randolph and Kelly Fields. The arrival of his much-anticipated letter from the Army Air Corps was a relief. He was requested to report on January 13, 1938 to "appear before a board of officers for examination for appointment as a second lieutenant, air reserve, and the military rating as Airplane Pilot." Tip was back in California by November 1937, and already flying passengers out of Clover Field. He was ready.

Louise said goodbye to Verna, and once back in San Francisco, enjoyed her first real home in her newlywed life. She and Tip rented an apartment in the Russian Hill neighborhood. Their Vallejo Street address had spectacular views of the city and the neighborhood hosted some of the few homes that had survived the earthquake and fire of 1906. San Francisco was vibrantly alive to a social couple in their early twenties. They had numerous dinner parties and drinks almost every evening with friends and neighbors. Tip and Louise were fashionable and charismatic. Their apartment was close to Macondray Lane, a picturesque little pedestrian street with verdant gardens, lined with Edwardian cottages. Louise was able to walk everywhere, and take cable cars anywhere out of walking range.

The Golden Gate Bridge had been finished just one year earlier and the Treasure Island World's Fair was being readied for opening in 1939. After the fair, Pan American Airlines intended to use Treasure Island for their international flights, but the navy would commandeer it as war drew closer. It was an exciting time to be living in San Francisco. Louise was a watercolor artist and had the entire city to inspire her work.

Within a month I had completed my flight tests and requested my final exams for commission in the Army Air Corps Reserve. I was told that the results and the commission might take six months or more to be approved. The part-time flying that I was doing was not supportive and once again, job hunting was the order of the day. An ad appeared in the morning paper stating that the Owl Drugstore was hiring a short-order cook for their new lunch counter. I applied for the job and was hired. Being the chef at a lunch counter was pretty much like my night stints in the Port Clinton restaurant. Fried eggs and hamburgers were about the most complicated dishes that were served. Weeks passed, and I was flying whenever time permitted and working the counter when on duty.

One morning, after I had just started working at the Owl Drugstore lunch counter, a Chinese gentleman asked if he could speak to me for a minute. Thinking he wanted to order something special, I moved toward the end of the counter where he was standing. He handed me his card, which read "Won Goon Dick" and had Chinese writing at the bottom, which meant nothing to me. He asked if I were Lieutenant Tippett, and I answered in the affirmative. He then said, "Would you consider flying for the Chinese government?" I answered that I would certainly consider it, after I learned the details. He said an American volunteer group was being formed of new pilots who would fly with Chinese pilots against the Japanese. He said the salary would be $1,500 per month ($22,500 today) payable in advance each month. He asked if I would meet with him to discuss the details the next day. I met with Mr. Won Goon Dick in an area in Chinatown, San Francisco. The details as outlined were most interesting and I accepted the job.

The job put me in charge of the first class of students to be trained in the US, but who would fly in China. The base of operations was to be a portion of the US naval base near Oakland, California. I was to inspect and purchase several planes within the next few weeks in order that classes could commence within a month. Following the graduation of the first class, I was to take this group to China and supervise their advanced training in fighter aircraft.

Within the next week, three Kinner-powered Fleet training aircraft had been purchased, and one Pitcairn Wright-powered Mailwing. The Pitcairn was to be used as a more advanced, heavier trainer. Three instructors were hired to assist, and our classes got underway. Several of the first groups of students were from various colleges and universities in the US. We had students from Harvard, Yale, and several from California universities. Within several weeks, we had students soloing and progress was being made in their ground school courses.

One incident occurred that could have been more serious, but ended being a minor problem involving the big Pitcairn. As we were operating off a paved runway, the Pitcairn needed a tail wheel instead of a tailskid, which it now had. I flew the ship to the Oakland airport to have a tail wheel installed and took one of my advanced students with me. As he had been checked out in the aircraft, I let him fly back to our Alameda naval base after I had checked out the new tail wheel. The tail wheel had been rigged to be steerable and worked in conjunction with the rudder pedals, which also served as brakes. Only the pilot cockpit had brakes. The landing at the naval base was acceptable, although a bit fast. As he had touched down slightly with the main wheels first, he pulled the tail down with some force that incited a violent vibration caused by the tail wheel wobbling. Instead of easing the brakes to stabilize the vibration, the student slammed on the brakes. This caused the aircraft to nose up on the runway, teetering tail up and finally settling down on the nose and front wheels rather than going over on its back. As I had cut the power the minute the vibration had occurred, there was little damage to the aircraft other than the propeller. This was the only incident that the training course suffered during the entire mission. Arrangements were being made for the thirty-three graduates of the program and myself to leave for China in three weeks.

While Tip and Louise were honeymooning with Tip's mother in Ohio, Japan had invaded China by sea and air. The island nation of Japan wanted the land and natural resources of the gigantic, but technologically backward, country of China. In some of the first offensive military uses of aviation, Japan had succeeded in invading and gaining a foothold on China's coast. China was suffering under the onslaught as Japan backed up the air effort with a sophisticated navy, and could not stand alone against Japan's push toward the interior.

China's leader, Chiang Kai-shek, was impatient for America to provide help against the Japanese invasion in the form of trained fighter pilots and aircraft, and initiated governmental negotiations that were led by his American-educated wife. America was still vigorously neutral and the US government could not officially respond with support, but agreements were being carefully worked around US neutrality law with the cooperation of Claire L. Chennault, a US Army Air Corps officer who had resigned from the armed forces in order to accomplish the project. Chennault visited China in 1937 to begin what would become official military operations, but in the meantime, other Chinese agents, like Won Goon Dick in San Francisco, were getting things moving using civilian resources.

San Francisco's Chinatown was a center for Chinese-American politics and organization. It had a large Chinese population that was rocked by the Japanese invasion of their homeland. Money and influence turned from private enterprise to nationalism, and Won Goon Dick had become a leader in a dominant faction dedicated to supporting Chiang Kai-shek. Tip's job acquiring aircraft and training pilots was part of the earliest organized efforts. Money was no object. China urgently needed expertise, pilots, and aircraft. As 1938 dawned, Tip was training some of the pilots who would soon become members of the American Volunteer Group, which became known as The Flying Tigers.

Since the United States was not officially politically involved in China's conflict with Japan, anyone working with the Chinese government had to do so from a civilian position. Tip would soon run into this issue himself in working with South American countries, but for now, he was legitimately outside of any branch of the armed forces and had no bureaucratic entanglements. Prior to US involvement in World War II, which was still three years in the future, pilots volunteering for flight training or service intended for China were notified that they were doing so on their own. They were mercenaries and had no official government endorsement. But they did eventually have presidential sanction from Franklin D. Roosevelt, and as Tip had experienced, the pay was significantly more than the men could earn at home. Volunteers and aircraft were proving readily available to the generously funded private agents of the Chinese government. Once the United States joined the world war, diplomatic leaders were able to fully recognize the pilot's participation.

At the same time that Tip was training pilots for China, he was engaged in passing his certification test for Airplane Pilot. This was an exhaustive evaluation of a pilot's basic flight skills. The primary aircraft used by the Army Air Corps Detachment flying out of Oakland in 1938 was the Douglas BT-2B. First introduced in 1932, this was a widely used training craft in the program, and it had more powerful engines than other training planes, which gave an extra depth to the pilot exam. It was a biplane, with a single propeller at the nose. The two open cockpits were configured one behind the other, so that the instructor could evaluate and teach the student in the air, without necessity for a solo.

In this craft, Tip demonstrated proficiency in taxiing, take-off, climbs, level turns, climbing turns, straight glides, landing, straight and level flying, a gliding turn with power, a gliding turn without power, stalls, spins, two turns each way without power, three turns with power, stall landings, crosswind take-offs and landings, chandelles (a 180 degree climbing turn), forward slips, side slips, eights on pylons (a figure eight flight referenced around two fixed points on the ground), 100 degree landings (an instrument-based landing direction), 360 degree landings, 2500 foot spirals, forced landings, normal and steep climbs, normal and shallow glides, stalls in glide, and combination climbs and turns.

On January 14, 1938, Tip passed his exam in two hours and twenty minutes. Captain George E. Henry, who conducted the exam, gave him full marks and found him "basically sound and mentally alert." Tip also passed the physical exam and was now clear of the hurdle that had deprived Burholt of his own dreams to pursue the path that Tip was taking.

Before I could leave for China, my great day finally arrived. I received notification that I had passed my exams and was commissioned a second lieutenant in the Army Air Corps Reserve. I was ordered to report to the Oakland reserve base for a flight test and pilot rating. This was done the following day, and I was authorized to fly the reserve base aircraft that consisted of Douglas BT-2Bs, North American BCs and BT-9s. I immediately requested active duty and an appointment to the US Army Air Corps flight schools at Randolph and Kelly fields in San Antonio, Texas. I was told that there was a possibility that I might be approved for the class beginning in October.

WAR DEPARTMENT Washington

13 September 1938

Special Orders, No. 214. 20. By direction of the President, each of the following-named second lieutenants of the Air Corps Reserve is, with his consent, ordered to active duty, effective 3 October 1938. On that date each officer will proceed from the place indicated after his name to Randolph Field, Texas, reporting in person upon arrival to the Commanding Officer thereat for duty. Each officer concerned will rank from the date set opposite his name.

CLOYCE JOSEPH TIPPETT (0-365631), 3 October 1938. 1032 Vallejo Street, San Francisco, California.

By order of the Secretary of War:

Malin Craig

Chief of Staff.

Tip finally had his ticket to the advanced flight training he had been working for and he wouldn't be going to China. Louise was at wits' end preparing either for a move to Texas, a trip to China, or, more likely, an extended stay returning to her family in Venice, California. While Tip was working for Won Goon Dick and flying the irresistible line up of aircraft at the Oakland reserve base, Louise was settling in to a lifestyle she really enjoyed. She was a watercolor artist in San Francisco, and her husband was finally happily employed. Tip's work for the Chinese made up for the lack Louise found in an airman's paycheck in 1938. Tip had continued flight instruction for Mr. Dick right up until he and Louise packed the car and headed out for Texas. The assignment was temporary, but the couple didn't know how long they would be gone. They arranged to keep control of the Vallejo Street apartment by sub-letting it to friends. Tip had been warned that no public accommodations were available at Randolph Field, so they found a small apartment on Alamo Street, in San

Antonio, and Louise began to set up house once again. For Tip, this was the beginning of the life he had been striving for since he joined the army, five years before.

Chapter Six

1938

Randolph and Kelly Fields, Texas

San Antonio, Texas in October 1938 was not vibrant. The city had seen widely publicized labor unrest earlier in the year, and living conditions seemed dusty and backward when compared with San Francisco's modern and glittering society. The climate was dry and hot, and the culture was Southern where it was not Hispanic, something quite foreign to Louise's California and Hawaiian upbringing. Effects of the Great Depression were in evidence throughout the city and a critical source of income and industry was the nearby army installation, funded by the government and drawing on the San Antonio community for support and sustenance.

The flying schools at Randolph and Kelly Fields had been built in 1926 and officially dedicated in 1930. Most pilots who trained for the Army Air Corps passed through these courses. Randolph Field was where the more basic training took place. Kelly Field was for advanced aviation. Charles Lindbergh had graduated from it in 1925, and Major General Claire Chennault, director of the Flying Tigers, had just left his teaching post at the air base to begin his work with China.

As an army wife, Louise had a built-in social circle of other wives. Randolph Field had many facilities and Louise did most of her daily errands there. The city of San Antonio did not present as many attractions for her as had San Francisco. For Tip, it was an exciting time of achievement, intense study, and long hours of flying. For Louise, it was a challenge. She made friends, participated in clubs and parties, and made their tiny house as home-like as she could on Tip's un-supplemented Army Air Corps salary.

At Randolph Field, Tip was assigned to the Air Corps Primary Training School. An Air Corps Memorandum Receipt from Randolph Field shows that 2nd Lt AC-Res C. J. Tippett was issued one pair of medium-sized winter flying gauntlets, one pair of Type B-7 flying goggles, one large summer flying helmet, one size 38 Type A-2 flying jacket, one size 40 Type B-2 winter flying jacket, one pair of size 11 Type A-1 flying shoes, one size 40 Type A-4 summer flying suit, one size 40 Type B-1 mechanics' suit, one pair of size 44 Type A-2 winter flying trousers, and one size 38 Type C-2 flying vest. Suited up and ready to fly, Tip was looking good for the Advanced Flying School.

When I reported to the student assignment operations office for Air Corps flight training at Randolph and Kelly Fields, I had over fifteen hundred hours of flight time. Our class consisted of twelve 2nd lieutenants and, being officers, we were apart from the flying cadets and enjoyed the personal attention we were receiving from our instructors.

All of our class had previous flying experience. One instructor, Lieutenant Reynolds, better known around the base as "horse face," had flown in Spain with the loyalists and had two bullet holes in his jacket to prove it. Joe Mackey was there. I had flown with him in Ohio at air shows and he had won the International. Both Mackey and myself had twice the flight time that Lieutenant Reynolds held, but we paid attention in class and followed him through all the primary maneuvers that the army taught in those days. We proceeded through basics like figure eights, S turns over a highway, spins, stalls, forced landings, and spot landings. Lieutenant Reynolds was intrigued with some of the acrobatics that Mackey and I were doing on our own when we should have been practicing our standard maneuvers and suggested that we do some acrobatics on one of our morning lesson flights.

The next morning I spent my entire "learning" period showing Reynolds how to do an outside snap roll in a Stearman Trainer. Following that, we did Cuban eights, hammerhead stalls (a vertical loop roll), slow rolls, and loops. Unfortunately, unknown even to Lieutenant Reynolds, the Captain had scheduled me for a primary check ride the next morning. As the past few days had been spent betting twenty-five cents on who could land closest to a spot on a grass field, my primary maneuvers did not satisfy and, as a matter of fact, left a lot to be desired.

Upon landing, the captain said not a word about the flying but announced that he was scheduling me for another check ride the next day and was hoping he could wash me out of the class. After two hours of practice in the morning, I was ready for my check ride in the afternoon. Things went a lot better. When we landed, the captain said "I'm sending Mackey and yourself to Kelly Field for pursuit class starting day after tomorrow." This came as a shock, as I had requested bombardment, hoping to get some "heavy" twin-engine time, which I needed to be employed by an airline when I finished.

Kelly Field was not far from Randolph Field and still in the San Antonio area. Tip was able to report for assignment at Kelly Field and return home to Louise at the end of the long days of November 1938. In Joe Mackey, Tip had found a kindred spirit. The shared self-motivated drive for flying experience in every available aircraft had put Tip and Joe at the head of their class and ready to present a handful to any instructor coming their way. Joe Mackey was still engaging in every air race he could enter. He flew a sleek and powerful Wendell-Williams Special, a single-wing plane with every surface polished for minimal drag. He was finishing high in the races and had garnered a reputation for stunt flying before he showed up at the flying school. Joe couldn't resist the open air and high-power engines presented to him through the Army Air Corps, and with Tip to compete against, they were both taking the aircraft to new extremes. When Mackey graduated, he went immediately into commercial aviation and founded Mackey International Airlines, which would become a leader in travel between Florida and the Bahamas. Mackey Airlines would eventually merge with Eastern Airlines and Joe would go into politics.

In the meantime, however, Tip and Joe were doing maneuvers in the biplane Stearman trainers that were more reminiscent of barnstorming than pilot training. Their patience with the linear system of the flying school was at odds with their ebullient spirits, obvious proficiencies, and victorious celebration at having finally reached their goal of flying at Randolph.

Our first day at Kelly Field, both Mackey and I were assigned to fly a Boeing BT-2B observation plane. This was a gigantic biplane that was built for reconnaissance. I had flown the ship before at the Oakland reserve base. Having made several touch-and-go landings and some air work for an hour or two, I brought the ship back to the line. As I was walking into the operations office, Captain Bert Hovey, Chief of the Pursuit Section stopped me.

"You have five minutes to make your next flight schedule - check the board," He said. Wondering why I was scheduled to fly the BT-2 again, I went to operations board to check the ship number and found that I was assigned a Boeing P-12, a hot little biplane that we all were anxious to fly. Grabbing my parachute, I walked to the flight line where two of the P-12s were parked. Captain Hovey was standing alongside one and pointing to the other as my ship. "Captain," I said, "I have never been checked out in the P-12." "What do you want to do, sit on my lap?" Hovey replied.

His only advice was to open the throttle slowly, keep the ship lined up straight, don't over control, take forty-five minutes air time to get acquainted with the ship, and make a half dozen touch and go landings. I found those instructions very informative, but as he taxied out, I was left with only the crew chief to go over the fine details. Like, how to start it.

I discussed the ship with the crew chief for about ten minutes, which was about all the time needed to know the entire system of the P-12. It was all engine, with tiny wings it seemed you could reach out and touch from the open cockpit. The ship had an inertia starter, which necessitated the crew chief manning a large crank while standing on the ground and bringing the starter up to full inertia before yelling "Contact!" Sometimes the pilot standing on the wing and cranking did this operation. This was tricky, as you had to leap into the cockpit and pull the string before the starter lost its inertia.

Actually, my entire checkout on the P-12 consisted of the crew chief showing me how to start it. The P-12 (F4B-4 navy designation) was a stubby little fellow, thirty-foot wingspread and twenty feet in length. Its empty weight was around two thousand pounds and it was powered with a Pratt and Whitney 550 to 650 horsepower engine. It was agile, to say the least, and most of the pilots were very apprehensive of its characteristics, especially on landing.

Mackey and I were having a fine time getting acquainted with the little Boeing, as we were the only two officers assigned to fly the P-12s. We flew formation acrobatic maneuvers, took cross-country trips and generally had a ball. We needed a certain amount of pursuit time in the P-12 before we could move on to the new Seversky Fighter that everyone was in awe of, but during this happy time, we came within an inch of being washed out of advanced flight school because of a night flight that Mackey and myself were scheduled to fly.

We were the only two aircraft in the air in the Kelly Field quadrant. I was on the right side of the field and Mackey on the left. Our assigned altitudes were three thousand feet. We had a beer bet going as to who could get down the fastest from their quadrant after the tower gave the clear-to-land signal. We would split full throttle and dive for the line on which we had to land, over the hangars.

There was probably not an aircraft built that made as much noise as the P-12 in a full throttle dive. Apart from the noise, Mackey came in over the hangar line inverted, with his landing lights shining upwards. This greatly upset the tower operator, mostly because Mackey missed the tower by only about fifty feet. We finished our flying at about eleven p.m., and discovered that San Antonio citizens, including the mayor, had been calling the base to find out what was happening. Unfortunately, a general from Washington also happened to be visiting that night, and the landing party that was waiting for us exuded a rather unfriendly atmosphere.

After having the riot act read to us the next morning, we were told we were on probation. Two days later we were assigned to the Severskys, which were considered the "hottest" fighter the military was testing at the time. The Seversky had the ugly habit of snap rolling out of a tight turn, a kind of corkscrew roll, which generally occurred as you were practicing close in landings and short finals. We solved this problem by letting the ship continue its snap until it was level again. Probably an appalling sight from the ground, watching a snap roll completed five hundred feet or less on a landing approach. This maneuver was taught to the students who later flew the ship but at a much higher altitude.

I had requested bombardment training when we were first assigned advanced training, but the paper came back disapproved, and upon graduation from Kelly Advanced Flying School, Mackey and I were assigned to Barksdale Field flying P-26 "Peashooters."

It was no wonder that Tip and his fellow pilots were excited about the Seversky P-35. In their normal world of open cockpit biplanes, the Seversky was a sleek, silvered thoroughbred. One of the first single-seat fighter planes built for the Army Air Corps, it offered an enclosed cockpit, all metal construction, and retractable landing gear. These were huge advantages over the Stearman biplanes, or the Douglas BT-2B aircraft. The closed cockpit was much more comfortable, and the speed and maneuverability transcended Tip's previous experience with non-fighter craft.

The flying time in the fighter advanced Tip's skill considerably, but overall, the Seversky did not shine as a fighter aircraft. By the time it entered combat, well after Tip was training in it at Kelly Field, the Seversky was considered obsolete, outclassed by later fighter planes. The P-26 Peashooter was a metal monoplane like the Seversky, but still had an open cockpit and fixed landing gear. It was called the "Peashooter" because of its tiny size in comparison to many of the other fighter planes in the air at the time. Like the P-12, many pilots considered the P-26 more than exciting; they found it dangerous and refused to fly it if they had a choice. Tip thought differently and although the P-26 wasn't as sought after by pilot trainees as the Seversky, he found it to be a huge improvement over the biplanes for flight training and excitement.

Barksdale Field, however, was no improvement at all, at least not for Louise. The field was located in Louisiana, more than 350 miles away from the San Antonio apartment Tip and Louise called home. Tip doesn't mention if he stayed in the barracks at Barksdale and came home on weekends, or if he commuted the distance by air every day, but the move left Louise alone in a town she was unfamiliar with, and despite her activities with other base wives, she found it difficult.

Tip kept a dedicated attitude to his flying school studies despite his adventures in the sky. In January of 1939, he was certified in Instrument Flying, which was critical to his ability to fly any aircraft under challenging visual conditions. In contrast to his occasional performances outside the boundaries of the flight school curriculum, Tip continued to reach for every opportunity possible, using a combination of charm and patience to get what he wanted from the army.

Two weeks after the assignment to Barksdale Field, I was surprised to receive orders to report back to Kelly Field for Bombardment Training. My previous request had finally been approved. Bombardment training began by flying Northrop A-17 and A-17A attack planes. The A-17 was a long range, low wing, and all-metal aircraft. It was very comfortable to fly and had the ability to go long distances without refueling. The bombers were Douglas B-18s, a military version of the DC-3. They had a more streamlined nose section for a bombardier, and bomb racks in the fuselage over bomb-bay doors that extended a third of the length of the aircraft. Our training was serious and intense, and included long-range navigation classes, training on the bombing range, and a great deal of night flying. Finally, we completed our courses and graduated. My assignment was the 88th Reconnaissance Squadron, based in San Francisco, California, and Louise was very pleased to be going home.

This major achievement of graduation passed by in a flurry of governmental paperwork, relocation, and exams for another pilot rating in February of 1939. Tip and Louise went happily back to the Vallejo Street apartment and Louise resumed her life as wife of a second lieutenant pursuit pilot. Tip commuted across the newly opened Golden Gate Bridge to Hamilton Field, which was north of the city in Novato. Louise was able to join her parents on a tour of the Golden Gate International Exposition held at Treasure Island, at the foot of the also-celebrated Bay Bridge. For Harry, it was a special commemoration, as the Bay Bridge was a tangible manifestation of the work he accomplished bringing funds from government sources to job-generating public works at a time when such projects had never been more needed by American workers.

A novelty photograph from one of the Exposition's model streets caught Harry and Love, Louise's parents, strolling together, as they enjoyed both the modern marvels showcased at the fair, and their first introduction to Treasure Island.

As Tip passed another pilot rating, Louise took her parents to Yosemite National Park. The couple were now in their mid-sixties and Harry knew he would soon be posted to Washington D.C. The 1939 touring spree with Louise was part welcome home, and part final chance to see the sights of Northern California. The Hossacks did not know when they would return. Tip was now twenty-six years old and working on certification in attack and bombardment ratings, a task that required extensive study in long-range navigation, celestial navigation and armament handling.

Reporting to a squadron commander was a new experience for me. The first officer I encountered in the 88th warned me when I checked in at base operations that the 88th was the toughest squadron on the base, whose only redeeming feature was that it had almost every type of Air Corps aircraft in inventory. There would be plenty of flying time in bombers, amphibians, attack planes and pursuit aircraft. After my initial paperwork, I walked down from base operations to the squadron operations to introduce myself to my commanding officer. Major Newton Longfellow was sitting at his desk as I was ushered in. I walked up to his desk and saluted smartly.

"Lieutenant Tippett reporting for duty sir!" I said, and held my salute for about two minutes, while Major Longfellow did not look up from his desk. When he finally responded, I expected him to say something welcoming.

"You think you're a pretty hot pilot, don't you?" he said.

"That will have to be determined by the squadron, sir," I replied, modestly, I thought.

"We'll see how hot you are," He said, unimpressed, "Dismissed!"

Leaving his office, I stopped at the operations desk.

"What's the matter with him?" I asked the operations officer behind the desk.

"He hates reserve officers and will bust you out if he can," he replied. "Watch your step. You are assigned as his co-pilot for squadron duty, by the way. Scheduled to fly with him at 0800 tomorrow morning. Good luck!"

My first impressions of Major Longfellow were not favorable. He was a short, slender fellow and carried a cushion with him when he flew so that he could reach the rudder pedals. One stare from him would wrinkle your uniform. He was probably the meanest, most demanding military officer I ever ran into. After flying with the major for one month, I didn't know whether to go over the hill, resign my commission, or shoot him, but by the time I left the squadron, I had the greatest respect for him. We became good friends and correspondents after I left the service.

My first experience in flying co-pilot with Major Longfellow was a disaster. We flew an OA-8 amphibian built by Sikorsky. It was used as a rescue ship and flown when the bombers were flying, in case one went into the bay. The weather was foggy and our mission was to patrol the Bay Area until the mission ended. We flew until about eleven a.m., when he said we would try some landings, both land and water. We had a brisk wind blowing across the runway at Hamilton Field, necessitating a crosswind landing. My idea of how to land an aircraft crosswind and the Major's were not compatible. In coming out of his cant, the aircraft floated just long enough to pick up drift so that when he touched down, the aircraft left the runway and headed for the bay that paralleled the runway. The Major applied full throttle and we climbed out of the pattern. Not a word had been spoken during this flight.

"Raise the gear, we're going to make a water landing." The major said, and I did. We made several water landings into the wind with no incident. Returning to the field, he started his approach.

"Do you want me to lower the landing gear now?" I asked, about four hundred feet from the runway. He shot me a furious look and nodded silently. We landed, not very smoothly, but safely.

Returning to the hangar, the Major informed me that we would fly the same mission the next morning and that I would be flying from the left seat (the pilot position). With this information, I checked with other pilots in the squadron as to the flying characteristics of the OA-8 and spent the afternoon reading the ship's manual. The next morning, we taxied out with me flying

in the pilot seat and Major Longfellow riding co-pilot. I followed
the manual to the letter, calling out orders for the co-pilot. I was
permitted to take off and for over an hour we did air work and
two water landings. I did well in my field landings, and the Major
announced that I was now qualified on the OA-8. He added that in
addition to my duties as Transportation Officer I would now also
enjoy Mess Officer responsibilities.

Tip's commanding officer, Major Newton Longfellow, would
eventually become Brigadier-General Longfellow and move from
commanding bombardment units in the United States to overseeing
the transfer of US assets to England immediately after America
joined the war in 1941. He flew extensive combat missions in
Europe and was one of the Commanding Generals of the famous
Eighth Air Force in England. Major Longfellow was almost fifty when
Tip became his responsibility. He was four years into an army air
corps career that would take him to the top ranks of military flight
command. He was a professional and proved to be a good, if strict,
influence on Tip, who had a new distraction looming.

In the spring of 1939, Louise presented Tip and her parents
with the happy news that she was pregnant. Tip was hard at work
progressing his flying career and the baby's anticipated arrival in
November added a new dimension to the schedule. Tip and Louise
were in a good position to welcome the new member of the family,
as the San Francisco army facilities were some of the best in the
nation, especially the medical unit at the Presidio. Tip applied himself
to the task at hand, which was to distinguish himself in the 88th well
enough to gain the possibility of promotion. In April, Tip applied for
commission into the regular Army Air Corps, a step toward moving
out of the reserve, and strengthened his case by collecting both
Dead Reckoning Navigation and Celestial Navigation certifications.
Major Longfellow assigned Tip to assist the base Mess Officer, and
then wrote a supportive recommendation for his application out

of the Reserve. Longfellow described Tip as "conscientious, hard-working, adaptable to new ideas, and anxious to get ahead." Tip had originally moved to the Air Corps reserve to accelerate his training in the plentiful government aircraft, but now the need for secure and steady employment was changing his plans.

Major Longfellow had a mission of his own, and that was to make the 88th the number one squadron on the base. As I had completed an instrument training course preparing for employment with the airlines and the military was not flying instruments in those days, I became the instrument instructor for the squadron. A memorandum was issued advising that every member of the squadron would have to qualify as an instrument pilot or transfer out. Days and weeks followed of training flights, practice hooded flights, and "beam" flying (following an electronic beam using instruments without relying on visibility). Days when other squadrons were in the hangar because of bad weather, we were flying. Three blind landings to a full stop to get your instrument ticket. We were the first squadron to be instrument qualified.

The next memorandum declared that every officer in the squadron would have to qualify as a celestial navigator. Now followed weeks of classroom lessons and sitting under the stars with a bubble octant trying to determine our position on the ground. Finding a position sitting in a chair in front of the hangar was one thing, but to do it "shooting" out of a tiny bubble of a window while bouncing around in a B-18 was something else. Within three months, what was left of the squadron was celestial qualified.

As I was the junior officer in the squadron, I was assigned the honor of drilling the troops every morning at six-thirty a.m. I had no previous experience in marching or close order drill, so this assignment presented somewhat of a problem for me. Fortunately, the first sergeant of the squadron was well versed in this sort of thing and marched alongside me whispering the commands. The practice was called the "knife and ball" drill. I found it derived its name from the fact you were marching with a saber and if you made a quick turn as you shouted your orders, the scabbard would entangle in your legs and cause all kinds of embarrassment. I had this duty, amongst others, for one month.

Major Longfellow was benevolent about taking the base aircraft on cross-country flights. Every weekend, he would urge us to get out and go somewhere and practice our navigation and weather flying. He insisted we fly in pairs, so each weekend Lieutenant Irvin and I would requisition an A-17 and fly to Los Angeles to visit Burholt, who was now a civilian working for the Garrett Corporation. We would leave at the end of duty on Friday night, make a night flight to Los Angeles, and fly back Sunday night. Whoever drew the flight back on Sunday had to lay off the beer and drink cokes on Sunday.

One cross-country flight we made in the A-17 was particularly notable. Lieutenant Basye, (later to become one of General Doolittle's Tokyo Raiders) and I decided that we should fly back to Cleveland, Ohio, and attend the air races. As my home was Port Clinton, a short distance away, I would submit the request for the aircraft. I submitted a written request to Major Longfellow for the use of the aircraft, listing the reason as a visit to my sick mother. The major called me in to his office.

"I'm sorry to hear about your sick mother," he said, "but if you wanted to go to the air races, why didn't you say so?"

The trip was approved, and Basye and I took off at about five o'clock in the afternoon, headed towards Cleveland. I was flying the first part of the trip and at about eleven o'clock that night we were just approaching St. Louis when the engine blew. Oil covered the windshield so thickly that we had to open the hatch to see out. We were flying at thirteen thousand feet, so we had plenty of altitude to decide what to do. I called St. Louis radio and advised them of our emergency. I told them that we were going to make a dead stick landing at the military base a few miles east of St. Louis. We asked for lights to be turned on at the base for identification.

The tower acknowledged our message but the reception from the military base was garbled and unintelligible, and at an altitude of ten thousand feet we had still not located the military strip. We knew from the map it was a single runway with hills on one side and trees on the other. At six thousand feet, Basye yelled "'Dead ahead!" I thought that was a hell of a way to describe a field I was trying to reach with no engine and goggles full of oil. Over the field we made a 360-degree overhead turn and landed easily.

We were towed to the hangar line and after telling the line chief our problem, we saw a bright and shiny A-17 sitting in the hangar. As we had official orders to fly to Cleveland, I got the bright idea of borrowing that airplane to continue on to Cleveland and pick ours up on the way back after the engine change. The crew chief denied us use of the plane and refused to call the commanding officer at this late hour, so that we could get higher permission. He suggested that if I wanted the plane, to make the call myself. What the chief didn't tell me was that this ship was the commanding officer's pet and that he would not care to be awakened at midnight by a couple of second lieutenants wanting to borrow his airplane.

We were at the base three days while the engine was being changed and to add insult to injury, the CO made us fly the repaired airplane around the field for three hours before we could clear for departure to Cleveland. The delay in St. Louis cost us a landing in Cleveland. By the time we arrived, the field was closed to transient aircraft and we proceeded on to a small landing strip showing on our map at Camp Perry, Ohio, about five miles from Port Clinton. We arrived just after dark and although the strip was not lighted, I knew its location and made our approach with our landing lights. As I was about to land, I saw a five-foot high rifle target just ahead on the strip. I gunned the engine, cleared the target, and landed, braking to a stop as soon as possible. We secured the plane and hitched a ride into Port Clinton to stay at my parent's house.

Early the next morning, my mother got a call from the commanding officer of Camp Perry telling us to get our butts out to the field and get our airplane off the rifle range. When we left the plane in the dark we did not see that we were surrounded by targets. We missed them by inches while landing and never knew the difference.

The nearest military base from Camp Perry was at Mount Clemens, Michigan, about an hour flying time. We overnighted there and flew back to Hamilton Field without incident and without seeing the air races. With the A-17 trip under our belts, Basye and I requested permission to attempt a non-stop flight from Hamilton Field, California, to Mitchell Field, New York, in one of our B-IVs. We were qualified in dead reckoning, celestial navigation, and instrument flying, so the flight was approved. We flight-planned the southern route to avoid some heavy weather in the north, but headwinds still slowed our flight to a ground speed of less than one hundred miles per hour. Approaching Dayton, Ohio, shortly before dawn we were told that the thunderstorm activity we had encountered seventy-five miles west of Dayton would intensify east of Dayton, and the weather at Mitchell Field would be minimum or below at our estimated time of arrival. We had been in the air about sixteen hours, and we were exhausted. Our attempt at a non-stop flight across the United States ended in the rain and wind as we gave up and headed for the barracks in Dayton.

Summer and the days of mild flying weather were over. Louise was nearing the end of her pregnancy and Tip began to stay closer to home on the weekends. They watched with the rest of the world in the first week of September, 1939, as Germany invaded Poland and World War II began. Aviation's role in warfare promptly moved from support and observation to attack and bombardment

as Germany's well-equipped Luftwaffe bombed Warsaw into ruins.

President Roosevelt reaffirmed US neutrality with the support of Former-President Herbert Hoover and numerous senators. Charles Lindbergh broke a long media silence in a radio speech in mid-September to support the government's policy of non-intervention. That same day, Russia joined the German offensive and invaded Poland from the east. Anti-neutrality groups in America lambasted Lindbergh and cited his recent acceptance of an aviation award from the hands of Germany's Hermann Goering as evidence of his lack of patriotism. Lindbergh's warnings against US involvement in the war were based primarily on his opinion that German military organization and technology far exceeded America's – particularly in aviation. This perspective offended American pride, despite the fact that it was true at that time. But Lindbergh made comments regarding other aspects of German politics that were either gravely misunderstood, or revealed an unattractive borderline support of the Axis regime. Lindbergh's public comments tarnished his popularity in America and worked against him professionally when America did join the war.

Public opinion was split on the practicality of continuing the Neutrality Act. Throughout the world, countries were lining up on one side or the other, and America had influential voices speaking out for isolation or for allied support. Recent advances in science and technology weighted the issue of involvement far more heavily than in previous armed conflicts around the world. In August 1939, while Tip was flying Northrop A-17 Nomads and Douglas B-18 Bolos between San Francisco and Seattle, Albert Einstein sent a historically significant letter to President Roosevelt, warning the president about recent successful nuclear fission test results conducted in Germany and repeated in the United States. Einstein wrote that a nuclear chain reaction releasing vast amounts of energy might be possible. Without actually saying that this technology could make the most powerful bomb in the world, Einstein encouraged

Roosevelt to remain watchful. The Manhattan Project, devoted to
development of the atomic bomb, was secretly born that year.

The nation's armed forces, including Tip, were watching
every newspaper headline with intense personal interest. Tip
passed another exam and qualified with an "Expert Aerial Gunner"
rating. While Tip left no written opinions for or against American
involvement in foreign conflict, he was nonetheless flying for the
Army Air Corps. Whether he agreed with it or not, Tip was training
for war.

On November 13th, 1939, Louise produced a son. Michael
Charles Tippett was born at Letterman Hospital in the Presidio in
San Francisco. Tip's family was bigger by almost seven pounds, and
Tip returned to duty on the base with cigars for all. The proud
parents sent a joint telegram to Louise's extended family in Southern
California and Tip's mother in Ohio.

> Baby gram:
> Weight 6 3/4 lbs., date 11-13-1939. Arrived safely. Dad
> and Mother very happy. Glad to say my name will be signed *Michael
> Charles*.
> A beautiful baby after a hard struggle - Louise in labor three
> days - finally had him. *Tip*.
> I am exhausted but we will all live on. He has a head full of
> dark red curls. Looks just like Tip. *Louise*.

Two days later, Tip was flying again. He took a Continental
Cub from California to an Air Corps base in Maryland, where he
flew their line-up of aircraft for several days. The Lockheed 12-A was
a change from his usual tour in the North American BC-1 "Texan"
or his beloved Boeing P-12s. The long range and carrying capacity of
the Lockheed made it a good choice for making the return flight to
California, and home.

The latter parts of my years of active duty at Hamilton Field were not only pleasant, but also instructive. Flying with Major Longfellow kept me from getting bored.

"Lieutenant," he said, on almost every flight, "there's never a time when you're flying that there isn't something to do."

Woe to the pilot with Major Longfellow in the co-pilot seat who didn't know to the second when he would be over his next checkpoint. The major monitored course, heading, altitude, radio contacts, manifold pressures, and time over checkpoints meticulously. This training saved my life many times in the flying years ahead.

Rumors were flying around the squadron that examinations for permanent commissions would be offered shortly. Insofar as the 88th was made up of about 40% reserve officers, everyone was prepping to take the exam. There was not one reserve officer in the squadron that did not apply for a permanent commission, but after the exams were taken, only one officer on the entire base was selected. None were chosen from the 88th squadron even though it had the most qualified flight group on the base and perhaps the entire Air Corps. All the pilots were rated in dead reckoning navigation, celestial navigation, and instrument flight on several different types of aircraft. I was not the only one who was disappointed.

Base Operations then advised us that representatives of Trans World Airlines (TWA), Pan American Airlines (PAA) and the Civil Aeronautics Administration (CAA), would be on the base to interview reserve officers for employment and my disappointment vanished. This was exactly what I had been preparing for. My first interview was with Pan American Airlines, who offered $225.00 per month ($3,326 today), four dollars more than I was making as a 2nd lieutenant, plus the promise that we could probably make captain in about fifteen years. PAA offered increases in $25.00 increments for

each rating you would get from them. As I already had the ratings, I
felt that I should start out with the increments. That was not to be,
so I moved on to TWA to see what they offered.

TWA was interested in me as a celestial navigation
instructor for their pilots. Accepting this position would have
kept me off their pilot seniority list until I was assigned to line
flying. We could not agree on this, although their pay was $250.00
a month to start ($3,395 today). The representative of the Civil
Aeronautics Administration had the most attractive offer. $6,800 a
year ($100,527 today) including use of an airplane and automobile
to cover my assigned territory. This would be after completing
a Special Agent course in Washington, which would take about
four months, including flight exams. After a family consultation, I
decided to consider the CAA job more seriously. It offered the best
future for a permanent job, which up to that time had evaded me.

With a wife and baby at home, Tip not only considered the
CAA job; he took steps to secure it. Once again, Louise's father,
Harry Hossack, came through. Using Washington connections built
through his work with the Reconstruction Finance Corporation,
Harry wrote letters of recommendation and introduction that
helped Tip compete for the position. The CAA job was not
exactly what Tip had envisioned when he planned for a career as
a commercial pilot, but since the CAA had only been created the
previous year, it hadn't been an option. In fact, Tip was ideally suited
for the job. He would be creating aviation training systems, which
he had been doing for years already, and establishing international
relations with allied countries. His personality, experience, and
inclinations were perfect for this task and Tip got the job.

Facing an unknown tenure in Washington D.C., Tip and
Louise decided that Louise would move in with her parents and Tip
would start his CAA job alone. The decision was not difficult. Louise
could choose to be bravely alone in a new city with a newborn

in her lap and a husband occupied for long hours in training, coursework, and overnight flying, or she could move in with her mother and father and share the effort of caring for infant Michael with delighted grandparents in a city she knew and loved.

Tip completed his assignment with the Eighty-Eight at Hamilton Field and returned to inactive duty in the reserves by December of 1939. Had he stayed longer at Hamilton Field, he may have been piloting one of the bombers quietly sent on a training run from Hamilton Field, California, to Pearl Harbor, Hawaii, on December 7, 1941. Tip's most frequently piloted ships, several Douglas BT-2B biplane bombers and at least one Douglas B-18 Bolo, were secretly dispatched on a flight from Oakland, California, to Wheeler Field, Hawaii, early in the morning of December 7. Navy craft were strategically placed on their route from the Hawaiian side to provide them with radio beacons to aid their navigation, but their arrival was not widely publicized, even inside naval circles.

The facilities at Pearl Harbor needed bomber aircraft and military leaders thought it prudent to stay quiet about the aircraft fleet stationed at Wheeler Field. The timing of the flight was totally coincidental to the attack on Pearl Harbor and the pilots had no idea what they were flying into. When the bombers came within range of Hawaii, they encountered what they assumed were escort aircraft, but which turned out to be Japanese fighter planes. Under heavy fire, the unarmed bombers desperately tried to evade the Japanese aircraft. The ships that didn't go flaming into the ocean had no easy time coming in for emergency landings. The bombers suffered friendly fire because they were unexpected and unrecognized. The fact that most of the aircraft made it to walk-away landings was testament to the training and skill of the exhausted and horrified pilots.

But that was two years in the future; at the end of 1939 Tip was relocating to Washington D.C. The civilian and diplomatic efforts underway at the time in Washington were intimately connected with military influences. Civilian work did not mean working for peace. Tip did not sever his connection with the Army Air Corps, a decision that was beneficial to both the army and to Tip. There was a real need for civilian activity that the military could cooperate with, and Tip was a perfect candidate.

The Washington experience was full of unexpected surprises. The Civil Aeronautics Association (CAA) class consisted of about twenty-five agent trainees, mostly army air corps, navy and marine reserve officers. Our classroom was housed in the Department of Commerce, in a room with barely enough space to move around. Mel Perrin, an old timer with the CAA, was our instructor and well versed in the trials and tribulations of new CAA inspectors.

Our classes covered such things as basic aviation law, inspection procedures, engine and airframe, management of CAA offices and office staff, flight-testing, communications, airport weather reporting, radio navigation, and beacons. Flight training standardization was carried out at a small grass strip field near Hyde Park, Maryland. The CAA had thoughtfully provided the trainees with a list of housing options. One option was a private home owned by Sally, whose husband was a WWI pilot and was killed in an air crash after the war. Two of us elected to rent a room at Sally's, which was comfortable and near enough to walk to class. There was a conglomerate of guests staying at the house. In the room across from me was the famous "Monk Hunter," ex WWI ace, and Lieutenant Bernie, later to become a four star general. Frequent visitors were Major "Tooey" Spaatz, Major Ira Eaker, and many of the early army air corps veterans who had served with Sally's husband.

It was not coincidence that brought Tip into contact with

these figures of legend from World War I; it was war. Britain was already engaged in an air war with Germany and appealing loudly for US aid. While the US Commander in Chief maintained a public policy of non-involvement, and polls showed that 85% of the public wanted to stay out of the conflict, the men with their hands on the machinery of war were wasting no time preparing for what they saw as the inevitable day when they would be called into action.

Every aviator with experience and skill was needed to build an effective fighting force out of a still relatively new technology. The surviving ace pilots of World War I were gathering in Washington, responding to quiet requests from politicians who were actively, if covertly, preparing for a US deployment on British soil. While Tip was starting his career with the newly formed CAA and attending orientation classes, these legends in aviation were organizing an attack and bombardment squadron which would be stationed in England less than two months after the attack on Pearl Harbor. These were to be the commanders and support staff for the Eighth Air Force, whose quick European deployment would only be possible because of the planning and organization that was taking place in the early weeks of January 1940.

Frank O'Driscoll "Monk" Hunter was forty-five years old when Tip roomed across from him at Sally's in Washington D.C. Hunter had joined the Air Service in 1917 and had stayed active in the army after distinguishing himself with aviation combat victories in World War I. He would attain the rank of major general and command the Eighth Air Force in England.

Major Carl Andrew "Tooey" Spaatz was forty-nine years old and about to be promoted to colonel. He had European experience in both combat and organization. At the time Tip met Major Spaatz in the hallways at Sally's, Tooey ranked high in the office of the Chief of Air Corps and was just weeks away from traveling to England as a special military observer. General Spaatz would be involved in the highest levels of the Air Force throughout the war, and would be instrumental in the atomic bombing of Japan.

Major Ira C. Eaker would begin the war as second in command of the Eighth Air Force in Britain, but would join the ranks of unit commanders before long. He was a gifted strategist and credited with the plan of targeted bombing raids aimed at the enemy's war infrastructure, which was intended to reduce the impact on civilians and civilian structures. The British preferred to stage their bombing raids by night, which reduced their pilot losses, but also their accuracy, when they dropped the bombs. It was Major Eaker who convinced Winston Churchill to work the British and American forces in concert with the Americans flying precision daylight missions and the British continuing their night bombing runs. The daylight bombing strategy was applauded during the war, but called into question by historians afterward, as they counted the enormous loss of pilots and aircraft. Eaker's intended legacy of avoiding non-civilian bombing was also compromised as the war progressed, but at the time that Tip met him, Major Eaker had a plan he still believed in. He would become four-star General Eaker; he had a degree in journalism, and wrote several books about wartime aviation.

At the time of Tip's rooming house experience, the situation in Britain had become very bleak. France fell to Hitler's army in June 1940, while the United States was still officially uninvolved. China was totally absorbed fighting a war with Japan, and the Soviet Union was concerned about an invasion by Germany and unavailable for any kind of support. Britain faced the German air onslaught alone, and even after narrowly avoiding aerial defeat in August and September 1940, suffered under the unending pounding known as the London Blitz. The German Luftwaffe bombed London and other parts of England day and night for eight months. Germany claimed to be targeting war-related command and manufacturing centers, but in fact, the bombing was indiscriminate and unpredictable. More than 40,000 people were killed, and the citizen population of London took to sleeping at night in subway tunnels and any deep basement available.

Now that aviation had proven to be much more than simply an observation support platform, every major government of the world was developing an air force. Japan had been the first to use aircraft for attack purposes, and their invasion of China had hinged on the strategic offensive use of aircraft. Now Germany was executing an all-out demoralization and destruction campaign, having expected to defeat Britain with air strikes alone. Germany, supported through treaty by both Italy and Japan, and for the moment, Russia, felt invincible and sent wave after wave of bombing runs against England. In Washington D.C., the politicians debated and waited, but the aviators organized. Tip, in the meantime, did what he had been doing since he was sixteen years old. He found a way to fly.

Chapter Seven

1940

The Civil Aeronautics Administration,

Washington D.C.

As we were CAA *trainee* inspectors and not yet graduated, we were only permitted to fly the agency training planes on local flights. Most of our Saturdays and Sundays were spent at the airport going through standardization maneuvers. Our check pilot was the former head of the Cuban Air Force, Len Povey. He was an American hired by President Batista to form and train a proper air force for Cuba. He was a famed acrobatic pilot and the inventor of the maneuver "the Cuban Eight." We all enjoyed our flights with him. I had met Povey in Ohio when we were flying air shows with Joe Mackey's "Linco Flying Aces."

Upon completion of our two months of classes and flight courses, our graduation exercises were held in the little room at "Perrin' Prep." We all waited to hear what our assignments would be; large offices, small offices, Hawaii, Europe, etc. When my name was finally called, I was told that I was to remain in Washington as the senior check pilot for the next inspector class, replacing Len Povey, who was moving on. Although this assignment did not particularly intrigue me, it did entail a great deal of flying and an opportunity to know all the new inspectors being fielded.

One morning, I was called by a senior member of the accident investigation board to inquire if I had ever flown the Boeing P-12. Apparently, the navy had given the Civil Aeronautics Board (CAB) three Boeing F4B-4s (the navy version) and none of their pilots had flown the stubby little bird. In fact, several pilots had stated that they had no interest in flying it. The ensuing weeks were pure joy. I had three Boeings to fly at my leisure. They were based at Anacostia, across the river from the (now) National Airport, and although it was February flying, in the heavy leather winter flight pants and jackets, it was great fun to be flying the little rascals again.

Leonard James Povey was thirty-six when Tip worked with him as a CAA trainee inspector. Povey had caught the attention of a delegation of Cuban representatives during an airshow in Florida in 1934. They liked his daring and skill enough to bring him to the attention of Cuban President Fulgencio Batista y Zaldivar, who was on good terms with the United States and interested in building an air force. When Povey returned to the US after successfully completing his work in Cuba, he became involved in the CAA. Stunt flying had brought Len Povey into civil aviation as if on a crosswind, and he remained at the forefront of aviation for the rest of his life, eventually joining Joe Mackey's airline as Executive Vice-President.

Tip's delight in flying the Boeing P-12 was unique among civil pilots of his day. The powerful little biplane was already obsolete as a fighter and other aircraft were readily available that did not have such challenging responsiveness. Pilots who flew the P-12 successfully loved it, but the ship was not for everyone. The navy had been using it as a bomber and fighter, capitalizing on its size and performance by giving it a hook so it could use the cable arrestor system on aircraft carriers. The plane was being moved out of military use and inventories began to build up in out-of-the-way

places. The air corps was leaving them in training hangars across
the country, and Tip was finding plenty of opportunity to enjoy
flying the aircraft. By 1940, the plane was almost at the end of its
deployment. It would not be like the Curtiss Jenny and become the
staple of private hobby fliers. The engine it carried was oversized
for the weight and size of the aircraft, which was exactly what
Tip, and the military, liked best about it. It was deceptively robust
and maneuverable, despite being an outmoded biplane with non-
retractable landing gear. Tip's skillful delight in flying the P-12 ensured
that he had an aircraft at almost every airfield he visited, since the
P-12 was invariably the last airplane of choice for most of the other
pilots in these civil aviation organizations.

In 1940, President Roosevelt was in his final year in office
and faced the decision of whether to run for an unprecedented
third term. He was conflicted over the idea, and the nation was
divided between the desire for an experienced leader with
established international relationships in this time of impending war
and economic depression, or the fear that America was headed for
dictatorship.

Running on a promise of "no foreign wars," Roosevelt was
elected to his third term in office by 55% of the popular vote. He
was the first and only American president to serve more than eight
consecutive years in office. The passage of the second amendment
in 1947, limiting presidential service to two four-year terms,
ensured that he would remain so. Despite his public stance of non-
involvement in the deepening world war, Roosevelt was conducting
secret meetings with the newly-elected British Prime Minister
Winston Churchill, who was as warlike a leader as Britain could have
wanted.

Civil aviation was poised to support the military effort.
Commercial airline companies were increasing their flight ranges
and capacity, and sport flying was fueling small industries full
of innovative designs and breakthroughs. In March of 1940, the

US government quietly granted permission for private aircraft manufacturers to sell combat airplanes to any country supporting Allied powers. In his work with the Civil Aviation Administration, Tip was establishing a network of affiliations and personal relationships with important leaders in aviation. These connections would aid him in his future work, but they were also a natural extension of Tip's manner and the development of his career. He was moving into a theater of operations that, quietly and behind closed doors, was as involved with the coming conflict as was the military. Tip was already involved with the Civil Pilot Training Program for the CAA, which began in 1938 and was, on the surface, a way to standardize the training given to civilian pilots throughout the country. It was also an initial preparation for young pilots who would then be able to apply for military service, ensuring a ready supply of pilots for an increasing supply of military aircraft.

At the end of the third class to graduate from my Senior Check Pilot instruction, I requested reassignment as my family had not moved to Washington, and could not, because of the temporary nature of the job. My request was approved and I was assigned to the CAA office in Atlanta, Georgia. Our chief there was Bill Robertson, an old hand with the CAA and a great guy. As they were short-handed in the southern region, I only remained in Atlanta for about a month, learning the ropes and finding out about the region in general. I was assigned a Fairchild PT-19 for flight travel, a Chevrolet for driving, and put in charge of the Birmingham, Alabama, office with a staff of one secretary.

Louise arrived in Birmingham with our young son, Michael, and we immediately rented a house near the airport. She proceeded to put the place in order while my days were filled with flight tests, airplane inspections, engine inspections, and making up itineraries to visit towns, cities, and flight schools in my area. The Civil Pilot Training Program (CPTP) had just been started wherein every flight instructor in the United States had to be re-rated for his instructor's license to be valid. Fred Easly, an ex-army air corps pilot, and myself were put in charge of this program in the southern region.

To my intense pleasure, I learned that the Army Air Corps Reserve base in Atlanta had about ten Boeing P-12s for reserve officers to fly. As most of the reserve officers in the Atlanta area flew for the airlines and had no military experience, the ships were not being flown because the risk of crashing one of these powerful little planes was not worth the effort of trying to check out in one. I once again had a fleet of the little pursuit planes to fly as I pleased. After I spent an afternoon flying two of the ships to put time on them, the major in charge of the reserve center suggested that I draw a P-12 and fly it back to Birmingham for my travel use. I would be doing him a favor, as he had to have the ships flying to justify their existence in Atlanta, and I would be the center of attention at my flight test center, flying in a P-12, which many people had seen pictures of but never one "in the flesh."

Tip was transitioning from Army Air Corps military flying, and its commensurate access to some of the most exciting planes from the late 1930s, to civil flight. His flight experience had already encompassed more than sixty different ships, from the Curtiss JN4 to the Seversky P-35, and everything with wings in between. His continued access to the P-12 was a joyful balance to the slower, more stable, workhorse aircraft of civil aviation. But even though the more common airplanes were less glamorous, they were still important to Tip. Flying, in any form, was his personal mission and now he was able to incorporate his dedication to safety with his working life. In the course of his work for the CAA, Tip flew a long line of civil aircraft. The day before his twenty-seventh birthday, Tip piloted a Stinson Voyager 105 on a private flight test. He climbed back into a biplane trainer, taking a Verville Continental A-70 up with another private student trying for certification under the new rules for civilian flight. In March 1940, Tip took up a Luscombe Model 8, and the next day, an Aeronca Chief. Later that week, he checked out a pilot in a Travel Air 6000 B.

My Birmingham office was responsible for a myriad of projects. Flight schools were springing up all over the region and had to be certified. An occasional airline pilot rating had to be given, requiring most of an afternoon or morning. Violations had to be investigated and written up. Examinations had to be given at all state and private universities in the region for the Civil Pilot Training Program. The work and the flying were never ending.

We were having increasing problems with Eastern and Delta Airlines flying into our airport during instrument conditions. The normal procedure was for the Birmingham airport manager to call Atlanta and advise on the state of the weather. On this particular morning, the airport was completely fogged in, so I closed the airport to all traffic and reported that news to the airlines flying in from Atlanta. Eastern Airlines pilot, Paul Woolley, ignored the closing and landed practically blind. The first thing he and his co-pilot saw through his cockpit windshield was the hangar line and my airplane parked in front of my office. He ground looped the DC-3, knocked out two obstruction lights, missed hitting my plane by inches, and ended up with his wingtip a couple of feet from my office door. I walked out of my office and looked up at the cockpit where Woolley was peering out of the window.

"The administration building is down there," I said.

"Many thanks!" he replied and taxied away.

He later appeared in my office and picked up his violation report saying that he had not received the news that the airport was closed. About twenty minutes later, a Delta Lockheed 10 thumped down in the middle of the field and the first thing that pilot saw was the DC-3 and the administration building. He jammed on his brakes and went up on his nose and stayed there. There were no injuries to passengers or crew, other than another pilot showing up in my office to pick up his violation report on behalf of Delta Airlines.

One of the town notables had been bugging me for a ride in the Fairchild PT-19 and asked if I would do a loop with him as he had never done any aerobatics in an aircraft before. I had planned a ten-minute ride and as I did the loop with him, I threw in a snap roll for good measure. When the plane came out of the snap roll, the rudder was jammed full right and I could not release it. The airplane was on the verge of a stall with full power and it was almost impossible to hold a straight level wing-up attitude. Having no radio and fighting to keep the aircraft flying, I thought of ordering my passenger to bail out in his parachute, which would give me a bit more time to save the aircraft and, more importantly, discover why the rudder had jammed. I quickly discounted this as impractical, as my passenger did not seem to be the type to jump out of the aircraft and pull a ripcord. I was not able to determine the cause of the jam, but I could see that the rudder pedal itself was jammed full right, so the problem had to be between the rudder pedal and the floorboard. Unfortunately, I could not delve into the cockpit to see if the pedal could be released, as the aircraft demanded my full attention.

By this time, I was confident that I could keep the aircraft from stalling and spinning by keeping the right wing low. I felt that if I could approach the runway in this position, and at the last minute try to level the wings for a touchdown, we had a chance to land safely even though we would be at almost full throttle. Minutes later, we were down and my passenger walked away, pleased with his ride and ignorant of the close call. He thought that flying around with one wing low was great fun and provided a marvelous view.

I immediately investigated the ship and found that the cause of the jam was the cover on the rudder. It extended just below the floorboards and with the right amount of twist and pressure; the

cover would come over and catch on the floorboard itself. When
I came out of the snap roll, my foot was high on the right top of
the pedal, instead of being squarely on the rudder pedal. With my
twisting movement, the rudder guard extended over the floorboard
and locked itself. Due to the pressure on the rudder from the
slipstream, it was impossible to disengage the rudder cover in flight.

As soon as I determined that this could happen again, I
tried, successfully, to jam it on the ground and called the Atlanta
office to report my findings. They asked me to call the Fairchild
factory right away, which I did. I spoke to Fairchild's chief test pilot,
Dick Hensen. He held me on the phone until he and one of the
engineers succeeded in jamming the rudder themselves. Immediately
a grounding order went out to every training school and military
operation that was flying Fairchild PT-19s. Engineers worked to
remove the rudder covers inside the cockpit and when this was
done, the ships were released for flying. There had been several
fatal accidents in training with this ship, especially in and during
spin recoveries, and it was felt that the rudder jam was the probable
cause.

One of our most troublesome areas at that time was
the crop-dusting aircraft flying near Jackson, Mississippi. Finklea
Brothers, a local crop dusting and aircraft repair organization,
were known violators of practically every regulation in the book. I
was assigned the task of bringing them to justice in whatever way
possible. I was told that their private landing strip and hangar was
a fortress, and they had been known to shoot at trespassers. I flew
to Jackson to confer with the inspector in charge, Jim Shipp, as to
what course of action I should take. He advised that their standard
violation was constantly flying their ships at night into their landing
strip, which put them directly over a designated airway. The only way
to catch them would be to sneak onto their strip and wait for them.

For two successive nights, I lay along the riverbank adjacent to their landing strip waiting for some action. Finally, at about nine p.m., three of their crop dusters landed without lights, one after another, and taxied to the hangar. The pilots filed out the front of the hangar and I handed each of them a federal violation ordering them to appear in court. The meeting was a bit tense for a moment, while I also advised them that I would be at the hangar at nine a.m. to run a shop inspection on their crop-dusting aircraft for licensing compliance. The next morning, the brothers were at the hangar waiting my arrival. They had one ship in overhaul. One of the wing panels had just been re-covered and the others were already installed. I inspected and passed the wing panel that they had just re-covered, and punched holes in the newly installed lower panel where the wing covering had rotted. By this time, it was noon and the Finkleas suggested lunch at a small restaurant a couple of miles away. They spent the lunch hour expressing their hope that I would rescind the night-flying violations, as they were all first offenders. I explained that it was the first time they had been issued a violation, but that they were reportedly continually in violation.

We returned to the hangar for the final inspection of the aircraft that was being assembled. They produced a wing saying that it was the replacement wing for the one I turned down in the morning. On close inspection, I found it was the same wing I had approved, and it had been taken off during lunchtime and placed on another ship. Needless to say, the ship was not re-licensed and I issued another violation. Although it took about a year, eventually repeated violations, shoddy work, and accidents finally put the Finkleas out of the aircraft repair business.

Tip felt that the most important aspect of work in civil aviation was in creating and enforcing safe practices. Although he had learned to fly in the early days of freedom, he had also seen the fatal consequences of inadequate training, poor maintenance, or confused communication. Tip flew safely and required all pilots he trained to do the same. If he took a risk in the air, it was based on his hours of experience, the conditions, and the purpose of the flight. For Tip, there was great satisfaction in completing his duties well. He was seeing progress in every aspect of his CAA duties, and making a name for himself in the world of aviation safety.

For Louise, at home with baby Michael, who was not yet one year old, Alabama was an odd place. Segregation was a fact of life in 1940, but black America was beginning to push back and there was racial unrest throughout Birmingham. Tip's duties as an aviation lawman kept Louise awake at night, and the couple acquired a serious-minded companion, a Doberman Pinscher, who was a formidable guard dog and devoted to Louise and the baby. Domestic life in Alabama at the time would not have included many of the modern conveniences that even the apartment in San Francisco may have had. Louise's days were spent housekeeping and mothering in true Southern tradition, from scratch and by hand.

While Tip and Louise were fighting their own respective battles for aviation safety and domestic tranquility, England was fighting the biggest air battle in aviation history. The Battle of Britain, in late summer and early fall of 1940, was the German Luftwaffe's attempt to smash the British Royal Air Force (RAF) prior to Hitler's planned invasion of the British coast. The London Blitz had taken a toll on life and property, but the Battle of Britain was even worse. The resistance from the RAF unpleasantly surprised the Luftwaffe, and the British proved that organization counts even in the face of an aggressive, well-equipped enemy. Hitler and Goering, commander-in-chief of the Luftwaffe, had expected an easy win, but the battle didn't go their way.

Since Britain refused to surrender after the fall of France, Hitler ordered that the British homeland be battered. Attack by sea was unfeasible because the German Navy, already inferior to the Royal Navy, had been damaged in its campaign against Norway.

Thus an air war was the next best plan. German aircraft began with attacks on English Channel convoys, then followed with sustained bombing attacks on British airfields, but as their campaign continued, they extended their targeting to aircraft manufacturing plants, ground support locations, and finally, to indiscriminate bombing of cities.

As Charles Lindbergh had so unpopularly maintained, German aircraft design and manufacturing were significantly advanced. While the Allies also had fast, agile aircraft and enormous manufacturing ability, British pilots were in short supply and had less combat experience overall than their German adversaries. If it had not been for the progress in radar science, the Germans might have won the 1940 air war. The British network of radar installations along their channel coast gave them a much-needed advantage against approaching German bombers. The early warning enabled them to scramble an air defense and sound the air raid sirens in populated areas. Germany ultimately responded to the British radar network with an almost successful attempt at the first jet-engine pseudo-stealth fighter, called the Horton 229. Named after the brothers that designed it, the plane would have been able to reach British targets so quickly that the Allies would not have had time to respond, even if they had been able to recognize it on radar. But progress on its design and manufacture was too slow to make a difference in the war. Meanwhile Britain still refused to surrender, and while unofficial aid and support from defeated but resisting nations helped, the country was becoming exhausted.

Back in Alabama, Louise suffered a terrible loss. On October 22, 1940, while Tip was flying multiple instruction flights, Louise's mother died in San Francisco. Louise Lines Hossack was in her mid-sixties when she died. If she had been thirty-five years old when she had Louise, as reported on Louise's birth certificate, or even if she had been five years older, as rumored by family, Love was still not yet seventy. Her death was unexpected and Louise was only twenty-six. Baby Michael was one month from his first birthday and Louise's only consolation was that her mother had been able to spend time with him in his early months. There is no record of whether Louise travelled back to California for her mother's funeral, and Tip's pilot's log shows no west coast flights. Louise dealt with her grief by herself.

At that time, as Tip pursued his instructor duties, he noticed that the local Alabama National Guard had aircraft parked on their field that were seldom flown. Always looking for opportunities to broaden his flight experience, Tip completed National Guard admission paperwork and joined the 106th Observation Squadron in the Alabama National Guard. He easily qualified for their flight certificates and rank as second lieutenant, same as he held in the Army Reserve.

The Alabama National Guard was based at the Birmingham airport with an aircraft inventory of eleven new North American O-47B aircraft, but only five pilots on their roster. They were local commercial pilots who had gotten a National Guard commission. The O-47B was a monstrous machine, with a thousand-horsepower engine. It was a big potbelly observation plane that operated with the pilot sitting forward and two other crew members in tandem behind. At that time, it was the fastest aircraft in the inventory and cruised at two hundred miles per hour with a tremendous range. The National Guard commander kindly invited me, as an Army Air Corps Reserve officer, to fly with the guard as I had military experience that could be useful to them. Between the National Guard and the CAA, I was flying over one hundred hours a month.

The Civil Pilot Training Program had grown out of proportion to the number of qualified inspectors. It, and the instructor re-rating program, kept all inspectors flying practically day and night. The need for new, well-trained inspectors had become critical, and Washington was toying with the idea of setting up an inspector standardization training center in Houston, Texas. The center would train new inspectors and standardize current ones, so that everyone in the field was standard in their procedures. Much to my surprise, I received a call from my chief, Bill Robertson, in Atlanta requesting that I fly in to report to his office the following day.

Fred Easly, one of our top inspectors and my re-rating partner, was also in Robertson's office when I arrived. The reason for the meeting was that Washington wished to transfer me to the new Houston Standardization Center as Chief of the Advanced Flight Section, and the move was to take place immediately. Easly was to head the primary flight section. Bennett Griffin, a former World War I pilot and an old time car-man, was to be the director.

Tip returned to Birmingham and the family began to pack for Texas, but before the move, he had one last important job. The Civil Pilot Training Program was only a year old and several colleges and universities had quickly applied for access to the government-funded program because it allowed them to offer pilot training to their students. The schools saw every advantage to sponsored training and one university in particular had a dream.

Aviation had its class distinctions. The British considered it the exclusive purview of the elite upper class, and therefore suffered in 1940 from a shortage of pilots as the high death and injury toll decimated its aristocratic ranks. Aviation training was available for the British working class, but British officer appointments were still a closed rank. The RAF drew on pilots from the colonies to fill cockpits during the Battle of Britain, and took a hit because their experience level was lower than that of the German pilots.

American record-setters were primarily educated white men, with the rare, much-celebrated white woman. By advertising the funding for the Civil Pilot Training Program at specific higher education locations, the government had increased the likelihood that the ranks of future pilots would continue to be made up of educated white men. But in February 1941, Alabama's black leadership was ready for change and dedicated to taking full advantage of this new civilian aviation opportunity.

One morning, I received a call at my Birmingham office from our boss, Bill Robertson, in Atlanta asking if I would fly over to Tuskegee, Alabama, and flight test a group of students who were engaged in the Civil Pilot Training Program at the Tuskegee Institute. Tuskegee should have been under the Jackson, Mississippi office.

"Why me?" I asked.

"All the Tuskegee students are blacks," Robertson said, "And none of my Southern inspectors will ride with them."

"Bill, I can't believe what you are telling me!" I said.

"It's true," he said, "You'll get a call from the Chief in Washington officially asking you to do this."

Within twenty minutes, I received a call from Fred Lanter, our Chief in Washington. He asked if I had any qualms about flight-testing the Tuskegee students. He said that it was a really hot political issue and I would be doing a great service if I would fly over there and give them their written exams and their flight tests, as they were now two weeks overdue. I assured Lanter that I had no qualms about flying with the black students, but that they would have to meet the same standards that all my students met or no license. Lanter agreed and I said would I fly over there as soon as possible. Fortunately, I had a P-12 in Birmingham at the time and arranged to fly over to Tuskegee to first discuss giving the written exams, then return another time to give flight tests to those who passed the written and oral exams.

The landing at Tuskegee was a grass strip about 1200 feet in length. I flew low over the strip a couple of times to be certain that it was clear, landed out of a side slip, and taxied to the one hangar on the field. There could have been no more excitement created by my arrival than if I had flown in without an airplane. None of the students had ever seen a Boeing P-12 close up, let alone have one land in front of them. I got out of the cockpit and was surprised that no one came out to the ship to meet me. Finally, an elderly gentleman with two black men accompanying him walked to the plane where I was getting out of my heavy flying clothes. He walked up to me.

"Welcome!" he said, "I am Dr. George Washington Carver, and this is Dr. George Washington, and Dr. Jones."

I had read about this famous educator and scientist, discoverer of peanut oil and many other things. Dr. Carver invited me to his office at the university and in the company of the other two black leaders, we discussed the questions and problems at the Tuskegee flight program. Dr. Carver and Dr. George Washington pointed out how important this program was to the institute, and how the outcome of these flight tests would be watched by the entire country. I assured Dr. Carver that they would have my full cooperation in the forthcoming flight and written examinations, and we set the following week as a deadline for the exams. I was escorted to my plane and after a couple of high speed (160 mph) flybys and a slow roll, was off to return to Birmingham.

The following week I returned and conducted the written examinations for a class of about forty students. I personally remained in the room during the test to be certain that no discrepancies occurred. I returned to Birmingham that night with the examinations. Much to my surprise, Tuskegee had passed the exams with the highest overall grade of any university in the US.

I telephoned an elated Dr. Carver with the good news that his students had passed with just over a 97% average. We scheduled the flight tests to begin the following day, and Dr. Carver invited me to stay overnight in their unfinished girls dormitory. The next day, the students all failed their flight tests and I realized that to continue as usual was foolish. They were so nervous that on two occasions I returned to the hangar without taking off. That night, I conferred with Dr. Washington and we agreed that I would stay for a day or two more and fly with the students as an instructor, rather than an inspector, in an effort to relieve their tensions.

Dr. Carver was very appreciative of this suggestion. I had the Boeing P-12 parked on their hangar line and invited several students to sit in the cockpit and have their pictures taken, which they were anxious to do. We relaxed and got acquainted, and after awhile, I found them to be joking about their role in military aviation, suggesting that when their squadron was formed, the airplanes would be painted black and fly at night so that no-one could see them. Ironically, the first all-black military squadron was in fact a night fighter squadron, flying Northrop two-seat fighter/reconnaissance aircraft.

I flew with one or two of the students the next morning and we went through the entire private pilot exam without a hitch. When we landed, I issued them their private certificates. From then on, the tests went much better. The students were relaxed and about eighty percent passed their flight tests, which was about average for any university student in the country. I am happy to say that this group was the foundation of the 99th Fighter Squadron and produced one four-star Air Corps general.

These students, and others with them, went on to become the Tuskegee Airmen, the first all-black squadron in the US Army Air Corps. The students took their civil pilot training certificates to the Tuskegee Army Air Field one year later and enlisted. Recent legislation in Washington D.C. had forced the reluctant US Army to make room for black recruits. The Army Air Corps had responded by creating high educational and pilot certification standards that they hadn't really expected the squadron to meet. But black leaders both in Washington and in Alabama had seen their chance and applied every effort to meeting those standards and gaining the foothold the legislation had offered.

Dr. George Washington Carver was seventy-six years old when Tip met him on the airstrip in Alabama. He had been teaching agriculture at the Tuskegee Institute for more than forty-seven years. Dr. Carver had made enormous contributions to sustainable agriculture, motivated primarily by his desire to see African American former slaves establish themselves as self sufficient, successful farmers. With his intense involvement in the American inter-racial cooperation movement, he was instrumental in bringing the pilot training program to the Tuskegee Institute, and was personally dedicated to its success. He lived long enough to see the establishment of the Tuskegee Airmen before his death in 1943.

Tuskegee's strategy in positioning itself to take full advantage of military positions for black airmen was only the beginning of their racial battle. The segregated unit posed logistical difficulties for the Army Air Corps in all of the support positions necessary for a functioning, yet segregated, squadron. There were no black doctors in the US military at that time, and so the army had to open its doors to enough black medical personnel to support the 99th Squadron. One enlistment at a time, the racial barriers in the military were being broken down, but the effort was tremendous. The black military men often felt they were fighting two wars, one for the world against the enemy Axis powers, and one for their race against bigotry and injustice inside their barrack walls.

The creation of this squadron of black pilots started a cascade of consequences that arguably accelerated the cause of racial integration. The Army Air Corps had already begun to apply psychological evaluation and testing methods to pilot training programs in an attempt to identify suitable pilots before they got into the cockpits of expensive air craft. They were using some of the first tests designed to evaluate IQ and personality. Most importantly, the results were standardized. These tests were applied to all units, including the new black squadron, and the results tallied regardless of race or geographical background. These test results were a direct blow to the fundamental assertions of segregationists, who held that black men were less intelligent or less capable than white men.

By 1947, seven years in the future, all white units throughout the army would be running short on qualified, trained support personnel and unable to pull from the growing numbers of proficient and capable black personnel because of the policy of segregation. President Harry Truman had the power to order equal opportunity within the armed forces because of his position as Commander in Chief, although he could not order such an action throughout the rest of America. In 1948, he enacted an order that abolished segregation in the military, an action that is considered to be the first step towards the end of segregation in America. But segregation would not be legally outlawed in America until 1957, seventeen years from the time that Tip certified the Tuskegee civil pilot training participants.

The Tuskegee Institute, and Dr. George Washington Carver, had made a start. One of the newly certified civil pilots watching Tip fly away was Daniel "Chappie" James Jr. He was twenty years old when Tip awarded him his civil pilot training certificate on the Alabama airfield. He would graduate from the Tuskegee Institute, join the army, and begin a distinguished Air Corps career with a tour as an instructor for pilots of the 99th Pursuit Squadron. In 1975, he would be the first African American to be awarded the rank of four-star general.

Chapter Eight

1941 to 1942

The Houston Standardization Center
Houston, Texas

Once again back in Birmingham from Tuskegee, Tip discovered that active duty orders had come through from his Army Air Corps Reserve commanders. These orders threatened his upcoming work for the CAA and his new posting to the Houston Standardization Center in Texas. In addition, both the Army Reserve and CAA anticipated movement on the part of the government to federalize the National Guard, making personnel and resources available to the military in case of war. Tip was asked to begin the paperwork to resign his National Guard commission. He had originally joined the Alabama National Guard to access the range of aircraft on the National Guard airfield and to boost the ranks of pilots. Now that Tip was fully engaged and moving up in civil aviation, his hands were full helping the country prepare for war and domestic aviation success. He had no time to work for the National Guard as well.

Tip's superiors in the CAA in Washington jockeyed with their Army Reserve counterparts to have his active duty orders rescinded, and he breathed a sign of relief when their efforts were

CORINNE TIPPETT

successful. Tip, Louise, baby Michael, and the Doberman finally
headed west for Texas in May 1941. At twenty-seven, Tip was about
to become Senior Advanced Flight Instructor at the Civil Aviation
Administration's Standardization Center. He would be at the heart
of the civil aviation movement. The job description for Senior
Advanced Flight Instructor CAF-12 at the Standardization Center,
Flight Branch, Advanced Flight Section was spelled out in five parts:

"...Under the general direction of the chief, Flight Branch,
with wide latitude for the exercise of independent judgment and
action.... Plans, develops, directs, and personally conducts courses of
instruction... demonstrates to subject flight personnel, while flying
Civil Aeronautics Administration aircraft of all categories, the various
standardized advanced and acrobatic flight maneuvers required...
prepares reports certifying that the subject flight personnel meet
the standards required... makes suggestions and recommendations
as to changes in the advanced flight standards which will increase
the efficiency of the operation..."

Suitable housing in the form of a small ranch-type property
near the airport was leased and the family moved in, complete with
the new dog. The center was staffed with a myriad of CAA experts
who acted as instructors in their fields. Everyone coming to the
Center had to start from scratch, from primary flight maneuvers
through acrobatics and instrument flight. We had two Lockheed
aircraft for the flight training. One was a Lockheed 10 and the other
a Lockheed 12. We had the only government-owned DC-3 at that
time, and one Stinson 450 hp Gull Wing for instrument training.
There were also three PT-19 primary trainers and one Boeing 247
airliner.

The training at the center was severe and purposeful. The
Army Air Corps requested ten students who had finished their
advanced training at Randolph Field to be trained as co-pilots to be
sent to fly "The Hump" in China. Crews were critical and needed

great skill to fly the weather that they encountered on this run. We also received several foreign students that were to be trained to go back to their country and retrain their instructors. (These foreign students were to have a profound bearing on my future, as it turned out).

"Flying the Hump" in China in 1941 meant navigating a dangerous and arduous 530-mile air route over the Himalaya Mountains from India into the Chinese mainland. Hundreds of men and aircraft would be lost to this effort by the end of the war in China. It was no pilot's first choice as a flight plan. Five years earlier, in California, Tip had trained some of the very first pilots to fly against Japanese bombers on the behalf of the Chinese well before they were officially sanctioned. During the intervening five years, China had fought to keep Japan from the interior, but failed to push Japan out of Chinese territories. Now Tip was once again training members of the American Volunteer Group, who were still considered civilian mercenaries, but were beginning to have solid political backing. Once they took to the air in China, they would come to be known as the Flying Tigers. The dangerous route was necessary because Japan still controlled China's Pacific coastline by air and sea.

Flying over the Himalaya Mountains challenged every piloting skill, regardless of experience. Navigation was critical because getting lost was a death sentence. The aircraft were heavily loaded, large commercial planes, often carrying gasoline or troops for the Chinese army. The organization that pioneered the route, the China National Aviation Corporation (CNAC), was credited with being efficient and skilled, and along with the Flying Tigers, made a critical effort against the Japanese to turn them out of the Chinese mainland. But flight over the tallest mountain range in the world never became routine. It was incredibly difficult.

Lighting-laced thunderstorms, headwinds, icing, and extreme

turbulence that could develop without warning were normal conditions regardless of the season. The Indian monsoons were something American pilots had never encountered before. Pilots flew in constant rain and zero visibility to landings on flooded runways. There were frequent crashes, and the toll it took on pilots and crews guaranteed a constant need for replacements from the US. Winter brought more stable conditions to India and Burma, but also deep cold, ice, and snow on the Chinese side. Pilots flew at the height of Mount Everest and fought the hurricane-force winds that were common at that altitude. The losses were tremendous for every nation that flew The Hump, whether Chinese, American, or other Allied powers.

To meet the need for a variety of aircraft standardization protocols, the CAA center had plenty of aircraft and Tip kept busy in all of them. The Douglas DC-3 at the CAA Center in Houston in 1941 was the first one owned directly by the government. Tip, at age twenty-eight, was the first and only pilot in government employ certified to fly the DC-3 at the time. It was a tremendously reliable plane, with the capacity to carry more than thirty passengers, and it required both pilot and co-pilot. It had a range of one thousand miles and could fly at 24,000 feet and speeds of 150 miles an hour.

The Lockheed 10 (Electra) was the same type of aircraft that Amelia Earhart was flying when she disappeared over the Pacific. It was also a dual-engine, metal-skinned plane and while faster than the DC-3, it could take only ten passengers and had less range. The Lockheed 12 carried six passengers, and The Stinson Gull wing was smaller still. These were the workhorse aircraft of civil aviation at the time and thus were the aircraft available for training and certification at the center.

The Boeing 247D was making passenger flights all over the country. It was the model of aircraft that had crashed on Lone Peak in Utah the day before Tip could interview for the copilot job with Western Air Express in 1936. He was now flying it in the role of instructor. A smaller plane, the single-engine Howard DGA-15, was prized as an instrument trainer, and Tip enjoyed its executive style as he certified students in Instrument Flight Rules (IFR). The Center also had the Stearman trainer and Fairchild trainer, and Tip was familiar with both.

Tip was kept frenetically busy with his duties as Senior Advanced Flight Instructor. The requirement for all pilots coming through the center to be re-certified from scratch ensured that the resulting CAA certification promised thoroughly-trained pilots, but carrying out the mission was a tall order for Tip and the other personnel. Tip was rarely at home during this time, and then only to sleep. Michael was now a year and a half old and Louise was once again tasked with creating a home in a semi-rural area whose main attraction was its proximity to the airport. At some point during the move, Louise discovered that she was once again expecting a baby. This was encouraging news for Louise in her role as homemaker and mother, and in a way, matched Tip's progress in his work. But, several months into the pregnancy, Louise miscarried. Again, she handled the event and its emotional aftermath in isolation, far from both her family and friends. Louise's cousin, Mary Jane, who was as close as a sister to her in childhood, wrote later that Louise "handled it very well." Louise wanted a Christmas with family and so Tip and Louise embarked on a driving trip from Houston to California in the first week of December.

On December 7, 1941, my wife and I were driving to spend a week in San Francisco with her father. Immediately upon hearing of the Japanese attack on Pearl Harbor, I called the Houston center and was told to continue my leave, but call in every day as they expected orders as soon as the picture cleared. I returned to Houston after ten days' leave and continued our inspector and co-pilot training for the military.

Early on Sunday morning, December 7, 1941, Japanese aircraft began a surprise bombing and strafing attack on the US Pacific Fleet that was moored in Pearl Harbor, near Tip's first Army Air Corps assignment at Wheeler Field, Hawaii. The Japanese had intended the attack to cripple America's fleet enough to keep them from interfering with a planned Japanese expansion into Asia and the Pacific, but it had the opposite effect. The devastating damage on American soil blazed away American isolationist attitudes. The US military was ready, and mobilized into combat weeks after the Japanese attack. Plans that had been in process behind closed doors were now openly discussed.

Once again, aviation had been the means to deliver a turning point in the war. The air attack on Pearl Harbor delivered devastation by surprise, something no naval or ground-based troop offensive could have done as effectively. And similarly to the Battle of Britain, and Japan's original air attack on China, a plan that had looked good in the planning stage failed to accomplish the intended goal. Japan expected to remove the United States as a threat in the Pacific, just as Hitler had expected to destroy England's defenses. But damaging as the air bombardments in these offensives had been, shock and anger resolved into determination. The United States mobilized not only to her own defense, but also finally reinforced Britain and the European Allies.

Tip returned to Houston by air, leaving Louise and little Michael with Harry Hossack in San Francisco. Although Tip had not yet received orders changing his civil assignment at the center, he was acutely aware of his reserve officer status and was expecting a call to active duty at any time. While he waited, he went back to his pressing work in an arena changed profoundly by the American entry into the war.

Louise and Michael returned to Houston by car accompanied by Mary Jane, who was a teenager at the time. They were determined to celebrate as merry a Christmas as possible under the circumstances, and the little house in Houston was full for the end of 1941. After ringing in the New Year of 1942, Mary Jane returned to San Francisco by Greyhound bus. Tip continued to fly the DC-3 with regularity well into the spring, still watching for orders. Life in Houston returned to a strange regularity in the face of this new wartime tension. Louise settled into her now normal routine of keeping house with suitcases out, ready to pack. She arranged a future home for the Doberman with the local police force, but kept him close for as long as they were still Texas residents.

We were training much-needed navigators, and I was making three to four long-distance navigational flights a week in the DC-3, carrying ten to twelve trainees per flight. One such flight took us from Houston, Texas, to Fort Wayne, Indiana, on to Oklahoma City then back to Houston. We departed Fort Wayne on the second leg of the trip at ten a.m., cleared non-stop to Oklahoma City. Our weather reports showed a cold front lying east of Oklahoma City and reported to be heavy with rain, some ice at altitude and moderate turbulence. Radio reports indicated that Oklahoma City was pretty much in the clear so we continued on. The first few minutes in the front was very heavy rain and after about fifteen minutes, I requested an altitude change due to turbulence. A few minutes later we suffered a lightning strike, which took out our radios. By this time, I had decided that our best course of action was to let down slowly, hoping to avoid the turbulence and if possible, land at a CAA emergency field this side of Oklahoma City. We broke out of the overcast at about two thousand feet. Everywhere I looked the black purplish clouds were visible. The emergency field was flooded. We once again took up a heading for Oklahoma City and activated one of our voice receivers. We were told we should proceed with caution as there were seven tornados reported in our area. As we climbed back to a safe four thousand feet, we must have run into one of the tornadoes, as the ship was practically uncontrollable.

After about five minutes of the most violent turbulence that I had ever encountered, we flew into relatively smooth weather with nothing more than heavy rain. Taking count of our casualties, we found everyone shaken up but only two with bumps and bruises. Two seats were ripped from the floor and although the ship flew well enough, I could feel that it was out of rig. We made a normal landing at Oklahoma City and were not surprised to learn that we were the only aircraft to fly into the airport that afternoon. A rough inspection of the ship showed that we had numerous broken wing bolts on the right and left wings. The force of the turbulence had put five degrees of dihedral in the wings.

Late one afternoon in May, I was just closing the hangar doors on the DC-3 when I received a call from Colonel Wallace Reid, who was commander of Ellington Field just a couple of miles from our base. He informed me that he had a group of musicians on the base that had to be flown to entertain the troops in Wichita Falls, Texas, that night, and we had the only aircraft big enough to take them. I told Colonel Reid that I wasn't running a taxi service and that I could not use the DC-3 for any such flights without express permission from Washington.

"I thought you would say that," he said. "You will hear from Washington any minute now." The telephone rang and the Assistant Secretary of Commerce was on the line authorizing the flight and any subsequent flights they needed to make. The only pilot at the hangar at that time was one of my co-pilot trainees. I told him to call weather and prepare a flight plan to Wichita Falls.

"Sir," he said, a few minutes later, "there's a hell of a cold front laying between here and Wichita Falls. Heavy thunderstorm activity as far as Dallas, but Wichita Falls will be clear by the time we get there about 1:00 a.m.." About that time, several military vehicles drew up in front of the hangar and seventeen people walked into my office. Much to my astonishment and consternation, the troupe was Bob Hope, Frances Langford, Jerry Colonna, Barbara Jo Allen (Vera Vague), and Skinnay Ennis with his entire orchestra. Bob Hope walked up to my desk.

"I'm looking for the pilot that is to fly us to Wichita Falls tonight," he said.

"I'm your pilot," I said, and introduced myself with a handshake.

"You're just a boy!" Bob said in surprise. I was twenty-nine years old.

I advised Mr. Hope that we were going to fly through some bad weather the first part of the trip, but I hoped to avoid as much turbulence as possible. We took off shortly after ten p.m. and hit the front about an hour out. It was a beauty, with lots of lightning, moderate turbulence and heavy rain. As we had no radar in those days, we picked our way through a nighttime front by watching the lightning flashes. We had taken quite a pounding and as soon as we were in clear weather, I went back to see how the passengers were faring. I had the ship on automatic pilot with my trainee co-pilot monitoring the instruments. Bob Hope and Frances Langford were sitting in the two front isle seats reading scripts. The rest of the group seemed comfortable and none the worse for the rough trip we had. I sat on the floor between Bob and Frances and we chatted about their schedule and their arrival time and if could we fly on to New Orleans after the show at Wichita Falls.

"I've never flown in a government DC-3 before," Bob said.

"No wonder," I said. "It's the only one they have."

I decided at this point that I would let Bob ride the co-pilot seat, but in the meantime we would have a little fun with him. I went into the cockpit and told my trainee to quietly walk through the cabin and sit down in the very rear of the aircraft. After a few minutes, I turned out all of the cockpit lights except the "black lights " for the instruments, checked the course and autopilot and walked back to Bob.

"If you would like to see what it's like up front," I said, "go on up and tell the co-pilot you're going to sit in my seat for awhile."

"I would like that!" Bob said and jumped up. "You look after Frances."

I warned Frances after Bob had disappeared into the dark walkway that there was nobody in the cockpit and in about ten seconds, Bob came flying back to where we were sitting.

"Nobody is flying this thing!" he screamed, "There's nobody up there!"

"Damn!" I said, leaping up, "It's that new co-pilot! He has a girlfriend in Dallas and he must have bailed out when we passed over!"

I took Bob into the cockpit again and put him in the co-pilots seat.

"You're the co-pilot for the rest of the trip," I said.

We were about thirty minutes out of Wichita Falls when I called the airport on the radio and got an instant reply.

"Use caution landing," the tower said, "A B-25 just crash-landed, caught his wing on the edge of the runway."

Bob was listening to this conversation and said, "What did they say? Who crashed?"

"You're the co-pilot Bob," I said, "You handle the radio. Tell them we're not going to crash."

"We're not going to crash! We're not going to crash!" Bob dutifully said into the mike.

The tower operator, probably a bit surprised by this non-professional reply said: "Roger, NC-14, try not to."

The show went on at about one a.m. before at least ten thousand troops and lasted for over an hour. Following the show, the commanding officer offered us coffee in his quarters and advised us to spend the night to no avail. Bob wanted the group in New Orleans for another show that night. We took off at three fifteen a.m. for New Orleans. Fortunately the weather was good and there was no repeat of the thunderstorm activity that we encountered previously.

Form 203
Revised 3-1-39

Civil Aeronautics Authority
WASHINGTON

RELEASE

HOUSTON, TEXAS
(Place)

5/15/42
(Date)

KNOW ALL MEN BY THESE PRESENTS that, Whereas, I

Bob Hope   N Hollywood Cal
(Full Name and Address)

am about to take a flight or flights on the above-mentioned date in certain aircraft of the Civil Aeronautics Authority ; AND WHEREAS I am doing so entirely at my own initiative risk, and responsibility, and am not acting upon the orders or suggest-ions of the United States Government or of any of its officers or agents; NOW, THEREFORE, in consideration of the permission extended to me by the United States through its officers and agents to take said flight or flights, I do hereby for my-self, my heirs, executors, administrators, and assigns, release, acquit, and forever discharge the Government of the United States, any and all of its officers and agent from any and all demands, claims, actions or causes of action, of whatever nature, arising out of any injury or death that may occur to me by reason of the said flight or flights, irrespective of death or any degree of injury that may occur.

This flight is to be made on official business and without expense to the Government.

Bob Hope
(Signature)

Mrs. Bob Hope
(Name of person to be notified in emergency)

N Hollywood Cal
(Address of person notified in emergency)

(Witness)

C. J. Tippett
(Name of Pilot)

NC-14
(Number of Airplane)

The signed release will be attached to the authorization for the flight or flights and carefully filed by Inspectors, or other officials or agents of the Civil Aeronautics Authority for future reference. A separate release will be signed for each day's flight or flights.

The CAA required passengers to sign a waiver, and Bob Hope politely complied.

Bob Hope, born Leslie Townes Hope, was thirty-nine years old in 1942 when Tip flew him and his United Service Organization (USO) troupe to entertain the troops. By then, Bob Hope was already well established in his entertainment career, but had been doing the USO tours for only a year. He would go on to perform for the troops in every armed conflict the US was involved in, up to the 1991 Persian Gulf War. Tip stayed in touch with Bob for the rest of his life, and saw him again socially and at several future embassy functions. At the time of Tip's flight, Bob Hope was married to his second and last wife, Dolores Reade. He continued to entertain audiences well into his nineties and lived to be 100 years old. The troupe that flew with Tip were all solid friends and professional partners of Bob Hope. Their individual dedication to the USO tours was a major feature in all of their careers. When they weren't appearing in person on military bases at home and abroad, they were working together on radio broadcasts that were immensely popular throughout the country during the war years.

In 1942, the Civil Aviation Administration was primarily concerned with making civil aviation safe and standardized. As governments watched war bloom across the globe, there was a clear mandate for the CAA to position itself to help Allied powers withstand enemy aviation efforts. Training foreign students in the protocol that the CAA was developing for aviation ensured not only the safety of American pilots and craft in foreign countries, but it also opened lines of communication and goodwill with nations that might otherwise be watching the world conflict from a neutral or enemy viewpoint. The US government poured resources into the CAA with this purpose in mind, and many of the foreign students passing through the Houston Standardization Center in 1941 were from countries in South America that were either neutral or being courted by Germany.

Brazil, in particular, was deeply interested in aviation, having already gained worldwide recognition for the accomplishments of Alberto Santos Dumont at the turn of the century. Santos Dumont was Brazilian-born, although France also claimed him once he won the Deutsch Prize for rounding the Eiffel Tower in 1901. He also made the first fixed-wing flight in France. At a time in history when

aviation pioneers were celebrities, Brazil offered strong competition
for headlines in the form of their own female pioneer aviator, Anesia
Pinheiro Machado.

Tip was introduced to his new trainee in October 1942,
when she was thirty-eight years old and already world famous. She
had been the first woman in Brazil to qualify as a pilot, soloing in
1922 at the age of eighteen. Brand-new pilot's license in hand, she
promptly set the record for a solo single-engine flight from Sao
Paulo to Rio de Janeiro by a woman. Her accomplishment gained her
instant celebrity and the personal attention of Santos-Dumont. She
took that attention and her own ambition directly into the work of
promoting and advancing civil aviation in Brazil. When she married
the Air Marshal of Brazil, General A. Appel Neto, she was able to
influence civil aviation policy even further.

Anesia Pinheiro Machado did not need to learn how to fly.
Like many of the students Tip was working with in Houston, she
needed certification that she knew how to teach. The instructor
certification program offered by the CAA in Texas was a solid
foundation in building a network of properly prepared instructors
throughout the world, and a first step in influencing international
standards. Anesia would learn the CAA's method, and then apply
it through her own extensive influence in Brazil's skies. She was
also taking the next step in her own pilot training by going for an
instrument rating. She had already made the leap from visual flight to
instrument, but Houston was where Tip would certify her.

Anesia Pinheiro Machado went on to earn a commercial
pilot's license in the US with both instrument and flight
instructor ratings in that same time period. Ten years later, she
set transcontinental and Andean flight records with her Brazilian
copilots. She worked so extensively for the enhancement of flight in
Brazil that she earned a long list of military and civilian medals and
awards throughout her lifetime. Tip stayed in contact with Anesia
throughout his life and they would meet frequently in the courses of

their careers.

Tip was immersed in his CAA routine in 1942 when the active duty orders he had been anticipating since the attack on Pearl Harbor suddenly came through. The Army Air Corps ordered him back to active duty, but before he could even respond, he received another letter notifying him that he was being loaned back to the Civil Aviation Administration, which in turn, was loaning him to the Defense Supply Corporation. The Reconstruction Finance Corporation had recently established the Defense Supply Corporation. Harry Hossack had been busy.

For the next three months, a flurry of paperwork and behind-the-scenes negotiations followed as the CAA firmly insisted that Tip retain his civilian status and not be listed in any official capacity as being on active duty. This was critical for the mission they were planning. These layers of civilian corporation employment would conceal Tip's military connections and enable him to be US Advisor to the Director of Civil Aviation of Argentina, a country flirting with the idea of abandoning neutrality in favor of Germany. A member of the US Armed Forces would be unsuitable for this diplomatically sensitive civilian approach. The Defense Supply Corporation was an independent private entity and Tip would be an employee. Civilian activity covering military objectives was widespread during the war years. The pool of experienced aviators in 1942 was small enough that the experts almost always had ties to military or diplomatic branches of their own governments. But countries that were undecided about which side of the world war conflict they supported could not be seen interacting with anyone's military.

The civilian status was not entirely a mask, as Tip was already well established in the advancement of civil aviation, but it was also not entirely true. Tip had firm connections to his military leadership, and was officially a reserve officer. The mission needed him to downplay his military connection, but it was both active and important in the deep background. Many of the pilots, leaders, and operatives who took these kinds of assignments would spend later years trying to untie the paperwork knots that the layers of subterfuge caused, and Tip would join them.

There were similar civilian military crossovers going on throughout the world as governmental departments tried to make political progress under complex conditions. Lieutenant General Claire Lee Chennault and the Flying Tigers in China would be the best example of this complexity.

To Tip, this was active military service, and he followed his multiple chains of command with discretion. In the meantime, German influencers were already active throughout Argentina and Tip would be starting from behind.

Announcements went out to family and friends, and Tip packed his own bag for Buenos Aires, Argentina. The position was not expected to last more than two months, but Louise was adamant about not staying by herself in Houston. Her father was now living in Washington D.C., and he had invited her to visit, but she had another invitation. Tip's father and stepmother lived in Luckey, Ohio, and Louise had never met them. Charles, Tip's father, had remarried around the same time as Verna married Adolf Eyth, but Tip had never spent time in his father's home as an adult. Charles and Alice Tippett were anxious to spend time with both Louise and Mike, who was the only grandchild for any of the couples. Louise went to Ohio. For her, it was an adventure in family relations as much as Tip's travel to D.C. was an adventure in political aviation.

When Louise arrived in Ohio in April 1942, she stepped into a furor of news and tangled speculation. Newspaper headlines in nearby Port Clinton announced the painful rumor that "Burholt May Have Been On Corregidor." Ralph Burholt was Tip's best friend and had been best man at Louise's wedding. The Burholt in question was

Ralph's brother, Arthur. Corregidor was an island at the entrance to Manila Bay in the Philippines, and was the scene of heavy fighting between US marines and Japanese forces. Louise may not have known Arthur Burholt directly, but Tip certainly did. The US soldiers had held out for as long as possible as the Bataan Peninsula fell to the Japanese in 1942.

The Burholt family was frantic to find news of their son; Arthur Burholt's letters to his wife had stopped. The newspaper article described Arthur's mother's desperate attempts to view a newsreel of the Corregidor footage because a family friend had claimed that it showed an image of her son. The Burholt family would not know for many years, but Arthur Burholt had survived the battle and then been captured by the Japanese. He had joined Father John E. Duffy, Tip's Jesuit priest football coach at St. Wendelin High School, on the march to Bataan. Both Father Duffy and Arthur Burholt survived the horrendous conditions of the march, but Burholt died in 1944 while still a prisoner of war in the hands of the Japanese. Father Duffy survived and returned to Ohio. He was awarded both the Purple Heart and Bronze Star.

Louise kept clippings of the news events in a scrapbook for Tip, and focused her energy into caring for young Michael. There was very little she, and the families in Ohio, could do otherwise. In 1942, food rationing was a fact of life and Louise would have joined her own ration books to the Charles Tippett household's for weekly meal planning. None of the Tippett family in Ohio were farmers, and so butter, milk, and meat were commodities bought at the local shops.

Although small family farms surrounded the Ohio townships, Louise's lifestyle was more similar to city conditions for shopping and cooking. Louise had to carefully steward her supply of nylon stockings, as there were no new ones to be bought, and she kept an eye out for rubber goods to contribute to the scrap rubber drives. Strict fuel rationing ensured that Louise and Michael stayed at home in Luckey, Ohio. They thought often of Tip, now far away in Buenos Aires.

Chapter Nine

1942 to 1943

A Record-Setting Flight
Buenos Aires, Argentina

In the summer of 1942, Argentina was walking a precarious path of neutrality regarding the world war, but the main concern for Argentine leadership was, and always had been, Brazil. The two countries had historically been in a tense standoff, wavering between friendly trade and unfriendly arms build up. Brazil had been receptive to American interests and was a vigorous American ally. Argentina was uncomfortable with the recent advances in Brazilian military capability that were the result of that relationship.

Brazil's northeastern seacoast was a critical access point for the US. It was the only way Roosevelt could get troops to the front lines in West Africa and Europe due to the German submarine threat in the Atlantic. Brazil happily accepted US arms and equipment to defend the Brazilian coast from German submarine attacks, and to build up a military that had always lagged behind Argentina's. Washington was conducting a dedicated behind-the-scenes effort to bring Argentina into alignment, but Argentina's government was skittish and unpredictable.

The civil aviation standardization effort, which was a

legitimate concern on its own, was a good way for the US to gain supporters in Argentina. Every country in the world was flying both private and commercial aircraft by 1942, and each country made its own rules. This was not only unsafe; it was also an obstacle to the economic success of international flights whose pilots and radio tower operators spoke no languages in common. Airport runways and signals were incomprehensibly laid out with no clear standard. Flight routes were company secrets, and radio beacons that could have boosted aviation safety were jealously guarded as private assets.

Tip's bosses at the CAA were open to the funding and support available from branches in the US government which needed access to Argentina. Civil aviation would be improved at the same time that political goals were accomplished. While there were no official sanctions against Argentina in July 1942, President Roosevelt was unhappy with Argentina's refusal to declare allegiance with the US. Roosevelt was keeping diplomatic channels open, but looking coldly on Argentina's continued contact with Nazi sympathizers. How to get money from the US government to the civilian mission was a problem, because the Roosevelt administration could not be seen to be funding advances toward Argentina. Money and equipment had to come from a source separated from the main channels of government. That was just the sort of thing that Harry Hossack did for a living with the Reconstruction Finance Corporation (RFC).

The wartime mission of the RFC had a different focus than when it first began operations to combat the Great Depression. The RFC was now driven to build businesses that could supply items like rubber, tin, and hemp, which were all in short supply as Japan controlled their Pacific sources. The RFC controlled The Defense Supply Corporation, and it was the perfect business to help the CAA extend aviation goodwill to Argentina, and Tip was the perfect person to do it.

Orders came from the Pentagon to report for work at the Defense Supply Corporation and to assist the Argentine government in a pilot training program similar to our Civil Pilot Training program in the US. I was also advised that I would be expected to flight test their airline pilots and bring them up to date on our latest instrument procedures. After a lengthy briefing at the State Department and the Commerce Department with the CAA, arrangements were made for my travel to Buenos Aires in July 1942. Dr. Samuel Bosch, Director General of Civil Aviation for Argentina, met me at the Buenos Aires airport. I had been thoroughly briefed on Dr. Bosch. An avid private pilot, his enthusiasm exceeded his ability to safely fly the sophisticated equipment he controlled. He had recently purchased a Beechcraft Staggerwing in Wichita, Kansas, and attempted to fly it back to Argentina. Three months, five minor (and one major) crashes later; he arrived in Buenos Aires without the Beechcraft. He had to order up another one.

Bosch was very pro-American in a country that was very pro-German at the beginning of the war. The next few days were dedicated to meetings at the civil directorate, planning the priorities of the program. Dr. Bosch offered his replacement Beechcraft Staggerwing for me to fly to all the airports of Argentina to survey the area and set up an instructor standardization flight course. As I had an unrestricted privilege of flying anywhere in the country, I was able to observe the activity of several shipping ports in the south that were suspected of harboring German submarines for refueling and supply. Observations finally indicated that the submarines were being supplied at sea by a mother ship.

Tip's observations from the cockpit may have averted a Brazilian attack on Argentina's southern shipping ports that year. German submarines were devastating the shipping lanes that Brazil depended on, and Brazil had been convinced that the submarines were resupplying in Argentine waters. Information about Argentina's

military capacity, and the extent of German activity at her ports and runways, was badly needed by the US. The German-supported Argentine press immediately began to run hysterically-worded articles accusing Tip of being a "Yankee spy, very clever and dangerous who should not be permitted to fly un-chaperoned around the country." Tip was amused and the press was not entirely wrong. Tip's helpful information about Argentine military activity was being passed along to the US Embassy over cocktails and brunch in the elegant capital city every time he landed.

Dr. Bosch's leniency in allowing Tip unrestricted access to the entire country by air could not have been an act of ignorance. He was one of the dwindling members of his government dedicated to advancing closer ties with the US. He also understood that his own time in office was limited. Tip was amenable to being a Yankee spy, as long as the spying could be done while he was otherwise occupied in aviation-related activities. The opportunity to fly a Beechcraft Staggerwing anytime, anywhere in Argentina was an unparalleled delight. The Staggerwing was a special kind of biplane. It was built for luxury and was out of reach of most working pilots. It was a 1942 version of a private personal jet, and fast for its time. The top and bottom wings were staggered to increase pilot visibility and improve stability. Tip settled in to his extraordinary circumstances and began to make enormous progress improving the conditions of civil aviation across Argentina while political and military tensions raged in the background.

Plans were made to re-establish a small airport near Buenos Aires named San Fernando. This was the base of Aeroposta, an Argentine airline flying Junkers-52 aircraft to Patagonia in the south and on to Punta Arenas at the tip of South America. Allocated to the school was a conglomerate of training aircraft. Three Focke-Wulf 44-J German trainers, one French Dewoitine twin-engine aircraft, five locally manufactured light aircraft modeled after Piper

Trainers, a Messerschmitt Me-108, a single-seat Junkers Fighter Parasol Trainer, and two old Waco cabin planes that had been imported years ago.

The first few weeks of the program were very confused. There were no proper books or flight manuals. I arranged with Washington to send materials to Buenos Aires for our translation. Classroom and blackboard drills consisted mostly of discipline in flight and on the ground. Airplanes were parked according to who got to the flight line first (causing chaos) and language was a problem. My Spanish at that time was practically non-existent. Fortunately I had an interpreter who kept things on track for the first month or two. By government decree, every instructor in Argentina was required to complete the instructor standardization course that I had established or lose his rating.

The ground school and flight course kept them at school for two weeks. I picked ten students from the class on the basis of their years of experience and flight hours. I personally flew and instructed these first ten students myself. I was flying an average of ten hours a day, seven days a week. Our flight course commenced at seven a.m. and continued until dark. I found the majority of that first class to be excellent pilots, but they had little knowledge of the aerodynamics of flight. Figure eights over a point, precision spins, 180 and 360-degree overhead landings were also troublesome for them. Of the ten students, I passed seven and recommended that the other three stay on for more training. Of the seven, I selected three to remain at the school as my assistants. I then relegated myself to the position of check pilot at the end of the course. I learned quickly that busting the nephew of an important politician was not easily explained, especially by an American instructor. I let my Argentine assistants take over those types of duties.

As the school became a precision operation, I was able to visit the aero clubs throughout the country and fly with some of the students that were being taught by my trainees. The results were more than pleasing. The Argentine pilots were enthusiastic about their new talents and drilled the new program into every student in the country. At the request of the director of civil aviation, I flew acrobatic demonstrations on weekends at various clubs throughout the country. I was using a German Focke-Wulf two-place model, a great acrobatic aircraft and far superior to our Stearmans.

The Argentine government asked me to evaluate a fleet of aircraft stored at an airfield near Buenos Aires. The planes had been confiscated from foreign governments like France, Germany, and Italy. I was expected to report back whether any of the aircraft could be used as trainers in our program. I agreed to fly them and determine their usefulness and condition. I was surprised to find that the aircraft consisted of some of the latest German trainers such as the Focke-Wulf 44J, and a Junkers Ju-52 transport. The Italian planes were not flyable. I sent my report to Dr. Bosch.

Tip successfully set up flight training, procedures for control tower operators, selected essential communications equipment, designed airports and airport lighting, and established weather reporting sequences and weather stations. One of his greatest achievements was persuading Argentina to accept English as the language for aeronautical voice radio communication, a standard that later became worldwide. He did it at a time when German was the language in vogue on the streets, and many of the most popular newspapers were written and run by German interests. Tip was Dr. Bosch's shining example of US benevolence and generosity, and Dr. Bosch made the most of him.

Now that Tip had more aircraft at his disposal than he had ever imagined possible, he could take on issues that had always concerned him professionally. The war and politics took a distant position in the back of his mind while he turned his significant talents to accomplishing exactly what the CAA hoped to do, standardize civil aviation in Argentina.

Dr. Bosch called me into his office one morning and suggested that the United States should donate some training planes to our program. I'd had this thought in mind for some time as all the aircraft that were being used were German or French designs. I discussed this with Norman Armour, the US Ambassador to Argentina, and he agreed that it would be useful to show the flag by donating a training plane to the program. A wire was sent to the State Department detailing my request with a copy to the Chief of Staff, US Army Air Corps. The request was approved for one Fairchild PT-19 training plane to be issued to me for use in Argentina. I immediately requested the date of probable arrival by ship to the port of Buenos Aires. Much to my consternation, I was told to come back to Hagerstown, Maryland, to pick up the ship at the factory and fly it to Argentina. German subs were sinking too many ships to send it by sea.

The PT-19 is a two-place, low-wing, 180-hp trainer. It has a cruising speed of about 110 mph. I would have to make careful preparations for such a long flight. The factory notified me that I could arrive anytime, so I immediately returned to the US by commercial airline. I met Rick Hessam at the Fairchild factory in Maryland where I had the PT-19 modified with a shading hatch (because of the heavy rain expected to be encountered) and a voice radio, which refused to work shortly after take-off. The plane had a range of three hours and in planning my route and distances, I determined that without extra fuel there was no way to fly this machine to Buenos Aires. The factory installed an extra tank in the rear cockpit, which gave me seven hours of fuel. An extra compass and a gyro-direction indicator completed my instrument panel and immediately ceased to function.

I flew from the factory in Hagerstown, Maryland, to Washington D.C., where the ship was christened by the Argentine air attaché and blessed by a State Department secretary. It was to be

the longest solo single-engine flight attempted to date, over some
of the roughest flying terrain in the world. At that time, there were
very few airports in South America and the few radio beacons had
been set up by airlines that jealously guarded their use. Overflight
and landing clearances had been approved at the last minute
through Central America and South America and the flight take-off
scheduled.

Only four years earlier, the two-seat Fairchild PT-19 had
become the standard for pilot training. It had two sets of controls
– one for the student and one for the instructor. Most pilot training
before WWII was done in biplanes because although they were
slow, they were stable and more tolerant of student mistakes. But
aviation technology had advanced quickly under the needs and
finances of war. The training that pilots received in the biplanes left
a steep learning curve when they were faced with the faster, high-
performance aircraft that wartime pilots were expected to fly. So
the PT-19 Fairchild had replaced the Stearman biplane as the most
common primary trainer.

Tip knew both the advantages and limits of the aircraft. He
had been flying them for years. With the hatch installed, the plane
took on a designation of PT-19A. The standard PT-19 windshield was
about as wide as a motorcycle shield, and so the hatch was essential,
but it also made the narrow cockpit even more constricted. The
single wooden propeller was at the nose, and both pilots sat directly
over the wing. Visibility to the ground was a peek over the side and
either forward or aft. The narrow, bare, cockpit of the PT-19A was
a stark contrast to the luxuriously spacious Staggerwing Tip had
been flying recently. Pilots of 1943 protected themselves against the
temperature extremes with heavy leather and wool flight jackets.
On the ground, there was no air-conditioning, other than an open
hatch. The extra fuel added weight and took up any space Tip would
have used for equipment or supplies, which made his packing list

very short.

> January 6, 1943
> Memorandum for Captain Wm. Barclay Harding
> On January 4, 1943, I received from you one parachute seat
> pack with jungle equipment, less one box of .45 caliber ammunition,
> which was returned to you. I will use this parachute on a flight to
> Argentina, at the end of which, the parachute will be turned over
> to the United States Army Air Mission to Argentina. I will ask
> the Senior Air Member of the US military mission to Argentina
> to advise the Military Attaché Section of the Military Intelligence
> Service when the chute is placed in his possession.
> > Cloyce J. Tippett
> > Approved:
> > s/ Wm. Barclay Harding
> > Chief, Contact and Operations Section
> > American Intelligence Command.

Aviation navigation had developed significantly since the early days when pilots used a compass, a Rand-McNally road map, and a key on a chain dangling from the control panel to determine their flight attitude and direction. But in January 1943, visual flight rules (VFR) flying was Tip's only choice, other than a few radio beacons and voice radio communication he might not be able to rely on. VFR meant that Tip would have to fly below the clouds, so that he could keep the ground and mountains constantly in sight. But Central and South America were notorious for rain showers, thunderstorms, and mile after mile of low hanging clouds, no matter the season. There were also few landing strips, and the ones Tip would use were separated by either jungle or mountain ranges, without the usual emergency landing options of open fields or roadways. The flight plan presented layer after layer of challenging details that Tip could not compensate for. He would simply have to do it.

Louise had traveled to D.C. to see him off, but, by her own admission, was less than enthusiastic about his journey. For Louise, the significance of the flight was overshadowed by her long-delayed move to join Tip in Argentina. She and Michael, now three and a half, had been perched anxiously at one family member's home after another for more than six months. Louise had gone from Charles and Alice's house to Tip's mother Verna, also in Ohio. Harry Hossack was now established permanently in Washington, and Louise left Michael with Verna to stay with Harry and see Tip begin his journey. Louise wrote:

> My father was living in D.C. when Tip returned from the Argentine. I traveled by train from Toledo to spend a few days with him. I have to confess rather sheepishly that I do remember that he was to fly a trainer to Buenos Aires, but he was so casual about it, and I was so disinterested in aviation, hazy in geography, and deeply disappointed that his sojourn was to be extended, that I didn't pay much attention. The first crack in the marriage might well have been my total lack of concern for the hazards ahead, and my subsequent lack of enthusiasm for the done deed.

Tip knew at the time that what he was doing was going to set a record. He also knew that it was going to take all of his training and skill. He had watched distance, speed, and endurance records set and challenged since he was fourteen and Lindbergh made his famous solo Atlantic flight, but made no comment on them in his notes and letters. Tip did not seem to purposefully set out to capture a record for himself, nor did he refuse the task set before him.

11,500 miles solo, Hagerstown, Maryland, to Buenos Aires.

Thursday, January 14, 1943. The weather in Washington D.C. was clear, with fair visibility and a headwind. There was smoke and a cold front to the west and heavy snow on the ground, but the ship was okay. The flight to Greensboro, NC took 3.05 hours and there was no heater in the cockpit. It was miserable. The weather in Greensboro was no better, landing at 16:25 and taking off again at 16:50, still ahead of the weather with a two-degree temperature improvement bringing it to 34 degrees Fahrenheit. I flew an hour to Charlotte, NC, where it was much warmer, and I stayed overnight in warm relief.

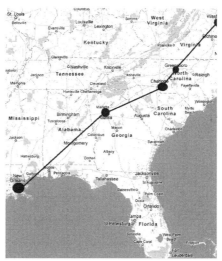

I took off to clear weather and a headwind and flew two

hours to Atlanta, GA, then on almost five hours more to New Orleans, Louisiana, fighting high head winds over scrub pine the whole way, with no emergency landing sites in view, something to get used to for the coming trip. Overnight in New Orleans.

The log for this record-setting solo flight consisted of 9 sheets of handwritten data and notes. Despite water damage and rips, the log is clearly legible and full of Tip's brief commentary.

Tip's precious original flight log, guarded through the years with impressive zeal, shows the passage of seven days in New Orleans. There are no notes regarding why, but it was New Orleans and Tip was a man with a nose for a good time. His story is made possible by his meticulous record keeping and habit of storing letters, newspaper and magazine articles, photographs, flight logs, flying certifications, orders, and anything else remotely pertaining to his adventures.

Friday, January 22. I left New Orleans for Texas in the

afternoon and flew 2:20 hrs. to San Antonio, Texas, all clear but turbulent weather. The temperature was warmer, 68 degrees Fahrenheit. After being grounded by weather for four days, I took off in an overcast afternoon and flew 2:05 hrs. to Brownsville, Texas. There I was delayed again, my Mexican clearance was dated wrong. The next day I had clear weather and clearance in hand, cumulous to the east and west, and a slight headwind. It was marshy wooded country and 72 degrees Fahrenheit. I flew into Mexico, landing in Tampico after a 2:45 hr. flight. The next flight to Vera Cruz, Mexico was the best so far, practically no wind, good weather and finally warm. The field was excellent.

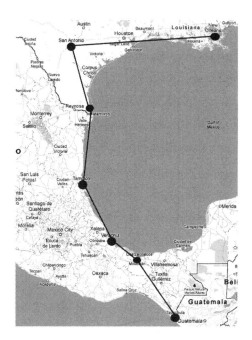

The next day was bad weather with a 300 foot ceiling. No forward visibility, heavy rain. 100 miles out of Vera Cruz on the way to Punta, I had to turn back, landing again at Vera Cruz after a 1:45 hr. flight. Minutes after I landed, a three-hour tropical rainsquall closed the airstrip. Sleeping quarters consisted of one small room with a broken window. I moved the bed to keep from getting soaked by the rainsquall. Food was tortillas, refried beans and quesadilla. As they had no bottled water, I drank beer.

Once again at daybreak, I took off from Vera Cruz for Minatitlan and was fortunate. After dodging rain squalls the entire trip, I landed just as a heavy thunderstorm engulfed the airport. As usual, daybreak brought high ceilings with a foreboding that within a few hours the tropical rains would be back again. Although the final hour of the flight to Tapachula was in heavy rain, the flight was much smoother than the previous days. Sitting in a tiny bar in Tapachula near the airport (a grass strip with no hangars), I was drinking a beer and trying to decide if I had the courage to order some food. The bartender had disappeared behind a flap of dirty canvas which hid the one burner stove when a huge rat jumped up on the back bar. The back bar contained a couple bottles of wine, two religious pictures, and what appeared to be a rosary hanging from a nail just above the pictures. The rat became entangled in the rosary and knocked the wine bottles into the pictures. The bartender came dashing out from behind his canvas with a spatula in hand and began hitting the rat with the spatula. The rat finally eluded his abuser, and I retired to my mosquito-netted cot without appetite.

The relatively short flight times of Tip's journey were determined by factors like fuel, weather, pilot fatigue and navigation. Piloting a PT-19 in 1943 was an active endeavor with constant course checks, corrections, and altitude variations to avoid weather. Tip made calculations on hand-held dials and mechanical calculators. He had a small metal clipboard strapped to his thigh with a pencil tied to the frame. He relied on mental and written calculations because the electronic calculator would not be invented for another twenty years. He navigated by compass and his own ability to maintain speed, estimate drift, or compensate for terrain.

Tip sat in the forward cockpit. The rear cockpit, equipped with a full set of controls for pilot training, was filled with a second fuel tank. This tank, and the sliding hatch covering the cockpit, were essential for Tip's journey.

The configuration of the cockpit required the pilot to experience every element the plane encountered, and temperature, weather, and visibility were constant demands on his attention. These planes did not insulate against the sensation of flight, and they were not quiet. It was a contact sport. A six-hour flight was the maximum Tip planned for safety reasons. There was no margin for an error caused by a tired pilot.

Emergency landings were a very different prospect than they had been over the open fields of central Texas. Tip, along with all the pilots of his day, kept a continual eye out for possible landing sites as they flew. Open pastures, country roads without power lines, or stretches of open land were a flier's insurance policy. The mountains of Mexico and jungle canopies of Guatemala, Honduras, and Nicaragua presented no option for landing a distressed plane. Tip was flying from airstrip to airstrip with no good landing opportunities in between. Engine failure or a navigation error would end the trip.

After a year and a half of World War II, the airfields throughout Central and South America were primitive, but they did exist. During his months of work in Argentina, Tip had been creating systems for airport identification, equipment, facilities, and communication, but as he flew the Fairchild south, he had none of that to rely on. He overnighted at almost every stop, staying at whatever accommodations were available at the tiny airports, which often had little more than a grass strip, a shed, and a bar. The cockpit of a Fairchild PT-19 offered no room for a tired pilot to stretch out for a night's sleep.

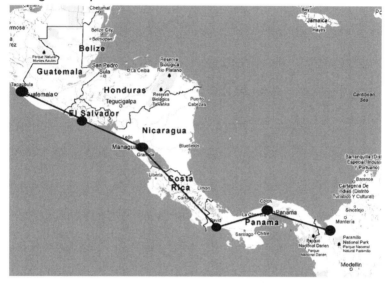

Tuesday, February 2. The flight from Tapachula to San Salvador was made in heavy rainsqualls over high jungle. My average altitude was perhaps fifty feet over the jungle trees as there was no forward visibility, only vertical. Flying by compass heading and elapsed time and allowing myself about a three to five degree downwind drift, I could arrive in the vicinity of the airstrip and know which way to turn to find the airstrip with little or no visibility. This system worked perfectly during the entire trip, although finding the airport after a six hour flight in heavy rain always seemed to be pure luck with a little bit of guardian angel thrown in.

The flight from San Salvador to Managua was extremely turbulent with heavy rain showers during the last thirty minutes of flight and downdrafts throughout. Central America during the rainy season has beautiful clear weather from daybreak until about noon, but anyone flying small aircraft or aircraft not equipped for instrument flying should beware. The heavy rain clouds quickly formed out of nowhere and many small aircraft, especially pilots not familiar with the area, had been lost. From Managua, I flew to David, Panama then on to Rio Hato, Panama, where I overnighted at the military base and did minor maintenance on the aircraft.

Tip was delayed for five days in Rio Hato, Panama. His log only notes "delayed service" and that it was hot. As an experienced pilot, Tip carried his own chamois cloth, a soft piece of leather for filtering the gasoline as it went into the tanks. This was a slow process, but the pores of the leather cloth were the right size for filtering out water and dangerous particles that contaminated the gas. A fuel line blockage while under way could stop the engine, and with no emergency landing sites, could prove fatal.

The Fairchild PT-19A carried fuel in both wings as well as the cockpit tank.

February was the dry season in Panama, meaning only that flying was physically possible, not that there was no rain. The Rio Hato airfield would become a significant airstrip in modern times, when it played a key part of the American military action to oust

Manuel Noriega, ex-President of Panama. But outside of the airstrip in 1943, Rio Hato was a rough town. When Tip was finally able to continue his trip, he was headed across the Panama Canal and into Colombia. The Panama Canal was so critical to the Allied Forces that the United States maintained strict control over the region. The canal was most vulnerable to air attack, so the air space was closed. Commercial flights flying high above were required to order the stewardesses to pull the curtains over the passenger windows when crossing the Panama Canal. Private aircraft, and Tip was considered private on this mission, had to be escorted by fighter aircraft, which had to be scheduled.

Wednesday, February 10. I was finally cleared for Turbo, Colombia and had an escort of four P-39s from the US air base across the isthmus at six thousand feet altitude. The flight to Turbo was uneventful, and after landing there, I flew on to Barranquilla, Colombia over heavy jungle and scattered rain showers and was able to maintain two thousand feet altitude during most of this leg. Barranquilla boasted a hotel that I found very poor and expensive.

At daybreak, I was off again from Barranquilla to Maracaibo, Venezuela, with clear weather and very strong headwinds complicated by the high mountains surrounding the flight course. The land looked like West Texas now. Pushing myself, I flew on to La Guira, Venezuela. It was another rough and windy flight and the overnight at the comfortable airport hotel was welcome after a day of nearly eight hours flight time.

The flight from La Guira, Venezuela, to Barcelona, Venezuela, was the roughest and longest flight of the trip. It was over desert land with a huge sandstorm in progress and I thought of returning to La Guira, but the weather had closed in behind me, forcing me to continue. I was in the air a total of 4 hours 25 minutes, and my ground speed averaged about sixty miles per hour. Once I cleared the desert, I was over the sea and could see natives below on the rough shoreline with dugout canoes on the clear water. It reminded me of Hawaii from the air. The weather cleared enough, coming in to Barcelona, to continue to Ciudad Bolivar, Venezuela, and apart from a few rainsqualls, the weather remained good. The scenery was becoming very tropical with many palm trees and scrub jungle.

Without weather reports, it was difficult to determine just where to head for and when to take off. For Venezuela, it was the rainy season and there would be hard and heavy rain. I could maneuver around squalls, but solid front tropical storms would have to be penetrated. I was anxious to arrive at Atkinson Field in British Guiana, as I had planned to spend a couple of days there, resting and doing minor maintenance to the aircraft.

I cleared for Tumeremo, Venezuela, with six hundred feet and light rain for openers, until once again, at the point of no return I ran into a huge tropical storm. I was flying at full throttle about fifty feet above heavy jungle, barely maintaining flying speed due to the tremendous weight of the rain upon the wings of the aircraft. I was amazed that the engine could continue running in such a downpour. It was instrument flying with no instruments. After three attempts to reach Waller Field, British Guiana, I made it. I waited until early afternoon to take off again, but after an hour and a half of flying through heavy rain, I had to return again to Waller Field, and sit out more foul weather.

The service ceiling of the PT-19 was thirteen thousand feet,

so Tip could not consider flying over the sixteen-thousand-foot mountains in Venezuela. His constant observations of cloud ceiling indicated how high he would be flying that day. If the cloud ceiling was 300 feet above the ground, then his maximum flying altitude that day would be no higher than 300 feet. Going up in altitude to calmer air, which is a technique common in modern aviation that can rely on radar and satellite technologies, was no option for Tip in the PT-19A. If he lost visual contact with the ground, he had no way of knowing what he would descend into. There may be a mountain mid-cloud or he might find himself out to sea, displaced by a crosswind impossible to detect without continual visual reference to the terrain below. The freedom in these early flights was intoxicating, but the margin of error was impossibly small. Pilots in these jungle skies were skilled, or they were mourned.

Monday, February 15. I took off for Atkinson Field in British Guiana. For most of the flight, I was flying at 200 to 300 feet, clearing the jungle by 100 to 150 feet with vertical visibility only. I had flown exactly two hours and forty-five minutes, my estimated flight time to the field, and had allowed myself a few degrees drift downwind. If my calculations were correct, I would make a ninety-degree turn to the left and fly until I saw the airport. As my forward visibility was practically nothing, I began to get a bit apprehensive when I had flown ten minutes on this course and had not sighted the field. Mentally retracing my course and time en route I could not see where I had erred. The only problem could be the drift factor. Knowing that it would be fatal to start flying in circles to locate the field in such heavy rain, I decided I must fly on my ninety degree heading for another few minutes. Almost like the rising of the sun in early morning mist, the airport came into vertical view. After I landed, I heard that the operations officer could not believe that I had flown from Tumeremo to Atkinson with no radio in such weather.

I remained at Atkinson Field to catch up on my sleep and eat some decent food. I was able to send a wire off to Washington advising them of my position and assure them all was well to date. The aircraft needed very little maintenance but we did install a new set of spark plugs and changed the oil.

Tip quietly celebrated his thirtieth birthday at Atkinson Field. In early 1943, Atkinson was an active US military base and a haven for Tip as he followed his flight plan. The US had established the field a year after it joined the war through a lease agreement with Britain. Atkinson Field was home to bombing squadrons that patrolled the Atlantic Ocean hunting submarines and protecting shipping. On the ground at Atkinson Field, Tip was under the protection of the United States and had at his service all of the technology, supplies, and support the base had to offer. But despite the comfort and security, he did not linger. Atkinson Field was not one of the long stops on his voyage, and he took off again after only two days.

Tuesday, February 16. At 8:40 am, I left for Zandery Field in Dutch Guiana. The weather was rainy with visibility about two miles, and the terrain looked marshy and tropical. The Dutch officials were very pleasant and permitted me to dry off in their barracks on the field. As the inter-tropical front was stationary in this area and extended several hundred miles in either direction along the coast, I needed to plan my flight to French Guiana (Cayenne) to arrive as early in the afternoon as possible to avoid the height of the storms.

I departed Zandery Field in light rain and about 400 foot ceiling. The weather was a bit better over the ocean, so I stayed about two miles off-shore just able to keep the shoreline in sight. I finally had to angle in to the shore and inland, which meant jungle flying once again. Luckily, I arrived at the Cayenne Air Base just as the heavy rains and thunderstorms moved in, and was well received

at the base. My French was non-existent, so we managed with
English and a bit of Spanish. I remained at the base the following
day. The weather was not flyable, even for the little Fairchild. The
base was zero-zero all day.

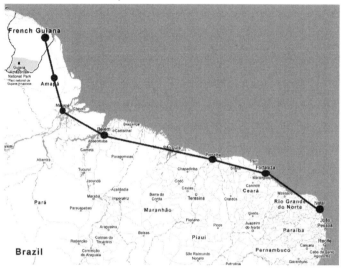

Zero visibility forward and zero visibility below, total cloud
coverage all the way to the ground. In these tropical regions, it
was not likely to be fog that was keeping Tip on the ground, but
the vigorous and almost constant thunderstorms. Cayenne, French
Guiana, was right on the coast of the Atlantic with clear access to
far away Europe. It was a heavily contested settlement in 1943, but
not a prosperous place. The French had been using it as a penal
colony as recently as five years before Tip landed, and the region had
a dangerous reputation. France's defeat by Germany precipitated a
temporary claim of the jungle territory by a pro-German regime.
At the time of Tip's overnight stay in the guard barracks at Cayenne,
the field was in enemy hands. Only a month after Tip departed, pro-
Allied forces retook the region in a quick coup.

While the war had made the PT-19A flight possible by
boosting the existence of adequate airfields throughout the route, it
also added to the tension and hazard of the journey. Tip's charisma
and charm, and the airfield's distance from the heart of the war,

figured in Tip's peaceful passage. But it was more the basic nature of civil aviation and the fact that Tip was a solo pilot in a small plane that saw him through. There was nowhere else to land, and the base leadership had no clear orders to stop him. Nonetheless, Tip never left his aircraft unattended for very long in these tenuous conditions.

Wednesday, February 17. The ceiling was about 400 feet and light rain when I decided to leave for Amapa, Brazil, and I had about two miles visibility. My alternative field, Macapa, was a grass emergency field for Pan American Airways DC-3 aircraft in the event Amapa and Belem were closed because of weather. The trip was the usual; hard rain, thunderstorms, gusting winds and moderate turbulence. After two hours and fifty minutes of buffeting, I arrived at Amapa. The staff of two was surprised to see me, but pleased to have the company. The field was in the heart of the Brazilian coastal jungle and about one hundred miles from the Amazon River. It was not a nice place to live. We slept under mosquito netting as there was a yellow fever alert, and I was there for a full additional day due to weather.

I left Amapa mid-morning for the short flight to Macapa, which lies at the edge of the Amazon River. The distance between the two points was about 160 miles over heavy jungle and swamp. The usual headwinds and heavy rain prevailed, which forced me once again to fly at tree-top level to maintain any kind of visibility. At about the halfway point, the rain became torrential and I experienced my first in-flight problem. The engine became exceedingly rough and began losing RPMs; I immediately reversed my course and applied carburetor heat, hoping that by some miracle it might be ice in the carburetor. No such luck. I lost a few more RPMs with the heater on. I cut it off and checked the magnetos, which made no difference in the vibration. I had definitely lost one cylinder. Although the vibration was constant, it did not increase and I continued on course back to Amapa, barely able to hold my altitude against the heavy rain and loss of power. The jungle field was a welcome sight. I landed in what seemed to be a shallow lake of water. The field mechanic was kind enough to push the aircraft partially under a large tent where he changed the spark plugs and checked the mags. The run-up after this work indicated the engine was back to normal. I celebrated by staying overnight in a tent next to the aircraft.

The airfield at Amapa, Brazil, was far inland, deep in rainforest, on the north side of the Amazon River. To turn back, heading away from the safe, well-supplied landing field at Macapa, and to fly back over the impenetrable jungle was nerve racking. If the ailing engine had quit, even glide time would not have helped. Tip would have crashed into the Amazon jungle a hundred miles from any help. Tip's log of this part of the flight indicates a cloud ceiling of between 75 to 200 feet, meaning that he was just clearing the top of the jungle canopy, giving him the additional hazard of having no room to maneuver or try any kind of in-flight restart on the engine should it quit. But turning back was the proper procedure, based on Tip's careful calculations. Tip's training dictated that trouble at the halfway point required a 180-degree turn back, and he held to the plan. His experience with aircraft engines and his experience through his hours as a pilot gave him an additional edge in judging what to expect from the ship. Skill, as well as luck, was seeing him through the journey.

Saturday, February 20. I started the leg of the trip that held the most apprehension for me. Once I got to Macapa, I had to cross the Amazon River from Macapa to Belem, Brazil. The delta, or mouth of the river, at this crossing is a bit over 200 miles. The course takes you over the Isle of Marajo and its swamps and jungle, then over open water about a distance of thirty miles to Belem. The early morning take-off was in light drizzle and visibility

of about three miles. Once again I flew at tree-top level to avoid
the low scud. At one time during the crossing over Marajo, I saw
hundreds of alligators basking in the rain along the small river banks
that make up portions of the Amazon delta. In Belem, I stayed
overnight in the Pan American "hotel" and was anxious to get
under way at daybreak the next morning. I was hoping to get into
some better weather, as I would be flying along the coast to Rio de
Janeiro. Unfortunately, going around the coast added another couple
of thousand miles to the trip, but flying direct across the middle of
Brazil in this aircraft was impossible.

One advantage to coastal flying was the relatively flat land.
Gone were the hundred-foot jungle trees and impossible emergency
landing areas. The weather was still lousy, but that was expected
until we were further down the coast. I refueled at Sao Luis and
it took longer than usual, as we had to bring the gas in five-gallon
buckets from drums off the field and pour it through chamois skin
to assure that no water, sand, and other corrosive elements would
enter the fuel tank.

The next day I took off in the early afternoon in light rain
and strong headwinds, and landed in Parnaiba after a flight of two
hours and ten minutes. The overnight accommodations in Brazil
took on a completely different nature both in food and lodging. The
Brazilians were most affable and hospitable and seemed amused
that I was flying a "tico tico" (butterfly) such a long distance. The
small hotel was clean and the food was a typical Brazilian "feijoada,"
consisting of pork, black beans and rice. I stuck to beer because I
knew it was pasteurized rather than attempt their local water supply,
although they assured me that it was "pura." I was amazed at the
number of local Brazilians that spoke usable English. On several
occasions, if I could not make myself understood, a small lad or girl
was sent for and acted as translator.

I made the trip to Fortaleza and the next day, on to Natal.
It took almost six hours of flying each day and although the rain

was not steady there were thunderstorms that proved bothersome and required me to alter my course. The overnight at Recife was at a Brazilian military base and was most comfortable. The ship was refueled and washed down, although it didn't need it after all the rain we'd been through.

The following morning was bright sunshine, almost the first of the trip. Although the headwinds were still there, it was a pleasant flight over sandy rolling plains. Sao San Salvador is a pleasant city and I stayed overnight at a lovely small hotel overlooking the sea. The food was outstanding, with several kinds of fresh fish offered as well as shrimp and lobster. Once again, the weather the next morning was bright sunshine and although there was no lessening of the headwinds the flight to Caravelas was about 4 hours 45 minutes elapsed time.

Five weeks into the journey. The day's flight was seven hours and thirty minutes to Rio, and both the aircraft and I'd had enough flying for a day or two. I checked into the American Embassy and briefed them on the flight so that they could inform

Washington. I called on the air attaché and planned to dine with him on my second night in Rio. A quick tour of the city, a few hours on the Copacabana Beach, and I was ready to depart on the final leg of the journey to Buenos Aires.

Rio de Janeiro, Brazil, in 1943, was as impressive from the air as it is today. It has many distinctive landmarks that are easily identified from above, but most of all, it is an enormous modern city and Tip had been flying into tiny towns, barracks, and bare airfields since leaving the United States. By reaching Rio, he had set a solo record in itself, but by continuing on to Buenos Aires, he was setting an even longer record, solo or not. Buenos Aires, Argentina, was still 1200 miles away. Tip wasn't finished, but the accomplishment of having reached Rio was a huge relief. He had been out of communication not only with Louise, but also with the rest of the world. Tip's visit to the American Embassy in Rio was the first chance he'd had in over a month to catch up with current events and to determine if Argentina was still expecting him. Argentine political unrest was rising and Tip knew of the instability before he left, but the embassy assured that his mission was still in force.

Sunday, February 28. I flew out of Rio toward my overnight, Florinapolis, a pleasant little coastal town. The first tailwind of the trip in bright sunshine was welcome. The six hundred mile flight was made in a few minutes over five hours. From Florinapolis to Porte Alegre was a coastal flight paralleling a five thousand foot mountain range most of the way. The weather again was clear with a fine tailwind, which brought me into Porte Alegre in a little over four hours of flight time. Porto Alegre lies about forty miles inland from the ocean, in a lovely clean valley. The city itself was attractive and predominately settled by a German community. The field where I landed was maintained by Air France, who had been offering service to this area since the early 1930s.

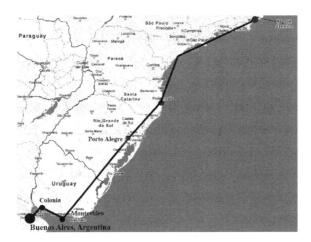

Finally, my good weather luck ended and I awoke the next morning to a light misty rain with low overcast. The Air France weatherman told me that the coast would probably be higher ceilings and better weather. I flew to the coast at a reasonable altitude of eight hundred feet and found the coast to be clear in that area so I climbed to six thousand feet to take advantage of the brisk tailwind. About an hour down the coast the low clouds moved in, and I was flying on top of an undercast, which I did not like to do normally. As the flight was a four-hour flight, I decided to continue and hope for dissipation. Fortunately, about an hour out of Montevideo, Uruguay, breaks in the clouds appeared and I let down cautiously through them. The weather was definitely deteriorating and I felt fortunate to be able to continue on to Montevideo. I telephoned Dr. Bosch at his home and he was elated to know that I planned to arrive in Buenos Aires the following day. He said he would have a tremendous welcoming party to greet the ship and me, and that all the newspapers would have representatives at the airport.

I could not leave Montevideo until late morning, as the weather had closed the airport earlier. I finally took off at about ten thirty in light rain and about two miles visibility with a five hundred foot ceiling. Fortunately the terrain was flat with very few obstructions. I had cleared for Colonia, Uruguay, because crossing the hundred-mile mouth of the river directly was too much open water for me at this stage of the game. Flying parallel to the Rio de la Plata river almost due west, I could see I was paralleling one of the blackest, most formidable thunderstorm fronts I had ever seen. I ducked into Colonia just before the fury of the storm hit.

For a while I thought we might lose the airplane. Wind gusts were estimated at seventy-five miles per hour. The storm ripped off shed roofs and overturned two small training aircraft that were not properly secured. Fortunately, I had the Fairchild headed into the wind and securely tied down, and three Uruguayans helping me hang onto the ship. In Argentina, Dr. Bosch heard about the fury of the storm and wired Colonia to inquire if I had landed there. The report went back to him that I was safe in Colonia and would fly over the next morning.

On Wednesday, March 3, 1943, I arrived at my destination. My reception when I landed in Buenos Aires was heartwarming indeed. Most of the representatives of the interior aero clubs had stayed overnight and were there at the airport with the instructors that had been students at the school. Banners and bands were in bright and noisy evidence. After hangaring the aircraft and about half the population having had their picture taken in the cockpit, we left for a giant asado that had been planned for the evening before. The celebration continued on into the early evening and after devouring a couple of beef carcasses and a few cases of hearty Argentine red wine, the crowd dispersed. Dr. Bosch dropped me off at the Plaza hotel and informed me that I would have one full day to myself before our flight to Mar del Plata, a resort casino city about 250 miles south of Buenos Aires. He also indicated that he would like me to check him out in the Fairchild prior to flying to Mar del Plata as he wanted to land the ship at the airport, where another "grand homage" had been planned.

Tip's flight log reads "Finished by God!" for the March 3rd
entry. He had flown forty-nine days, over 11,500 miles, and set the
solo North America to South America flight record. But he was
allowed no time to rest on his laurels on arrival in Buenos Aires. The
Fairchild PT-19A was a true prize for the Argentine Civil Aviation
Group, which was under heavy pressure from portions of Argentina's
military with Axis sympathies. German-supported newspapers were
condemning Dr. Bosch's American-backed handling of the whole
Argentine civil aviation department. There was a political urgency
about Dr. Bosch's desire to celebrate the aircraft's arrival by showing
it off all over the country with him at the controls. The plane was
given a work-over, and the extra fuel tank removed.

The Fairchild was a relatively simple plane to fly and I had
no trouble checking out Dr. Bosch to fly the aircraft. Of course, I
would be in the rear cockpit where I also had controls, so there was
really no danger in letting Dr. Bosch fly into the airport at Mar del
Plata as the pilot in command. We remained in Mar del Plata until
late the following afternoon when we returned to Buenos Aires and
formerly christened the aircraft before turning it over to the flying
school.

As this was the first modern US trainer that they had seen,
and since it had been donated by the US government, the German
press had a field day in denouncing the acceptance. They ran long
articles once again calling me a Yankee spy who was permitted
to fly over the sacred territory of Argentina without control. Dr.
Bosch came under attack and they called for his resignation as
director general of aviation. In the meantime, the Argentine air
force officers that held posts within the civil aviation directorate
were interested in flying this new machine. The next few days, with
Dr. Bosch's permission, were spent in giving some of the initial
observation rides in the aircraft. Once the military was involved, the

press backed off in their criticism of the program.

Tip was greeted in Buenos Aires by Dr. Samuel Bosch, pictured to Tip's right, and members of the civil aviation clubs. In addition to the flight record Tip set in the Fairchild PT-19A, the newspaper coverage also noted the fact that the aircraft had a plastic skin, instead of metal or fabric. This was a new feature of the trainer, and considered experimental.

Tip's successful flight in 1943 was one for the record books in aviation. He had done it simply to get the aircraft to its destination in Argentina, not for the publicity or the fame, but it was still a first-in-flight requiring considerable skill. Tip had contributed to the annals of aviation almost as an afterthought. This would become his personal style in both his professional and personal life.

Chapter Ten

1943

Flying and Spying in Buenos Aires, Argentina

During the months of March, April, and May 1943, Tip was absorbed in the Argentine program. He flew all over Argentina, training pilots and building the infrastructure of the civil aviation organization. Back home, Louise was consumed by her own struggles with their family life and was missing Tip bitterly. She was living in a series of unfamiliar towns with extended family who, although pleasant and generous, were not her own beloved mother and stern but supportive father. Louise was feeling frustrated and isolated. She didn't know when Tip would return or where she was going to be living next.

During Louise's separation from Tip, she had watched war accelerate throughout the world. Major battles, victories, and setbacks were happening monthly. The pivotal Battle of Midway had taken place six months earlier, when Tip first travelled to Argentina in early June 1942. The battle, near the island of Midway in the Pacific Ocean, was the first significant victory by the United States against Japan and buoyed a worried nation. The US Navy led the fight, but aircraft flying off aircraft carriers had struck the critical blows. World War II was progressing or retreating on the wings of air battles.

Flight was also touching civilian life in more extensive ways. In January 1943, while Tip was navigating through blinding rainstorms over Central and South American jungles, President Roosevelt became the first American president to travel by airplane. He flew to Casablanca, Morocco for a conference with Winston Churchill and other Allied leaders on war strategy and goals. Aviation's most famous hero, Charles Lindbergh, had offered his services to President Roosevelt at the outbreak of the war, but Roosevelt had coldly declined Lindbergh's help. Charles Lindbergh's extensive time in Germany and his undisguised admiration of German technology, in addition to recent speeches he had made had earned him accusations of anti-Semitism. To many Americans, he was no longer a popular figure. Undeterred and unapologetic, Lindbergh continued to make pioneering aviation contributions with United Aircraft. He worked closely with Henry Ford and Igor Sikorsky, and quietly flew unofficial combat missions in the Pacific for commanders more interested in his professional knowledge than his private opinions.

As Tip was grounded by storms in Guiana and flying over the tops of jungle trees in the Amazon, J. Robert Oppenheimer had already secretly appropriated the Los Alamos Ranch School in New Mexico as an operations base for the Manhattan Project, in the race for the atomic bomb. The Los Alamos National Laboratory was established in 1943 and the group of scientists worked frantically to make progress against what they imagined were similar advances in Germany.

Newspapers and magazines were full of war news, and despite patriotic optimism, the outcome was not certain. Every country had staggeringly high numbers of casualties. Rosie the Riveter, a painting by Norman Rockwell, graced the cover of the Saturday Evening Post. Louise's communication with Tip as he made his solo flight was sporadic, and she was mainly dependent on the American Embassy in Argentina and the State Department in Washington for news. It was an anxious time for her, with many days passing without word. When Tip arrived safely in Buenos Aires, Louise was finally able to relax, but the sporadic communication continued as Tip immediately began touring the interior of Argentina and resumed his duties to his CAA mission. Louise still had no idea when she and Michael could join Tip.

The flying school was a huge success and was operating very well under the supervision of my Argentine instructors and inspectors. I spent more time in Dr. Bosch's office drafting and revising sections of his civil aviation directorate. I had brought all these new innovations with me from our CAA. The regulations concerned both domestic civil flight and international airline operations. Setting up primitive airways required me to fly to every part of Argentina and personally inspect their aerodromes. For these flights, I sometimes used Dr. Bosch's Beechcraft Staggerwing, as it was the fastest civilian plane in Argentina. I made other flights in a Waco cabin plane owned by the directorate, and occasional short flights in the Fairchild.

The American Embassy was calling on me more and more for information on certain areas of the country. Germany was sinking all freighters in the South Atlantic that were not from a neutral country. Because of this, some Argentine businesses, like the Dodero shipping line owned by Alberto Dodero, were making millions shipping beef and grain to Europe under Argentina's neutral flag. The embassy wanted to know more about interactions between German and Argentine civilians, as they suspected collusion. One day, as I was leaving the Plaza Hotel where I was residing temporarily, much to my surprise and seemingly to his, I met my German air attaché friend from Washington. He had been recently posted to the embassy in Buenos Aires and seemed disturbed about the way the war was going, particularly the fact that the US had entered the conflict. We exchanged pleasantries and before parting, I invited him to visit our flight school at San

Fernando. The following day he appeared again and we had lunch at the small commissary. I later took him for a flight in the new Fairchild training plane, which I permitted him to fly once in the air, and he remarked that the plane was much better than his early training planes in Germany.

Before leaving, he invited me to have dinner with him and we agreed to dine at the "Boca," a restaurant on the Rio de la Plata waterfront not generally populated by the Argentine social crowd. The discussion during dinner was unimportant local topics, and reminiscing of his early days in the German air force. He told me how he longed to go to war if the battle prolonged. His feelings were that a peace proposal would be made which would halt US aid to England. We made a friendly parting, but were somewhat saddened by the turn of events. I found him to be an interesting gentleman and pilot, an occupation that ordinarily lowers many barriers regardless of country or doctrine. It was obvious that he was alerted by the German Embassy to the existence of the flying school and sent to learn what he could about the US plans in Argentina.

The following afternoon, I received a call from the American Embassy requesting that I meet with the ambassador that afternoon. Arriving at the embassy, I was ushered into the ambassador's office where the ambassador, the first secretary, and the economic advisor (both FBI) were seated. The ambassador, reading from a sheet of paper, informed me that I was seen in the presence of the German air attaché at a restaurant, talking in a friendly manner and that we had been together for more than two hours. The report was obviously a FBI document from one of their agents posted at the "Boca."

I informed the group that the air attaché was a friend of mine whom I met in Washington when the German Embassy requested permission from the CAA to send him to our inspector school to learn our basic pilot policies and how we trained our CAA inspectors. The attaché visited my flight school and flew with me several times. I pointed out that he was intrigued with the little P-12 pursuit ship I would fly to the field from time to time, and had his picture taken sitting in the cockpit. We had no political discussions concerning information of any kind and the meeting was more of two friends meeting in a foreign country. I told the ambassador that if my meetings with the attaché were making the embassy nervous, I would cancel any further get-togethers.

The ambassador said that they had been trying to learn about the new German air attaché and I was the first person on his staff to know him. Rather than not meet with him, the ambassador encouraged me to continue seeing him, as it was a vital connection to the German Embassy and a possible source of information. At that time, Buenos Aires was the center of espionage in the southern hemisphere. The US had agents who had agents and every nightclub in town had spies. The big brassy night club "Faberes," which had girls from every country in Europe working either on the stage or serving food and drink, also had informers from every country in the world working there. I estimated that about a third of the girls were working the merchant sailors for information for the Americans, another third for the Germans, and the other third for the Japanese.

Having access to the only private plane in Argentina, and being the only civilian pilot with unlimited permission to fly, I made many Argentine friends. Most every weekend I would fly to one estancia or another, give the owners a flight, and take aerial snapshots of their beautiful properties. Polo was "de rigeur" and ponies were furnished and games played every morning and afternoon. I played badly on teams that would be playing two ten-goal players on opposite sides. They usually won against the likes of me and their eight-year-olds, who were learning the game. After a morning in the saddle, it was comfortable to get back into the airplane again.

Every Saturday, Dr. Bosch would report to the airport classroom for his instrument course ground school. Following an hour of ground school, we would fly his Staggerwing for two hours of instrument practice. One particular morning, the weather was clear in our area but overcast was reported in our Mar del Plata destination, so we thought we might get some actual instrument flying opportunities. As we approached Mar del Plata, we could see a bank of cloud extending to about five thousand feet in height with a thousand foot ceiling below. No thunderstorms were reported nearby so we entered the cloud at an altitude of about four thousand feet, Dr. Bosch doing the actual instrument flying. We were in the cloud about five minutes when there was a tremendous explosion. The cockpit filled with smoke and the radios went out.

I could smell burning rubber and fabric and immediately took over the controls. I checked the engine RPMs, oil pressures, etc. and determined that the aircraft was still under control and started a gentle turn. I was flying co-pilot in order to have better visibility in the turn. As we had been only a few minutes in the overcast, I knew there was clear weather just a few minutes on a reverse course. We broke out into clear blue-sky weather and began to evaluate what had happened. The aircraft was flying reasonably well and all engine instruments were functioning. Only the radio instruments and set had suffered. We decided to return to Buenos Aires rather than continuing on to Mar del Plata because we had a repair shop at our airport.

Upon landing, we found that about fourteen inches of fabric had been burned off the left wing tip, and that there were two puncture holes in the right wing tip. Our fuse box was seared and the trailing antennae missing. I had heard of static electricity problems from time to time flying, but had never experienced it before. We did have our trailing antennae out for long distance communication and it was always wise to reel it in when flying in thunderstorms to avoid a lighting strike. We had left it out as the conditions in which we were flying were cumulus clouds with no thunderstorms in the area. We could only deduct that a massive charge of static electricity had built up and explosively discharged into the plane.

While Tip was exploring Argentina's airspace in Dr. Bosch's scorched, but still luxurious Staggerwing, his exploits were keeping the American Embassy busy. On May 14, 1943, Merwin L. Bohan, Counselor for Economic Affairs under Ambassador Norman Armour, mailed a packet of confidential documents to the US Secretary of State in Washington D.C. Mr. Bohan had compiled a collection of Argentine dispatches written by Dr. Samuel Bosch that were causing an uproar among Argentine and international commercial airlines. Mr. Bohan was in the uncomfortable position of explaining Dr. Bosch's aggressive, though justifiable, actions requiring new government inspections and controls regarding commercial aircraft and pilots. These had recently severely interfered with much of Argentina's international commercial airline traffic.

Dr. Bosch was flaunting his American backing, support, and funding by publicizing Tip's name at every opportunity. As Dr. Bosch implemented the civil aviation program Tip had written, he called press conferences to promote the directorate's mission, referencing Mr. Cloyce Tippett on every page. These actions were causing diplomatic problems for the embassy, which was trying to uphold Tip's civilian status against increasingly angry, and substantiated, documentation by the local German-staffed "El Pampero" newspaper stating that Tip was observing Argentina's military infrastructure during his tours around the country and reporting back to the US government.

Pan American Airways, Pan American Grace Airways, and Condor Airlines had roared objections to Bosch's interference in their business processes and forced the embassy to intervene. Dr. Bosch quickly backed off from that approach and restricted his orders to domestic Argentine airlines, instead citing the North American companies as models to guide the progress of the Argentine program. Mr. Bohan's letter assured Washington that the disruption to international airline business would not reoccur, and detailed the embassy's attempts to convince Dr. Bosch to reduce his public references to Tip. Mr. Bohan wrote:

"…It is to be regretted that Mr. Tippett's name actually appeared either in the Bureau Order or the letter written by the Director of the Bureau of Civil Aeronautics to the Corporacion SudAmericana de Servicios Aeros S.A. This, however, is but an example of the direct way in which Dr. Bosch works. It has been explained to Mr. Tippett that the embassy feels his name should be kept very much in the background, especially in view of El Pampero's constant campaign against Dr. Bosch, in which it so often features Tippett. It has been suggested that it would be better were he to decline any official appointment and to explain to Dr. Bosch that he must restrict his activities entirely to those of advice and counsel, even though at the same time he will be perfectly free to perform the functions which Dr. Bosch desires to delegate to him…"

But Dr. Bosch continued to wave Tip's name like a banner to rally attention and admiration for his improvements in civil aviation, and he set Tip firmly at the forefront of the push for much needed regulation, improvement, and training throughout Argentina's aeronautical industry.

Aeroposta Argentina was a privately-owned airline flying from Buenos Aires to the south of Argentina, Patagonia, and Punta Arenas, at the very tip of South America. The owner of the airline was Don Ernesto Pueyrredon, whom I had become very friendly with through social contacts. Mr. Pueyrredon invited me to fly with his airline to Patagonia and evaluate his pilots insofar as their instrument flying was concerned, and their general handling of the aircraft. They flew German Junker Ju-52 planes.

The morning conditions of our take-off were heavy fog with visibility of just a few hundred yards. The captain invited me to fly co-pilot and prepared for take-off after the six passengers and two sheep were loaded into the aircraft. He advised me that this fog was local and the top of the overcast was only a few hundred feet. His blind take-off procedure was weird, but it worked. A large white line made of lime was centered on the grass runway extending about half way the length of the runway. Lining up on this white line to the left of the aircraft so that he could see the line clearly with his window open he would start his take-off, keeping the aircraft parallel to the line. The take-off run of the Junkers was only a few hundred feet, and the minute the aircraft was airborne, the captain shifted to his instruments and continued his climb out. Primitive, but workable.

Our first stop was a coastal city about 400 miles south of Buenos Aires. The landing field was unpaved and the terminal was a lean-to shack. By now, the weather had cleared and landing was textbook. Our next stop was Trelew, about 350 miles from Bahia Blanca and another small grass field. Passengers were dropped off and cargo loaded without shutting down the engines. I was warned that we were heading into a high wind area where the surface wind was a constant forty to fifty knots and required outside help in holding the aircraft on the ground while loading and unloading cargo and passengers. Landing at Trelew was windy but not unmanageable.

The next stop, Comodoro Rivadavia, would be with outside help in landing and loading and as we approached the grass strip runway I noticed two small jeep-like vehicles, one on each side of the runway. Standing up in the rear of the vehicles were two men, each with a hooked metal rod. As we floated over the fence at a

ground speed of probably ten miles per hour and still in the air, the
two men hooked onto the half circle of metal on the lower wing
and held us on the ground as we touched down.

    The aircraft was held on the ground until all passengers and
baggage were loaded, then power was applied to the three engines,
the hooks disengaged, and the aircraft lifted off with a ground run
of perhaps fifty feet. Our flight continued along the barren coast
to Puerto Deseado, then on to Santa Cruz and Rio Gallegos where
the flight terminated. Flight time averaged sixteen to eighteen hours
with a turn around the next morning.

    On one of the flights, I was presented with a pair of
penguins. They were in a small cage and I was told they were young
and would make good pets. I was not told that they had to be fed
about ten pounds of fresh fish a day. I kept them in the shower
house at the flight school with the shower turned on, as it was very
warm in Buenos Aires. The penguins seemed uncomfortable from
the heat and refused to eat the various plates offered them. About
a week after I brought them to Buenos Aires, one of the flight
students suggested that we let them take a swim in a small lake near
the airstrip. The property belonged to an absentee landowner and
it seemed innocent enough to exercise the penguins in his small lake.

    At the time, we did not know that the pond was stocked
with prize goldfish and other varieties of exotic marine life. We
watched the penguins for about a half hour diving and frolicking
in the pond, after each dive surfacing with a brightly colored fish in
their beaks. It took the better part of the morning to recapture them
and return them to their shower, but they seemed much happier
than usual. The next day they were given to the local zoo.

    There was much unrest among the labor unions and the
military in the Buenos Aires province at that time. Coups were
attempted within the military barracks, but most were quickly
stamped out with a few casualties and an officer or two deported.
Civilian mob scenes were almost a weekly occurrence. They stormed

the "Casa Rosada" (the Argentine White House) and were dispersed by tear gas and mounted police with sabers and whips.

On one such occasion, Tony Duke, Assistant Naval Attaché to the American Embassy in Buenos Aires, and I were on the outskirts of the plaza observing the gathering of the "descamisados" when the mounted cavalry moved in, swinging their sabers. The mob quickly began to disperse in small groups, one group crowding into our small niche along the sidelines. While pressed against the building walls, one of the group asked me politely if I had a match and I gave him a small pack of paper matches. He quickly ran across the street where a large bus was parked, removed the gas cap, lit the packet of matches, and tossed the burning packet into the tank. The resultant explosion blew my new friend practically back to where we were cowering, but he seemed unharmed and happy.

The mounted cavalry came charging towards us, riding on the sidewalk, and Tony and I decided that we were getting caught up in a situation that was becoming unpleasant. As we left our snug wall hideout and were more or less out in the open and walking away, we hoped we would not be noticed, but a mounted policeman came at us at full gallop, swinging his saber. Fortunately, I caught the flat of the saber, not the edge, but it was enough to knock me down for a second before I could get away to a more protected area and return to the embassy.

These were the weeks leading up to June 4, 1943, when officers in the Argentine military overthrew the Argentine government. It was a bloodless coup, but it was thorough. Every government official who had been urging closer ties with the US was either ousted or put on notice. Dr. Bosch's time as the Director of Civil Aviation was coming to a non-violent close, despite his attempts to hold on and keep US aid flowing.

The new Argentine government, known as the Junta, did

nothing drastic about the country's position regarding the world war, but persuasive members of the military forces made it known that they felt the Axis powers had a better chance of winning the war and wanted Argentine sympathies extended to Germany. The question of Argentine alliance had been answered and it was not to the liking of the US government. While the Allied countries eventually moved to recognize the new military government, they did so slowly and cautiously. After the coup, civilian and military operations alike went through a period of quiet uncertainty as the ramifications of the change in government settled in.

Tip's program in Argentina had been so successful that during his flight from Maryland to Buenos Aires, the US Army Air Corps had granted another plane to Argentina. This time, the craft was a two-engine Cessna, which would expand the Argentine training program into multi-engine aircraft. Tip had once again been requested to return to the United States to pick up his shiny new plane and take it down to South America, but before he could leave to begin what would have been another record-breaking flight (the first Cessna to be flown from North to South America), the Junta overthrew the Argentine government of Ramon Castillo.

This changed Argentina's relationship with the United States. The US stopped courting Argentine officials, and the transfer of the Cessna was put on hold. Tip's civil aviation work had lost one of its primary funding sources, the one that wanted to accrue sympathy towards the US. The bulk of his real mission had already been accomplished with the training programs underway and aviation infrastructure in place. His Argentine mission began to lose momentum, but Dr. Bosch was reluctant to give up the hope of expanding to multi-engine work and kept Tip on the job while forces in the government were in turmoil. The naval intelligence agency of the American Embassy also encouraged Tip to stay in place, adding a note to an intelligence report dated July 7, 1943, saying "...having Mr. Tippett in this position affords a continuous and valuable source of aviation information to the United States government..."

Argentina had very few pilots that could qualify to fly multi-engine aircraft. The multi-engine aircraft that I was invited to fly were owned by the Civil Aviation Directorate and were mostly German and French, not suited to be primary training aircraft. Dr. Bosch and I made a two week inspection trip around Argentina in his Beechcraft to determine how many aero club pilots could be made available for a multi-engine and instrument training course if one was offered. We visited the main aero clubs of Salta, Tucuman, Mendoza, and Cordoba in the north, and Bahia Blanca, San Carlos de Bariloche, Neuquen, and Comodoro Rivadavia in the south. All were very excited about the prospect of attending an advanced flight school.

During this trip, we visited one of my good friends in the Argentine military, Admiral Zar, chief of the naval base at Comodoro Rivadavia. Admiral Zar had attended graduate school in the United States and was a rated navigator. While still a captain in the Argentine navy, and commander of the base, Admiral Zar flew a Waco cabin aircraft back and forth from Buenos Aires to the naval base. He had been doing this for about four years. When he was promoted to admiral, he was given a twin-engine Lockheed Model 12, and I was presented as his pilot, as he was not qualified in the aircraft. I should mention that Admiral Zar had been flying for fifteen years, accident-free. On the first trip in his new Lockheed, I let him try a landing. He overshot the grass runway at the naval base, skidded into an embankment, wiped out the landing gear and came to rest on the railroad tracks bordering the airport. The train from Buenos Aires to the south of Argentina ran once a week, and as the aircraft came to rest on the train track, the train appeared. It hit the aircraft before the admiral and I could escape, breaking the admiral's leg. I was unhurt. The train was traveling at ten mph.

When we returned to Buenos Aires, I received a call

from my friend in the German Embassy asking if we could lunch together. We met at our usual spot in the "Boca" and discussed the general situation in Europe and the war. He advised me that he had requested and received orders to return to Germany and rejoin his squadron. I wished him well, we shook hands, and he turned and said, "I hope we can meet after the war and be friends again." I reported our meeting to the embassy.

The flight training school was operating at capacity and I was spending more and more time in the field inspecting airports, airplanes, and pilots. New manuals had been translated and there was a national enthusiasm spreading throughout the aviation circles to become a part of the new system of flight training. At the same time, the German press was becoming more and more belligerent regarding my activities. Threatening letters were received and anonymous phone calls advising that I must leave the country. The American Embassy cooperated with my request to advise Washington that my work was pretty well finished in Argentina.

Washington agreed to my recall and Dr. Bosch was officially notified that my work with them was being terminated. Dr. Bosch gave a farewell party to which all the aero club presidents were invited, as well as their instructors and pilot trainees. The party was held at the San Fernando airport and a huge "asado" was the entree of the day. An asado is a traditional Argentine barbecue. As the half-side of beef is roasting on stakes set downwind of the hot ashes, you decide what cut of meat you want, well done or rare, and cut it off with a razor-sharp knife about a foot long. This "asado" was special, as they roasted the beef with the hide on. This is called "befe con cuero." You hold the piece of "befe" that you have cut off by the hair on the hide and cut off the meat, or bite it off, depending on how much of their red wine you have consumed. Before the afternoon was over and the last speech made, I'd had one of their new training planes named after me, been made a member of every aero club in Argentina, and given a silver gaucho knife and belt inscribed "from your friends in Argentina."

El Pampero newspaper ran an article about Tip's farewell banquet titled "Aviator Tippett will return to United States with Baggage Crammed with Aeronautical Data." The article correctly, and disgustedly, referenced the fact that Dr. Bosch had been allowing Tip to fly for months over Argentina's restricted airspace, "thus carrying out in a brilliant manner his mission of *observer*."

A partial list of Tip's accomplishments, sent in an embassy dispatch on August 13, 1943, included setting up a system for standardization of flight training, the actual training of forty-eight instructors, the creation of a training course for inspectors and the actual training of three inspectors, the reorganization of traffic regulations for Argentine aero clubs, the organization of a system of aircraft inspections, the actual inspection of all airports and aero clubs in Argentina, the supervision of translation and adaptation of CAA written examinations and flight manuals for use by Argentine civil pilots, the flight check of Aeroposta Argentina, and the training of four instrument inspectors. Tip had accomplished an incredible amount in a short time, and even though Argentina's neutrality was heavily laden with enemy sympathies, his mission had been a clear success.

Chapter Eleven

1943 to 1944
Flight to Rio
Rio de Janeiro, Brazil

The Roosevelt administration declared an official policy of non-cooperation with Argentina. Brazil had not only cooperated enthusiastically with America, but had also declared war on Germany and so became the focus of American attention in South America. Brazil, with an anxious eye on Argentina's German-influenced neutrality, began to plead for military support from the United States.

Tip boarded a plane to the US expecting to rejoin the Army Air Corps, now that the US was engaged in World War II. He contacted Louise and asked her to meet him in Washington D.C. with Michael, who was not yet four years old. Louise traveled by train from Ohio, looking forward to seeing Tip and to visiting her father. Tip journeyed back from his sojourn in South America thinking that it had been a sideline adventure in his aviation career. He hadn't expected to be separated from his wife and son for so long and they had all looked forward to a happy reunion.

My flight from Argentina to Miami, and on to Washington

D.C. was made aboard a Pan American Airways DC-3. The flight originated in Buenos Aires, flew to Rio de Janeiro and overnighted, then went on the next day to Belem for another overnight. The following day to Trinidad and overnight, then on to Miami the next day. Pan American had their own small inns or hotels at the airports where they housed and fed their passengers. They also had their own radio communication system and in many cases, their own exclusive navigation beacons.

During the flight from Rio to Belem, the stewardess casually asked me if I had flown down to South America with Pan American. I told her that I had flown a Fairchild PT-19 down to Buenos Aires from Hagerstown, Maryland. A few minutes later, our pilot, Captain Kimball Scribner, came back to where I was sitting and asked if I was the person that the stewardess had told him had flown a single-engine airplane from the US to Buenos Aires. He said he couldn't believe it. I assured him it was quite true and that I wouldn't want to do the flight on a monthly basis, but I did it. To compound coincidences, after chatting a bit, I found that I had been the CAA inspector that had given Captain Scribner his commercial pilot rating flight test in Miami a couple of years previously. Co-pilots hired at that time were made captains in a little over a year. I flew the rest of the trip mostly sitting in the jump seat with the crew, exchanging experiences on flying in South America. Captain Scribner and I became close friends and agreed we would keep in touch.

I had expected that upon arriving in Washington and checking in with both the State Department and the Air Corps, I would be sent on to my reactivated squadron. Following a two-week leave, I reported back to Washington and was briefed by General Arnold, his staff, and the State Department, as well as the Department of Commerce Undersecretary for Air, Mr. William M. Burden. The gist of the meeting was that I was to go to Brazil and be named Civil Aviation Advisor to Dr. Cesar Grillo, Director

of Civil Aviation of Brazil, as well as Civil Aviation Advisor to
Air Minister Trompsky. My primary mission was to coordinate US
military flights through Brazil to Africa, but I would also establish
a flight school similar to the school established in Argentina to retrain instructors and inspectors in a newly established Brazilian Civil
Aviation Department.

General Henry "Hap" Arnold had been commanding the
US Army Air Corps since before it was renamed in 1941 as the
US Army Air Force. He would still be in charge in 1947, four years
later, when military aviation was finally separated from the army
and became the US Air Force. General Arnold was the guiding force
behind the organization of the now-official Eighth Air Force, active
in England. The leadership of the Eighth Air Force was comprised of
the aviators that Tip had met in the boarding house in Washington at
the beginning of his training with the CAA. General Carl Spaatz and
Lieutenant General Ira Eaker, along with General Hap Arnold, were
now publicly pursuing the plans they had made when Tip was passing
them in the halls. Their daylight precision bombing plans for the war
in Europe were in action and would become legend.

General Arnold was tasked with fighting an air war on
multiple overseas fronts, including new demands to support
operations in North Africa. The only way do this, given Japanese
aggression in the Pacific and German submarine predations in the
Atlantic, was to move military aircraft through Brazil. This required
diplomacy and political maneuvering, and so General Arnold turned
to the State Department for help.

The State Department and the Department of Commerce
had the successfully completed CAA operation in Argentina to
offer General Arnold as a model for Brazil. The program even had
a twin-engine Cessna that could be gifted to Brazil, now that it was
no longer destined for Argentina. The same multi-layered funding
approach used in the Argentine program for civil aviation and

diplomatic influence could be applied to Brazil, and the man who had pulled it off so well just happened to be available. Tip was back in the employ of the CAA and headed south again.

A small detail of my new assignment was that I would be flying the training aircraft to Brazil myself. The newest twin-engine trainer at that time was the Cessna T-50; a five-passenger wood and fabric aircraft powered with two 245-hp. engines. I was very familiar with the aircraft, as we had used the first ones at the Houston Standardization Center for the training of our inspectors. I received permission to refit the instrument panel with state-of-the-art instruments instead of the factory standard. Also, additional radio equipment was installed along with a comfortable interior. I was advised that I could leave when the aircraft was ready and that the civil and military departments had approved of my family flying with me. We would be accompanied by a State Department undersecretary named Anthony "Tony" Satterthwaite.

Tony was a Foreign Service officer and a diplomat of the first order. He was an aviation enthusiast and was anxious to learn first-hand the trials and tribulations of flying internationally. It must be remembered that, at that time, there were no international agreements between countries, only between airlines. Crossing borders without permission or proper clearance could ruin your whole trip with confiscations, fines, and even jail. It was not uncommon, even with properly signed clearances or visas, for the local constabulary to ignore these papers and demand payment for transgression. These problems could always be handled diplomatically and with understanding, as long as payment was made. Tony was as much a living visa as he was a trip companion.

The Cessna T-50 (military designation C-78) was delivered from the factory to Washington D.C. There was much work to be done in preparation for this trip. A new instrument panel was installed and checked, along with new radio equipment and auxiliary fuel tanks. All had to be tested carefully after installation. The ship checked out and I decided to leave on October 24, 1943. Louise, Michael, and Tony Satterthwaite comprised the crew. In order to make everything proper for the aircraft manifest, Tony was listed as co-pilot, Louise as crew chief, and Michael as the radio operator.

Tip had completed his first record-setting flight from Hagerstown, Maryland to Buenos Aires, Argentina, in January 1943 and he was about to set another record over the same terrain less than one year later. This time, it would be the longest flight by a two-engine aircraft the size of the Cessna. Regardless of the record-breaking details, it was still a flight over jungle and mountains in wartime. If Louise had not paid attention to the details of such a journey before, when Tip was flying alone in the Fairchild PT-19A, she certainly did now. Later in her life, Louise wrote the following as an account of the flight intended for magazine publication. It was never published, but she carried it through the various moves and storage conditions she encountered through her life.

Louise: My husband, Cloyce Tippett, a special representative of the Civil Aeronautics Administration in Brazil, met his son, Mike, and me in Washington on his return from his foreign assignment. One day he came in from the CAA office bursting with news and asked me if I'd like to go with him to Brazil. I said sure I would. But Tip had been sent the year before to Argentina for "six weeks" and he had stayed more than a year. All that time, I had one bag packed while I perched precariously on the assurance I was to join him, but I never did. So now I put a strong dash of salt on the Brazil talk.

He assured me patiently that this time it was different and did I, or did I not, want to go to Brazil? I played another card. He had flown down there in a two-seat Fairchild single-engine plane and I wanted very little of that. Tip was a patient guy; tall, good-looking, with smile wrinkles mixed in with the lines that usually frame a pilot's eyes. He described the Cessna that the CAA was turning over to him. Cozy, he said, as a small apartment. Long back seat where you and Mike could curl up and sleep. Now being converted from its military purposes at the factory. Make the trip in ten days. Magnificent scenery. New places. Rio's wonderful.

It took us weeks to get on our way. I found it hard to get my heart into the trip at first. We said goodbye to all our friends in Washington so many times it became embarrassing. I worked myself up to the point where I took the necessary vaccination and typhoid shots. I began to plan my clothes. I had a good taste of the incompatibility of hotel rooms and three-year-old boys. Things got a bit full in that hotel room and we shipped Michael off to his grandmother in Ohio so we could get into the going-away battle unencumbered. Mike and the hotel hadn't been getting along.

We began to pack. We had to play hopscotch over the suitcases in our room. I was completely ruthless with my things, throwing this and that dress to the winds. I listened, innocent soul that I was, to a recently returned American wife from Rio. Concentrate on dressy blacks, a dark suit or two, she said. And I can't decide whether stupidity or spite moved her, but it was a calculated crime. Don't bother about shoes, she said. Indeed! I say if you're going to Rio, take cotton, light silks, things that you can wash because you can't get them dry-cleaned and bring shoes, shoes, and shoes! Unless of course, you wear size four or five and enjoy concrete soles. In that case, you'll be well supplied down there.

As our preparation went along, I worried about this State Department man. Tip had broken the news that he was going along. I thought he might be a formal, forbidding sort. His full name was Livingston Lord Satterthwaite. I worried about other things, too. I inherited my father's Scots habit of looking on the dark side of everything, so I read the army's jungle survival books carefully, only to learn that you must eat white grub worms and get drinking water by lapping up dew on palm leaves.

Tip and I went round and round on parachute or no parachute. When it was obvious that there was no way to have a three-year-old child bail out, I declared firmly that I would go down with the ship rather than land alone in a tropical jungle, so we carried none. I had telephone conversations with my mother-in-law; she didn't help either. She had such strong ideas against taking a child on a flight over the jungle that I feared she had found one of those survival books.

Tip went merrily ahead, collecting the essentials: army K rations (they taste of sealing wax); a machete; a terrifying medical emergency kit full of sulfa and morphine and such; flare guns and such a good radio that he was in ecstasy about it. We staggered out of the hotel laden with two folding canvas army bags, my suitcase, a parachute bag packed with odds and ends instead of a parachute, the medicine kit, the jungle kit, one fur coat, two topcoats, and Tip's handsome tennis bag. And there stood Tony on the sidewalk, carrying one pathetically thin folding bag. I thought we might just get along fine.

The Cessna T-50, military designation AT-17, was a trainer.
Tip's students in Brazil would be able to log twin-engine hours.

Tip: After retrieving Michael from his grandmother, we left Washington National airport at eight a.m., on October 24, 1943, weather cold with high clouds and a brisk tail wind. All went well until we were about twenty miles north of Winston-Salem, North Carolina. The left engine suddenly started running rough and the oil pressure dropped to zero as the head temperature gauge went into the red. Not having feathering props, I immediately

called the Winston-Salem airport and declared an emergency.
The Cessna would not fly very far on one engine with the dead
propeller windmilling, but it would fly. We landed at the airport and
immediately found that we needed an engine change. It was a fine
start. Fortunately we were able to locate a new engine that day and
had it installed the following day. The "what else can go wrong"
attitude lasted as far as New Orleans, where we spent the night
after having refueled in Atlanta, Georgia. The crew thus far was
behaving very well. Our radio operator was intrigued by the sights
and spent most of his waking time looking out the window. From
New Orleans, we flew to Houston, Texas, then on to Brownsville,
where we spent the night and partook of the first of our many
Latin meals.

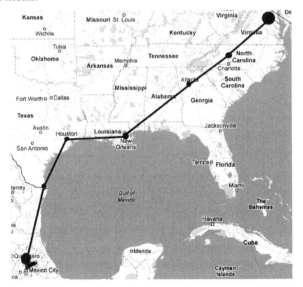

We were fortunate that the next morning held beautiful
weather with light winds. The flight to Mexico City took three hours
and twenty minutes, flying at twelve thousand feet most of the
way. Oxygen was provided although Michael seemed to be content
without it. Mr. O.K. Haley, the CAA representative based in Mexico
City, met us upon landing in Mexico City. Although we were urged
to stay a day or two in Mexico City, I was anxious to get out of the

high altitude country while the weather was still good.

Taking off at Mexico City at maximum load in a Jacobs-powered T-50 is an experience. With twenty-one inches of manifold pressure, 2150 rpm, we broke ground after a run of about twenty-five seconds, when our indicated air speed was ninety mph and rate-of-climb 500 fpm. I was glad that we left at seven a.m. rather than later in the morning when the temperature was higher, as we might have had to abort our take-off.

Louise: We got past Brownsville, Texas, without the CAA deciding that Tip's family had better stay at home, as I had been confident they would. We went up to 12,000 feet, getting above the cloud cover, my first introduction to the land of cumulus. However, the clouds broke as we started across the range of mountains that surround Mexico City. Popocatepetl, almost 18,000 feet high, loomed snow-rimmed in the distance. The range had a surprising number of villages tucked away on well-wooded slopes. After many miles above a cotton-tufted carpet of broken cumulus clouds, we settled down at Mexico City where I began to learn how expatriate Americans live.

The hospitality of the Haley's (he was the CAA representative in Mexico) made our stay in Mexico City very comfortable. We met the servants the family was able to keep on their government salary, and right there I was all set for Latin living. Mike found the Haley's older girl a perfect companion despite the fact she could speak only Spanish. This language problem threw me and, like many other Americans, I had to rely on my own resources. I found I could talk with my hands, my eyes, and even my shoulders. I found that Tip was right in warning me that "if you kick and scream, Latinos will kick and scream right back at you."

We were scheduled for three days there but weather held us up again. The delay gave me a chance to lose my money at the horse races. It didn't seem to matter whether I picked them by

the color of the jockey's cap or by the experts. As we prepared to
depart, I had enough personal flying experience to know that it
was an education to watch a master like Tip planning a flight. He
sent a load of our baggage by Pan American on to Guatemala City
because the Mexico City airport is more than 7,000 feet above sea
level, and that's no place to bring up a heavily-loaded Cessna. As it
was, it seemed that Tip merely drove the aircraft to the end of the
runway and pulled up his wheels. The Cessna had no choice but to
be airborne.

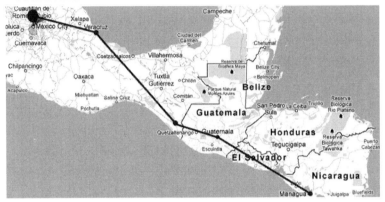

Tip: We landed at Vera Cruz, Mexico, for fuel and
immediately departed for Tapachula, Mexico, to take advantage
of the weather. Refueling at Tapachula took only thirty minutes
but weather built up while we were on the ground and we had to
overnight.

Louise: The tropical fronts, which build up in the
afternoons, caught us at Tapachula. We landed there to wait out
the weather before heading on. The town itself was definitely rural
Mexico, with cobblestone and mud streets, heavy tropical foliage,
and low-eaved adobe houses. Satterthwaite was an orchid fiend and
hung out of the station wagon on the way into town, spotting the
blooms.

Latinos apparently sleep contentedly on mattresses made
of stone and pillows stuffed with clay. They also like their coffee

strong, then diluted with hot milk. The sugar was a coarse gray, which seemed to be low in sweetness. You just never know what you'll meet running about the world in an airplane. Tip had been forced to sleep sitting up in his Fairchild one night at Tapachula in his previous passage, but we found that Cecil B. DeMille had filmed part of "The Story of Dr Wassell" here just months before we arrived. The movie company had built a hotel and then left it operational. There was a shower that was most effective even though it was right over the toilet.

What would you do with a three-year-old on a 10,000-mile airplane trip? I had it all planned. I took along blocks, small airplanes, and little cars. Mike paid them no mind. Occasionally, I could get him to dovetail with me on the big back seat and nap but most of the time he was on Tip's lap, flying the plane or talking for hours into the microphone like Daddy did. He couldn't have played even if he wanted to, because Tip had left about four inches of clear space on the floor. Tony aided and abetted any mischief Mike thought up, and I gave myself indigestion hissing at the undiplomatic State Department agitator. I can't convey the slightest idea of the grandeur of scenery while flying. It was overwhelmingly beautiful.

Tip: After Tapachula, we made a lunch stop in San Jose de Guatemala. This was a US military base and the soldiers were pleased to see anyone they could talk to besides themselves. They were overjoyed to see a little boy and took him in tow, much to Michael's delight, and disappeared into the village. As we were lunching with the commander of the base in his tent and enjoying a couple of hours of relaxation, we paid little attention to what was happening to Mike. As we were preparing to pack up and take off for Guatemala City, a caravan of soldiers appeared, carrying Mike on their shoulders. He was screaming with delight because he had a monkey on his shoulders, tail wrapped around his neck. The soldiers

had given Mike the pet monkey to take with him. This delayed our
departure for thirty minutes while I tried to explain to Mike, and the
soldiers, why we could not take the monkey with us. My lecture did
not satisfy Mike, who sulked for about an hour after we took off.

The flight to Guatemala City was most pleasant. We flew
through the pass into the city at eight thousand feet, in clear skies
with a few cumulus clouds hanging over the mountains. We refueled
and departed immediately for Managua, Nicaragua. The afternoon
thunderheads were already forming and I flew us straight to the
coast to avoid the heavy rain and turbulence that accompanied
these clouds. We had our first taste of instrument flying getting into
Managua. The heavy afternoon rains arrived before we did and we
had no choice but to continue. The buffeting wasn't too bad, but
even a small amount is too much if it can be avoided. The three-
year-old thought it great fun, bouncing around and squealing with
delight every time we hit a little turbulence.

Louise: We went into Guatemala City through a pass with
peaks towering on either side. I spent the next few hours with my
nose pressed against the windows, watching the coastline below us.
I saw the white frill of waves wiggle off into grays and tans and
then into emerald greens and finally, way offshore, blue. Thatched
roof settlements straggled along muddy streams and the volcanic
mountains loomed over everything. The mountains put little puffs
of steam into the air every now and then.

Suddenly the whole view was blotted out by a thundering
rainsquall. A solid sheet of rain curtained our entry into Managua,
which was a critical gasoline stop for the Cessna. We couldn't skip
it and fly another direction to get out of the rain. Tip began to let
down, talking furiously into the microphone, and Tony and I peered
futilely at the rain-enveloped wingtips. That's when you are thankful
for a good pilot. Tip found a hole in the clouds and we scooted
down through them. There before us, "right on the nose", was

Managua.

Tip: We decided to spend a couple of days in Managua
relaxing and checking over the ship. Since the engine change, there
had been no trouble with any of the components. Lots of oil on
the cowlings, but that is the life of the Jacobs engine. When it stops
throwing oil, you begin to worry. The two days in Managua were
spent peacefully. A long cable was sent to Panama announcing our
schedule in order to be escorted through the Canal Zone by fighter
aircraft. A bit of sightseeing and route planning took up most of
the time.

Louise: While Tip checked the weather, he installed Mike
and me in the army lounge where the soldiers had a pet fawn and a
chipmunk. Mike was entranced with the fawn's little hooves clicking
on the tile floors. The presence of men working to build the Pan
American Highway, plus the passengers overnighting with Pan
American Airways, left us without any hotel accommodations. Just
as the vision of sleeping in the airplane seemed about to materialize,
Tony's influence began to pay off. He had us jeeped to the home of
the military attaché, Major Duke and his wife, who won our fervent
gratitude by taking us in. Cozy little horse-drawn carriages were the
mode of transportation in Managua, so we rode one home from
dinner.

The town had no street numbers or names (at least, none
known to the Americans) but fortunately the Dukes lived next
to the Costa Rican Embassy, so we were able to give the driver
a destination. I learned a fascinating bit of information about
Nicaraguan communications. There was no device on the central
telephone switchboard to indicate when a conversation was finished.
Instead, an operator plugged in and yelped "Allo?" If you didn't
come back pronto and scream "Hablando!" at him, he would
cut you off. "Keeps all our phone calls to a minimum," our host

admitted.

Tip: Leaving Managua, we skirted the lake and spent most of the hour and thirty minutes in flight dodging cumulus buildups, and then finally sighted San José. Although we had sufficient fuel to continue on to David, Panama, I decided to top off the tanks, as we were certain to have some instrument flight time en-route. We stayed overnight.

Louise: We made San Jose, Costa Rica, the next day, which was Sunday, November 7. Satterthwaite, who had been stationed there ten years previously, returned with great fervor. We were immediately taken in tow by two of the embassy staff and whisked out to the country club, which lay ten miles outside the city. The valley was a shallow saucer heavy with greenery and frosted with clouds, which curled around the surrounding mountains.

At this time, one of those understanding women that every mother needs came into my life. She was an embassy wife and she prescribed for me a whole day of rest from Michael. Although he was a little darling, I had been living so close to him for so long, that you will know what I mean. It was blessed relief to leave him playing with her children for the entire day. I got an invitation to dinner and rushed back to the hotel and used the traveling iron to press out my one fancy dress. My hair had long since decided to go straight, so I wound a scarf around it and pretended I was the turban type. This help was typical of the graciousness that we encountered along the way.

The next morning, we got ready for our flight. I was beginning to become resigned to the delays at each airport. We went through the routine of up at dawn, a rushing taxi to the field, and then an hour or so while Tip scurried around after weather reports and clearances. Tony Satterthwaite would say, "He's after more wool!" The "wool gathering" as Tony put it, meant that Tip was making sure each ounce of gasoline was put thru a chamois before it went into the fuel tank. It was a chore and took time, but the meticulous care paid off in safety. Soon, we would have our military escort through the Canal Zone. In those war days, the Cessna was the only civilian plane that had been in that territory recently. The Panama Canal was so vulnerable to air attack that the military took no chances, and so civilian or no, we got our escort.

Tip: From David we proceeded on to Rio Hato, Panama, where we were forced to spend the night as the tropical rain and thunderstorms made it risky to continue. A daybreak take-off revealed the beautiful early morning sight of the four P-40 fighter planes that escorted us across the Canal Zone. Two ships flew in formation on each wing, much to the delight of Michael, who kept shrieking and pointing at the trim little fighters flying so close to us. How I envied those guys in the fighters. Perhaps, I thought, after this mission I can get back to fighting the war.

Louise: The entry into the Canal Zone was tops in excitement. The P-40s had to do a series of S-turns on our tail to keep their speed down to that of the Cessna. You may remember that airliners had their curtains tightly drawn when flying over the Panama Canal, but for us, the whole tremendous view of the canal was spread out. I got to thinking of the bored young men assigned to the anti-aircraft guns below and wished the P-40s would stay closer to us. Those gunners had been waiting a long time and nothing had happened. Just pulling a trigger would relieve the monotony. I wasn't too sure some trigger-happy soldier might not let fly with some flak. Our orange and black paint job was a far cry from army and navy camouflage.

Tip: Although we had fairly low ceilings and occasional rain, we flew on to Coro and then to La Guaira airport in Caracas, Venezuela. We remained overnight and prepared for an early morning take-off, planning to fly to Atkinson Field in British Guiana.

Louise: A heavy front played games with us going into our next landing. In one of the towering clouds, I saw my first sign of patterns that Tip called The Pilot's Cross. The clouds made a vast and awesome pattern of tunnels, peaks, and eerie tree-like shapes. Their innards contained those turbulent air currents that can tear a plane apart. We landed at La Guaira, Venezuela, and were greeted by the military attaché. He was on hand to meet some touring congressmen, but as they failed to show up, he took us up the mountain to Caracas in senatorial transportation.

The Caracas road has some estimated six hundred curves as it doubles back and forth, going up grades built on the sides of a deep ravine. There are very narrow streets with stores flush to the pavement, but only a few feet in depth. Homes clung to the upper slopes. I kept wondering how many stray children were lost each year off the backyards. The lovely residential district lies out further in a valley. Trees parade the avenues and lawns and gardens frame the houses.

Tony Satterthwaite knew the Oswald Watsons of the embassy, so all four of us landed on their doorstep. My admiration went rampant for a hostess who can weather four unexpected overnight guests without a quiver of an eyelid. We had drinks and dinner at the Tivoli Hotel and I had a dark moment in mothering that bothers me to this day.

At the hotel, Tip and Tony had cocktails while Mike squirmed on the barstool. The men had me trapped in the middle and I felt completely helpless. Tip, of course, left me to manage Mike at times like that. When Mike wants to go eat, and Tip is sounding off with some flying crony, Mike is my problem. And when I want to eat too, Tip is my problem as well. This time, Tony was problem number three, but after a long day of flying, the only problem I felt I could solve was Mike.

I looked at him, poor impatient hungry little kid, and I thought of the time he had gulped brandy from Daddy's bottle. The picture of his limp little form, I believe we adults call it 'out cold', came before me and I fingered my own cocktail. Wouldn't it be peaceful? Then I shook myself vigorously and downed my drink so fast I took on a coughing spell. I've been worrying about the matter ever since. It might have been just airplane nerves. It might have been Cessna claustrophobia. Anyhow, I'm glad to say the temptation didn't come again. I made noises about staying over to see more of the city but we were on our way to Trinidad by 7:30 the next morning.

Tip: Due to heavy thunderstorms throughout the area we gave up our plan to go all the way to Atkinson Field and cleared for Trinidad instead. We were guests of Pan American airways in their comfortable guesthouse for the night. A dawn takeoff was made with clear skies and light winds. The flight was to take about three hours, but due to later rain and thunderstorm activity, we flew almost four hours. Atkinson Field is located in a heavy jungle area just a few miles from the coast. Locating it this trip was much easier with the new radio beacon, which I did not have access to on my first flight in the Fairchild. After refueling, we dined at the mess hall and bedded down in the officers' quarters.

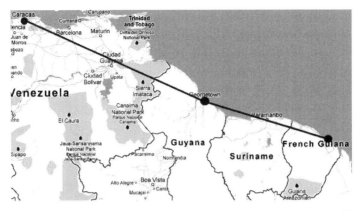

Louise: We caught up with the war again at Atkinson Field in British Guiana, where battle-camouflaged US transport planes and bombers were roaring away to Africa. Coming in, a steep bank of the plane woke me from a nap. Outside was a low blanket of darkish clouds licking our wings and hundreds of feet below was angry water. En-route to French Guiana, we had been asked to watch the jungle to locate, if possible, a plane that had been lost along that route. We saw nothing but unappetizing greenery with sluggish breaks of muddy streams and an occasional brave settlement of mud huts.

Belem was our next destination, but the gas stops at Atkinson Field in British Guiana and Galion Field, French Guiana broke the stretch. We crossed over the infamous Devils Island, but its inner horrors and tragedies didn't carry up to our altitude. It looked rather like a school. Mike suffered the first calamity of the trip at Galion Field. He ran into the edge of an open window and injured his ear. The bleeding alarmed me so much that the army doctor, Captain Steele, very kindly examined him. It was a minor cut, but the delay had cost us the remaining daylight. The army came to our aid with cots in their operation shack. We dined with the soldiers and saw a 16mm version of "The Three Musketeers."

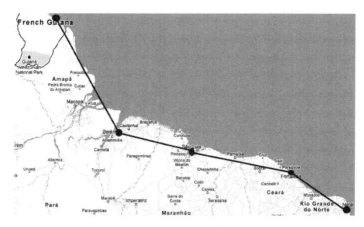

Tip: The weather was misty with low ceilings as we left Atkinson Field for the trip to Cayenne, French Guiana over Surinam, and the flight was uneventful. After refueling in French Guiana, we cleared for Belem and the one hundred mile crossing of the mighty Amazon River. All hands aboard were most impressed when they sighted alligators (caimans) lying on the riverbanks. From Belem we were blessed with clear skies flying along the coast of Brazil and landing and refueling at such lovely small cities as Sao Luis, Fortaleza, Natal, Recife, Sao Salvador and Caravelas.

Louise: On November 13, Mike turned four years old. What other four-year-old has celebrated his birthday with a crossing of the equator pretending he was on a roller coaster 8,000 feet in the air? Tip had me sitting up front, peering down at the approach of the Amazon, while Tony was mysteriously busy in the back seat. We were a little too high in the air to go through the Rites of Neptune, but he conceived an aeronautical version of the traditional ocean celebration and made a mask out of paper and lipstick, and then got set for a series of roller-coaster dips. Tony had rigged up an absurd King Neptune's mask and Tip kept the Cessna diving and zooming.

Mike never got enough of it, but I did. That same day we crossed the Amazon and for my money, this is all the space it deserves. It was a bitter disappointment because it was broken into so many parts and tributaries. Fortaleza was our first Brazilian town, one of gaily-colored stucco houses and stiffly trimmed trees and shrubs. Pan-American Airways had made arrangements for our use of their suite at the Hotel Excelsior. It was the only one in the place with a private bath, and once again, the deadly inflexible beds.

In Belem, Tip bought Mike a Brazilian comic book. Although I had been studying Portuguese for the last two or three weeks, I was not prepared for this. With no Portuguese, a dozen words of Spanish, and high-school French, I had fun trying to decipher the captions. I have since found that Portuguese is not a language you can master in ten easy lessons. My Portuguese was just strong enough to tell a frantic American woman at Natal whether to go in the room marked "Caballeros" or "Senhoras."

We had a little talk, she and I. I told her in delicate feminine phrases of my four and five-hour flights with two men and a boy in a five-seat airplane. Woman to woman, I told her how the plane came equipped with a relief tube for the male occupants, but no accommodation for the wife. I brought along a small enamel pan with a lid. To use it, I squatted and spread my skirts about me like a broody hen. Fortunately, I believe I only had to resort to that method once. Mike thought the relief tube great fun.

We overnighted in Bahia, or Baia, depending on which map you read, and it was one of the scenic plums. It was built on two levels facing a harbor partly screened by a low peninsula. There was a white concrete shaft housing an elevator, which transported the pedestrian traffic up and down. The upper city had narrow cobblestone streets. We had ridden the twenty miles to town with an army transport officer, but the taxi ride for the twenty miles back cost us a bundle. Gasoline was just as scarce in Brazil as in the United States. The road was a winding washboard crowded with wandering goats and stubborn burros. Each hazard gave our cabby a chance to blow his multi-toned horn.

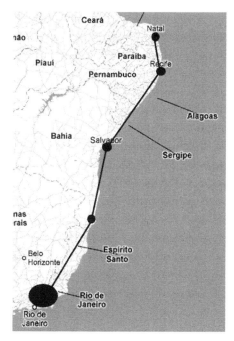

Airborne again, we sighted Rio at last. The view of the harbor wiped away my fatigue. It was quite beyond description with great peaks, blue water crusted with islands, sharp modern buildings, and wide tree-lined avenues. For me, there was a touch of nostalgia for San Francisco with the ferryboats plowing their awkward way through the bay. There were times when I had hated the Cessna with a deep, purple hate, and times when I wished for a soft and permanent bed. Or thirsted for unavailable water with an almost Sahara intensity, but I wouldn't have traded the trip for anything. Nothing in the world, no travelogues, no description, will ever prepare the traveler for the beauty of Rio's harbor from the air.

I treasured the view of the mouth of the bay with Sugar Loaf Mountain as sentinel, and the gracious winding of the flowered boulevards, and the austerity of modern apartment houses that bit into the mountain sides, and the airport of Santos Dumont that lay like a postage stamp at the mouth of the main thoroughfare. I saw the Christo, the tremendous statue of Christ, which stood on the top of Corcovada Hill and stretched out his arms in blessing.

Ferryboats, white-winged sailboats, clumsy freighters, and warships dotted Botafogo Bay. The air was soft, the sun welcoming, and the water very blue.

We landed on November 15, 1943, after twenty-two days en-route. We covered about ten thousand miles over country that I hadn't dreamed of being able to see. Now that we had arrived, I found that I was rather fond of Tony. I could look at Mike again with all a mother's love. I was grateful to Tip for his unfailing good humor, although at times it seemed indecent. I learned that a girl can get along if she puts her mind to it, and that it felt good to be the first American family to travel by air from the United States to Rio in what amounted to a private plane. And I paid my compliments to the plane. Once her digestive system was fixed in Atlanta, she didn't falter once.

On approach to landing in Rio de Janeiro, Brazil.

Tip: We landed in Rio de Janeiro, tired but happy, and were met by a contingent of State Department officials, Brazilian civil aviation officials, and representatives of the Brazilian air ministry.

We were packed off to our temporary residence at a small hotel on Copacabana Beach and prepared for our stay in Rio. Within a week a house was rented on Ipanema Beach and the family settled in, complete with a newly-hired Brazilian maid.

Chapter Twelve

1944

Flying to Rio Again, and Again, Brazil

Ipanema Beach in early 1944 Rio de Janeiro was a colorful place. The diplomatic life that Tip was now enjoying gave Louise a full card of social duties and responsibilities, and she was delighted. For an American woman just turning thirty, it was a fun position to be in. Home-making on the beach in Rio de Janeiro was a far cry from the small house by a Texas airfield. Louise had domestic help and a whirlwind social life. The embassy hosted parties and functions that dazzled. Dancing, drinking, and meeting people were considered part of the job. The American ambassador to Brazil at the time was Jeffery Caffery, who was an accomplished diplomat with an active after-hours lifestyle. Louise observed that the social lives of the South American Embassy personnel were on the wild side at times.

Civil aviation took a major step forward with the formation of the International Civil Aviation Organization (ICAO) in Chicago in 1944. The US government had invited fifty-five countries to gather and discuss an approach to finally bringing together all of the civilian aviation activities around the world. Safety was the primary concern, but commerce and communication were also on the table. This new officially-coordinated effort would soon affect Tip personally, but for now, he was absorbed in moving Brazil forward in the same way he had with Argentina.

In July of 1944, the famous pilot and author Antoine de Saint-Exupery disappeared over the Mediterranean. He was on a reconnaissance mission to support the Allied invasion of his native France. His loss was widely mourned throughout the aviation community, especially by the Lindbergh family. Saint-Exupery had just published his most famous book, The Little Prince, in 1943 and was only forty-four years old. While Tip had never talked about meeting Saint-Exupery, the flier's records and writings were as widely known as Lindbergh's.

Three out of four of the most famous pilots in Tip's time had now died in flight. Only Charles Lindbergh was still flying, and only one of these record-setting heroes had died as a result of war. Amelia Earhart had disappeared and been declared legally dead. Wiley Post had died in a well-publicized crash, and now Saint-Exupery was also gone. Tip was making his own risky and record setting flights. His emphasis on safety, preparation, and training was more vigorous than ever.

The war in Europe, which affected everything, still seemed very far away from Rio. The leadership of the US armed forces was beginning to understand that progress against the Japanese was going to take an enormous toll in human lives. The tendency of Japanese soldiers to fight to the death, and the frequency of Japanese civilian suicides, was an unexpected aspect of the Pacific theater. War among the blazing hot islands of the Pacific was very different from the war in Europe, where the Allies were close to victory.

In June 1944, General Eisenhower led an overwhelming force of nearly three million men up from the beaches of Normandy, France. By August, these Allied troops had liberated Paris from Nazi occupation.

President Roosevelt, concealing his rapidly failing health from the public, won re-election to his fourth term amidst war turmoil that encompassed the globe. He had encouraging news that the Manhattan Project, still a closely guarded secret, had made progress in its goal to develop an atomic bomb.

Tip took his Argentine experience and expanded on it, determined to accomplish even more with Brazil. He was absorbed and determined, and finally had a stable home environment to balance his work. This time, the diplomatic relationship was more established, so he could acknowledge his embassy connections and rely on his official ties with the CAA. Tip was heavily involved with the military and intelligence work that was an underlying purpose of his mission to Brazil. Similar efforts had been disguised as a social aspect of his work in Argentina, but everything was bigger in Brazil.

Louise and Tip entertained frequently at their apartment on Ipanema Beach in 1944.

A series of meetings were arranged with the Brazilian military, the Department of Civil Aviation, and the State Department. At these meetings, I outlined the various steps that would be taken to establish an advanced training center for civilian instructors and inspectors as well as translating all pertinent CAA manuals into Portuguese. An inspection trip to Brazil's principal airports would be necessary in the future, as well as a complete check of their radio communication system. I received total cooperation from all the entities and was surprised with the interest and vigor that the civil aviation personnel showed in the program.

The Department of Civil Aviation assigned to me one of their young engineers who had just been granted his private pilot's license. Eugenio Seifert was of German parentage and spoke very good English. Although he had never visited the United States, he was a student of the country and amazed me with his knowledge of the customs of the American people and our technology. He was a tireless worker and spent sixteen hours a day preparing the English flight manuals for translation into Portuguese so that we could start our flight school at the earliest possible moment. A small grass field a few minutes from downtown Rio was offered as a site for the school. Builders immediately set upon the airfield, and within weeks a new hangar and office buildings were erected. Students were bussed from a small hotel in the vicinity to the school for classes and flight training.

During the few weeks preparing the airstrip and the buildings, I was offered several aircraft to fly and inspect, which would then be used in our initial training courses. The aircraft offered were much like the aircraft used in training in Argentina. We had three Focke-Wulf 44 biplanes, and one high-wing parasol-type Messerschmitt, which was a single-seat fighter trainer powered with an inverted BMW twelve-cylinder engine. I did not release this ship for student flying but instead kept it for myself, as it was a joy to fly. Three Brazilian-made high-wing primary trainers and the Cessna T-50 twin that we had just flown down to Rio completed the inventory.

It became immediately obvious that the Brazilian program was to be much larger than the original plans called for. After conferring with State Department officials and our US military, I advised the Brazilian civil aviation department that I was requesting two American flight instructors to join the program. The Brazilians immediately approved this and the request was forwarded to Washington. Within a matter of weeks, the two instructors arrived and the program started. The pattern of the training program was much like the Argentine program, which had already proved successful. Out of the first class of ten instructors, three were selected for inspector training and were kept at the school to act as instructors and check pilots. For the first few classes, I flew with each student to determine his efficiency and the ability of the instructors to impart the new flight theory and technique to the students. The system was working.

More and more demands were being made of my time from the State Department, the US military, and the Brazilian Air Ministry. I had become very friendly with several high-ranking officers in the Brazilian Air Force. I had visited the headquarters of the Caribbean Air Command in Recife several times and knew the commanding general quite well. Relations between the Brazilian high command and the US were generally good, but in some areas were not working well. Brazil was, at the start of the war, firmly allied with the US, but there was a popular Brazilian opinion that Rommel in Africa was winning that war and it would be only a matter of time until England would surrender.

One morning I was called to the ambassador's office and told that the Defense Supply Corporation had once again commandeered me for an anti-Axis goodwill action on their behalf. The ambassador held a memo from US headquarters in Washington that I was being assigned, on memorandum receipt, one C-45 twin-engine Beechcraft to aid in carrying out duties that would be described later, including unrestricted access anywhere in Brazil. I was to fly back to Washington and pick up the aircraft to fly it back to Brazil.

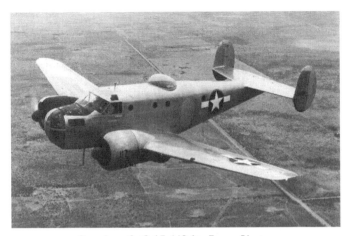

Beechcraft C-45, US Air Force Photo

This trip, which took place in June, 1944, would be Tip's third flight from Washington D.C. to South America in less than two years, but the Beechcraft C-45's power, and Tip's freedom to acknowledge his military connections, changed everything. The Beechcraft C-45 was a powerful, twin-engine, six-passenger aircraft that was being used for every imaginable wartime purpose. This time, Tip could fly the military route through Guantanamo Bay, Cuba, and rely on the Beechcraft's range of 1,200 miles. This made it possible to cross the Atlantic from Miami to the South American mainland using only a few islands to refuel and overnight. Tip could finally fly directly across the Amazon from Belem to Rio de Janeiro, something he had been eager to do ever since he started flying this remarkable route.

The Fairchild PT-19A, which Tip had flown down the first time, had a 430-mile maximum range. He had extended that range by installing an extra fuel tank in the second cockpit, but still had to work with a maximum speed of 132 miles per hour and his solo pilot status, which required him to hug the coastline of Central and South America. The Cessna T-50, which he had flown just eight months earlier, had a better range of 750 miles, again extended for safety by extra fuel tanks, and a top speed of 195 miles per hour. But he was still the only pilot and had to take the land route because of the aircraft's range. This meant frequent refueling stops and overnights. Now Tip was in the cockpit of an aircraft that rivaled the Douglas DC-3 for range and power. In fact, the Beechcraft C-45 had more than 100 miles greater range than the DC-3, and could fly 225 miles per hour, even without the modifications that Tip considered standard for flying into South America.

When I arrived in Washington to pilot the aircraft back to Brazil, I learned that one of the my most important assignments was to urge the Brazilians to permit the US military to fly combat aircraft through Brazil to Africa via Ascension Island to Dakar and on to military airfields. Another important project was locating raw rubber in the jungles and arranging to have it transported down the Amazon River to Belem, then shipped to the US.

At headquarters, I went to General Arnold's office and was given a letter authorizing me to call upon the commanders of any air force base for assistance or supplies in order to carry out my assigned duties. The letter was signed by General Arnold himself. I was advised that the new Beechcraft C-45 was being requisitioned from the Ferry Command and would be delivered to me in Washington within a week. I was authorized to make any changes in the aircraft equipment that I deemed necessary, including the installation of long-range fuel tanks. Within a week after receiving the Beechcraft, the long-range tanks were installed and the aircraft avionics and instruments revised for more precise instrument flying.

I was unaware that a Ferry Command officer would accompany me until the morning before departure. I was told that Lieutenant Colonel Paul Davis would be in command of the aircraft until it reached Brazil, because it was a Ferry Command aircraft. In checking out the lieutenant colonel's background, I found that he was a political appointee, former member of the National Guard, and had never flown outside the US. He had very little flying time. I protested the order, saying that decisions might have to be made flying that he would not be capable of making due to lack of experience. I invited him along for the ride, which is what he wanted, but I was the pilot-in-command.

We cleared the next morning for Miami and after we were under way, I turned the aircraft over to the lieutenant colonel, who was riding in the co-pilot's seat. He had trouble maintaining altitude and airspeed, as well as heading, which indicated that it was going to be a long journey, especially as I kept pointing out these discrepancies to him. His attitude was "what difference does it make? We're headed in the right direction."

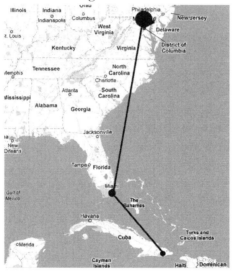

We landed in Miami only long enough to pick up our over-water gear, our medical kit, a rifle, and a pistol. I should mention here that the aircraft had a CAA aircraft license number (NC-1) painted on one wing and a military star on the other. I was planning to use the more convenient of the two designations, depending on where I landed. Davis asked if he could make the take-off from Miami, on our way to Guantanamo, Cuba for an overnight. Flying from the co-pilot's seat, his take-off was erratic. Direction control was a problem and his flying was generally sloppy. He said he had never flown a Beechcraft before and he would like to make the landing at Guantanamo.

The runway at Guantanamo at that time was a single strip paralleling the ocean beach. We had about a ten-knot crosswind, which I cautioned him about. The approach was a disaster; high and fast with a drift factor that he did nothing about. I let him touch down on the wheels and then bounce back into the air, and by then he had left the runway. I told him to apply power and go around for another attempt, but he decided that perhaps the crosswind was too much for him and I had better land the plane.

That evening, sitting in the officers' mess, we had a heart-to-heart talk. He confessed that he had very little flying time but would like to learn from the trip. It was agreed that I would give him dual instruction during the trip, in return for him assuming the role as student. From Guantanamo, we flew and overnighted in St. Thomas. Davis got carried away with his first night in the tropics and imbibed a bit too freely. I had recommended an early night, as we had a long flight the next day to Trinidad. The result of his partying was that he had a monstrous hangover the next morning and was surly and unpleasant throughout the flight, when he wasn't sleeping. His bad manners at our refueling stops were beginning to annoy me. I would need these people for assistance on later flights and I wanted a friendly atmosphere to prevail, but his attitude never changed, no matter what I said. Nothing satisfied him and he considered all the people he met to be stupid.

The flight from Trinidad to Belem was long, and we arrived in the middle of a rainstorm. We had flown on instruments about two-thirds of the way, and in some moderate turbulence. During

the flight, Davis insisted that we land and terminate the flight until
the weather improved. I told him to be quiet and that we were lucky
that the weather wasn't worse than it was.

After securing the aircraft at the Belem airport, I suggested
that we take a taxi into town rather than stay at the air base. There
was a very good hotel and restaurant in Belem named Madam
Zay Zay's. As we were riding into town in the decrepit old taxi (no
windows and one door wired shut), we passed a young lad who
had a small boa constrictor wrapped around his neck, who hailed
us. Davis was fascinated, having never seen a boa constrictor up
close, and demanded that we stop the cab so that he could have a
closer look. I got out of the cab and spoke to the lad in Portuguese
regarding the snake. He advised me that it was for sale and was
guaranteed to keep the river rats (about the size of a cocker
spaniel) away from our house. He advised me that the boa could be
purchased for three dollars. On the spur of the moment, I decided
that I would repay Lieutenant Colonel Davis for all the hours that
he annoyed me on the trip. I told the boy that my friend in the cab
might want to buy the snake, but he wanted to handle it first. The

lad walked over to the cab and thrust the snake through the open window onto Davis's lap. As the door was wired shut, there was no place to escape. I had never realized that a man could scream like that.

    The snake incident had a definite impact on our relationship, which was shaky to say the least. When Davis learned that we were flying direct to Rio de Janeiro over some of the worst jungle in the world, he almost left the flight in Belem. I assured him that the route we were taking was the route Pan American flew, and that we would be stopping to refuel in Barreiras, a halfway point. There simply were no landing fields in between and any alternative would add a thousand miles to the trip. The flight was uneventful and upon landing in Rio, Davis demanded that he be taken to the office of the US air attaché immediately to arrange his return via commercial aircraft.

    I did not linger in the attaché's office, but advised the attaché officer discretely that the lieutenant colonel was a politician and could be troublesome. The air attaché called me the following day and said that he had taken Davis to dinner and dropped him off at his hotel with the advice that some of the seedy nightclubs should be avoided, as they were off-limits for military personnel. Apparently, that did not deter our friend who reported to the embassy the next day that he had been beaten and mugged, losing his passport, money, and identification cards. He said he could identify the girl he had picked up at the bar and the place where she had taken him. He was not certain he could identify the person who slugged him. He was given a new passport, sufficient funds, and an airline ticket to take him back to Washington. I never saw or heard of him again.

As Tip settled back into his civil aviation work in Rio with this shiny new addition to the school's fleet, he began to take advantage of the unlimited access to Brazil that had come along with it. Tip had permission to fly anywhere in the country and this time, the muscle to get there fast. Tip had made a personal connection with General Hap Arnold and kept in touch with him by letter. The General wrote that he was gratified to learn that the Air Force and the CAA were working together so effectively in Brazil, and to thank Tip for sending him a novelty pen that would write both at altitude and underwater.

In the course of his civil aviation and diplomatic work, Tip naturally crossed paths with Paulo de Oliveira Sampaio, president of the giant Brazilian airline Painair do Brasil. Panair was the first airline outside of the US to operate the Lockheed Constellation, and its service record was extraordinary. Sampaio's English was perfect, and he and Tip formed a friendship that would last their lifetime. The work Tip was doing to establish and maintain the air supply route through Brazil to North Africa was parallel to Panair's establishment of airports in strategic locations critical to both commercial and military air transport. Painair built at all the sites Tip had used in his Cessna and Fairchild flights from North America, like Macapa, Belem,

Foraleza, Natal, and Recife. Tip and Paulo had plenty to talk about at their frequent asado and golf outings in Rio.

At the beginning of 1945, Tip pulled together reports to CAA headquarters in Washington D.C., detailing his progress and evaluating the present and future costs of the Brazilian civil aviation program. As chief of the mission, Tip personally visited each airfield in Brazil and summarized his findings with a write-up of the planes available and student experience in them. The first revelation from classes held at aero clubs throughout Brazil was that many of the Brazilian pilots needed access to modern training materials. Their main training manual had been a French book published in 1920.

The Brazilian training fleet included three Fairchild PT-19s that had been flown down in the spring of 1942 from Hagerstown, Maryland to Rio by a 58-member team of pilots, mechanics and support aircraft. They had taken a similar route that Tip had traversed almost a year later alone, but they had terminated their flight in Rio, while Tip had continued south to Buenos Aires. The planes were now in poor repair and Tip noted difficulties keeping them maintained and flying, but they were still the best trainers from the students' perspective.

In addition to the Fairchilds, there were three Focke-Wulf 44's, one Aeronca L3, and several Piper Cubs. The one Bucker Jungmann biplane with its swept-back upper and lower wings was irresistible for acrobatics. This fleet of foreign aircraft presented Tip with the challenge to keep as many of them on the line as he could, given their maintenance requirements and condition. He did have more aircraft to choose from, as Brazilian manufacturers had been busy making unauthorized copies of many of the foreign planes in use at the time, but some of them failed to meet Tip's standards. He carefully evaluated the Brazilian aircraft and wrote detailed reports for the CAA.

There was a single Instituto de Pesquisas Tecnologicas, (IPT-7) which Tip refused to fly after taking a close look at its internal condition. The program had twelve Companhia Aviacao Paulista 4s (CAP-4). Tip's primary concern was safety, and he decided that they were unsuitable for student use and grounded most of the Paulistinha fleet. He was worried about the Muniz M-7, M-9, and HL -1, all built by Companhia Nacional de Navegacao Aerea. An example of his primary criticism was the HL-1's door, which opened into the wind stream and was therefore difficult to bail out of in an emergency. The HL-6, a low-wing, all-wood, tandem-cockpit ship with a single Lycoming engine passed Tip's inspection, which was a comparatively high compliment. As Tip toured the Brazilian factories, he learned that ball bearings were impossible to obtain in Brazil. This led factory engineers to invent substitutes to fill the need, and some of the maintenance issues he encountered stemmed from these substitutions.

The Beechcraft had become the prize of the Brazilian fleet and made multi-engine advanced training possible for the program, but qualified students had to wait for Tip's arrival to get in the cockpit. The Beechcraft went where Tip wanted to fly it.

In February 1945, Allied bombing raids on Dresden, Germany resulted in a firestorm that consumed the city center. The ferocity of the attacks and destruction shocked Germany and the world. The incendiaries used were a wicked mix of chemicals with jellied gasoline that exploded and burned at a much higher temperature than conventional bombs. The resulting fire created an enormous updraft which pulled in a fierce wind, feeding an unstoppable inferno. The firestorm melted roads and ignited everything in its path. Military estimates of casualties put the death toll between twenty to fifty thousand people, but the city was packed with refugees fleeing the oncoming Russian army, and other estimates of those killed exceeded 100,000. Military advisors argued that Dresden was a major German transportation and communication center intimately engaged in war efforts. Other experts argued that Dresden was a cultural landmark and that the bombing was unjustified. Nazi Germany surrendered twelve weeks after the bombing. The strategy that Germany had once envisioned for bringing Britain to surrender had instead been effective against its own country.

Also in February, the US began the first operation in the eventual planned invasion of Japan by capturing the island of Iwo Jima. Japanese forces fought to the death and took a high toll on US Marines. Many military planners looked at the results of the Battle of Iwo Jima with pride, but with misgiving. The victory illustrated the difficulties and possible high casualty rate that lay ahead if the US invaded the Japanese homeland. President Roosevelt knew he had another option in the atomic bomb. He was weighing the use of the closely guarded secret weapon. If it would prevent the deaths of thousands of American and Allied lives, was he justified to use it? Secret consultations with selected military advisors had begun.

In April 1945, while Tip was engaged in overseeing the translation of critical flight manuals into Portuguese, Soviet and American troops liberated the largest of Germany's death camps and the full horror of the holocaust was revealed. Adolf Hitler committed suicide along with his new bride. The war in Europe was almost over, but the war with Japan continued to take up the majority of American attention.

While Tip was quietly distinguishing himself in the Beechcraft, the rest of the world was watching the political and wartime landscape change irrevocably. President Franklin D. Roosevelt died suddenly on April 12, 1945. He had taken office in the middle of the Great Depression and created reforms and programs that are still in effect today. He kept the US neutral in the face of worldwide war for two years, and then led the country into a war that was about to end in victory. He had served as president for twelve years. Many Americans at the time did not know that Roosevelt was paralyzed from the waist down by polio he had contracted at age thirty-nine. The newsreel and photographic footage of him always featured him in some natural sitting position. He appeared in army jeeps, at conference tables, or in open convertible vehicles. In the course of his presidency, he had been consistently portrayed as strong, capable, and resolute. He, and his wife Eleanor, had led the country through one of the most difficult times in US history and now Vice President Harry S. Truman was handed the office at a critical point in the war.

Following Germany's surrender in May 1945, President Truman had tried a strategy of firebombing numerous Japanese cities in a similar manner to Dresden. But Japan ignored all ultimatums and refused to surrender. The US military was massing for an invasion of the Japanese mainland and every officer knew it would wreak a disastrous death toll on their men.

At the embassy social gatherings in Rio, these events were widely discussed and victories celebrated. The embassy staff said goodbye to Ambassador Jeffery Caffery and got ready to welcome Adolf Berle as the new American ambassador to Brazil. Berle was an influential politician who had worked closely with President Roosevelt on many of the strongest reforms of the era and was part of his "brain trust". He had just finished his appointment as Assistant Secretary of State and was now taking up residence in Brazil. The appointment of this powerfully experienced man to the US Embassy in Brazil was a strong indicator of the importance of Brazilian cooperation to the United States. The army supply route was well established through Brazil and the potential end to the war in Europe did not lessen its importance to the US military.

Ambassador Adolf Berle had worked closely with the Reconstruction Finance Corporation, where Harry Hossack was still engaged, and was the president of the International Conference on Civil Aviation. Tip was on good terms with the new ambassador and kept in close communication with him as Berle took up his Rio post.

Frequent evening parties continued to be a feature of Tip and Louise's routine and a great deal of critical information was exchanged in these social settings.

In June 1945, during a week of particularly violent and continuous thunderstorms, Tip was at one of these parties when word came in of an emergency.

Due to the fact that I had unrestricted permission to fly anywhere in Brazil (also Argentina, Uruguay, and Paraguay), the embassy used me and the Beechcraft more than they used their military C-47 (DC-3), which could not land at some of the fields that I could get into. One such mission, more hairy than most, was a night flight from Rio to Asuncion, Paraguay. I received a call from Ambassador Berle about eight o'clock one evening at a dinner party for embassy personnel. An urgent cable had been received from the embassy in Asuncion that several of the embassy children had high fevers, were partially paralyzed, and had trouble breathing. Two adult members of the staff were also afflicted. Serum was needed immediately, as they were afraid that the virus was polio.

Airline travel had been halted for two days due to cloud cover so thick and low to the ground that it fell below minimum conditions for airline operation. No flights had departed or arrived in Rio, nor had any flights been able to land in Paraguay. Weather reports indicated that there would be no change for at least another twenty-four hours. I advised Ambassador Berle that I would attempt the flight if the embassy surgeon came along with the needed serum. Berle assured me that Dr. Starkloff, the Surgeon General of the South Atlantic Command, would be ready to leave within two hours.

I scheduled departure for two a.m., hoping to arrive over Asuncion, Paraguay, at daybreak. If there were to be any lifting of the cloud ceiling, it would be then. At the time we departed, the Asuncion airport was closed due to heavy rain and fog. Rio was estimating a two-hundred foot cloud ceiling and a few yards visibility, which meant that I wouldn't be able to see a thing until I could get above the cloud cover, but a blind take-off was no problem as long as everything kept running. As this was a calculated risk mission anyway, the take-off into solid clouds and rain that obscured all vision, and my heading for an airport destination that was closed due to weather, were only details. Dr. Starkloff arrived at the airport at one a.m. with about three hundred pounds of medical supplies. After securing the boxes and checking our weight and balance, we took on a full load of fuel. The aircraft showed to be about fourteen percent over allowable weight. Another calculated risk, but as long as we had no engine failures, we would be okay.

I received special permission from the Brazilian Air Ministry to take off at my own option. As there were no radio stations on our route, we would be unable to advise anyone of our position or emergencies until within a few miles of Asuncion. Dr. Starkloff was not a rated pilot, but I felt he would be more comfortable in the co-pilot's seat. As the Beechcraft was a single pilot aircraft with dual controls, I cautioned him against leaning on the controls during flight, as some turbulence was expected. The take-off was sluggish, but assisted by a gusty thirty-knot downward-sweeping tailwind that kicked in immediately after I cleared the runway. The wind was so strong that it was necessary to make a thirty-degree turn to the left to avoid smashing the landing gear on a two thousand foot rock directly on the edge of the airstrip.

We climbed out the pass slowly and blindly, gaining altitude over the ocean. My flight plan called for me to fly at five thousand feet along the coast for about an hour before climbing to eight thousand feet to clear the lower mountain range. At eight thousand feet, we were on top of the overcast by only a few hundred feet. Pan American Airways had assured me that they would turn on their non-directional radio beacon number five, at which time I estimated that I would be within one hundred miles of Asuncion. I had also requested that the local radio station activate their tower as a backup radio signal. I planned to maintain five thousand feet until I received a signal from one of the radio stations, at which time I would execute a letdown called "boxing" the station. This letdown, which was used by most of the airlines flying in South America at the time, permitted the pilot to be within two minutes of the radio beacon at all times and directly over the field where the beacon was located.

I was five minutes past the time that I expected to pick up a radio signal and could hear nothing. Due to the heavy rain, there was an annoying amount of static. My automatic direction finder was showing nothing to latch onto and I could raise nothing on my manual direction finder. I had no choice but to continue my dead-reckoning heading, as I could easily be further out than anticipated. Seventeen minutes past my estimated time of arrival, I started getting a faint signal on the automatic direction finder and in another five minutes I was getting a strong signal. Eight minutes later I was over Asuncion Airport. I made voice contact with the Pan American operations agent stationed in Asuncion, who advised me that there was an undetermined ceiling between two and three hundred feet and about one half mile visibility with moderate rain. The letdown was made very cautiously and we landed out of a close-in spiral from over the radio station.

Dr. Starkloff was hurried to a waiting car after we unloaded his medical equipment from the plane. It was beginning to rain again

and thunder could be heard in the distance. I decided to remain with
the plane to refuel and try to determine what our next move was. I
hoped that we would not be required to take any patients with us, as
we were very heavy with fuel and equipment and there was no sign
that the weather was getting any better. I must have slept for about
six hours lying on the floor of the airplane when I was awakened
by a pounding on the door. It was a Paraguayan air force officer,
who advised me that Dr. Starkloff was en-route to the airport and
needed to take off immediately in order to get blood samples to the
laboratory in Rio. It was now about one thirty in the afternoon and
the weather at Asuncion was moderate rain with a varying ceiling
of two to three hundred feet and wind gusting to twenty knots. Rio
had sent an earlier report indicating that their airport was still below
minimum and that no airline traffic was flying.

Fortunately, Dr. Starkloff had diagnosed the problem as a
virus very much like polio but a milder variety. Tests had to be made
immediately to be certain, and serum specific to the virus returned
to Asuncion. This was good news because with such prompt care,
the children might avoid permanent paralysis. Following take-off, we
climbed to seven thousand feet, which put us on top of the overcast
at that point. As we progressed northeast, on a direct course to Rio,
I could see heavy clouds building up in the distance, which indicated
heavy thunderstorm activity. Climbing slowly, I had hoped to be
able to top them but we were now flying at thirteen thousand feet
and barely topping the forerunners of the higher clouds ahead. At
fifteen thousand feet we penetrated the clouds once again, hoping
that we could punch through the front within a few minutes. We
began to pick up ice along with moderate turbulence and I realized
that we needed to get out of this weather immediately.

I attempted to lay out a new course heading by drawing
a line from our estimated position to Porte Alegre, to the south. I
could not find a pencil and I shouted to Dr. Starkloff to get me a
pencil or pen with which to draw a course line. The doctor looked

at me and refused to move. Lack of oxygen does strange things to people. I told him that if he didn't give me a pencil, we would fly into a mountain. He finally reached out shakily and plucked a pencil from behind my ear.

We broke out of the thunderstorms after clearing the coast. The top of the overcast had lowered considerably over the ocean, and was now at a comfortable six thousand feet. A garbled weather report indicated that Rio was still below minimums and a choice of let downs had to be made. I was flying about fifteen miles off the coast over the ocean because I knew the terrain and could identify the mountain peaks by sight. I decided to let down over the ocean and "scud run" into Rio harbor rather than to attempt a boxing of the non-directional beacon without help from a co-pilot. Both of these letdowns were risky, to say the least, but I felt my decision was the best.

I broke out of the overcast over the ocean at about eight hundred feet. It was raining heavily and the winds were gusty and turbulent. I took up a direct heading with my automatic direction finder and my manual direction finder both agreeing on the course for Rio Harbor. The ceiling was irregular and at times it seemed we were skimming only a few feet above the whitecaps. The entrance to Rio Harbor is quite narrow and rimmed by mountains and the airport lies nestled in them. It was common knowledge among pilots letting down into Rio Harbor that under five thousand feet, you were thirty seconds from the mountains on three sides of the airport. We were fortunate that the rain had let up a bit and the visibility improved enough that we located the airport and landed without incident. Dr. Starkloff regained some of his color and indicated that this trip had been beyond the call of duty, and from now on, he was keeping close to the hospital.

Our return flight to deliver the serum was less dramatic, but weather conditions in Rio were still extremely hazardous. We were invited to spend a few days at the Paraguayan estancia of the Caben

D'Arenses family while waiting for the weather to clear for the flight back. They promised a relaxing time of hunting, fishing, and touring some of the picturesque areas of the estancia. Gilberto Chufeta Caben D'Arenses had a several thousand-acre estate in the Chaco area of Paraguay with a good airstrip. The estate bordered a large navigable river that carried freight from the estancia to Asuncion for trans-shipment to Buenos Aires. Numerous lakes and streams dotted the vast area of the estancia, along with areas of intact rain forest. The jungle boasted of a myriad of inhabitants ranging from orzas (jaguars), pythons, alligators (caimans), deer, wild boar, as well as a variety of insects intent on carrying you away in small pieces. All the rivers and small streams were infested with piranha, which made swimming in the streams a bit dicey.

Our night flight had quickly become the stuff of legend in flying circles. Weeks after the flight, I realized that the most lurid detail of the story had nothing to do with the weather conditions or the aviation accomplishment. It was instead highlighted by the fact that, while alligator hunting one night on the estancia, I had shot myself in the bum by pulling a pistol out of my back pocket. In some versions, it was suggested that an irate husband had caught me, buck naked, going out a window. I always denied all reports of the shooting, but did have to spend some time healing from our relaxing trip to the Paraguayan estancia. It occurs to me that the frightful flight had been played down so much that it is only now, in retrospect, that I have any idea of the danger we were in.

As is so often the case with achievements born of necessity, the significance of what Tip had accomplished in flying Dr. Starkloff safely in and out of Asuncion in June 1945 wasn't recognized until much later. Dr. Starkloff had completed his duties with the American Embassy in Brazil and later in his career, went on to pioneer gastric bypass surgery. He wrote a letter to Tip in which he revisited the event and thanked Tip again for his extraordinary skill and courage in making the flight.

Dr. Gene B. Starkloff, Lieutenant Colonel, Medical Corps, and assistant military attaché to the Brazilian Embassy, wrote to Tip about how he had received word of the Asuncion Embassy's problem through his South Atlantic Command headquarters but couldn't get anyone to agree to make the flight because of the extraordinarily bad weather. He had been directed to request help from the Army and Navy doctors stationed in Recife, but Recife was under the same weather conditions as the rest of the South American mainland and they refused to fly. In desperation, Dr. Starkloff had left urgently pleading messages with anyone he could reach at the American Embassy in Rio. By the time Ambassador Berle had become aware of the emergency, Dr. Starkloff had gone in person to find the generals of the Army and Air Corps in Rio at the party they were attending that evening at the Copacabana Palace Hotel. Tip, also at the hotel for the party, had gotten the call from Ambassador Berle just as Dr. Starkloff was personally pleading with the generals. The generals had just refused Dr. Starkloff when Tip emerged from the crowd, in black tie and tails, and offered himself and the Beechcraft for the job.

"I will never forget that trip that you volunteered to fly when no one else would," wrote Dr. Starkloff. "I requested that you be awarded an appropriate decoration for being the pilot on that flight. I remember also, our having to fly without oxygen for a couple of hours trying to top successfully the mountains, in the world's worst thunderstorm. God Bless."

Chapter Thirteen

1945 to 1946

The End of the War and The Arrival of Sue

Rio de Janeiro, Brazil

On July 16, 1945, President Truman received word from the Manhattan Project that the test at the Trinity site, near Alamogordo, New Mexico, had resulted in a true atomic detonation. Truman faced an awful responsibility with the decision whether to use the atomic bomb against Japan. It would not be a case of dropping a new weapon on a purely military target. This would be a strike against a city and it was certain that more civilians would die than military personnel. But Truman felt he had to end the war. Reports from the Pacific, complete with color images of casualties and conditions, supported the military advisors' predictions of a victory that would be extraordinarily costly. The first and only nuclear weapon attacks in warfare took place on August 6 and 9, 1945, on the cities of Hiroshima and Nagasaki. The United States dropped two atomic bombs on the Japanese homeland. Despite the shock and death toll, Japan continued to resist and Truman was considering a third atomic bombing when Japan finally surrendered on August 15, 1945.

Radiation sickness was first discovered two days after the denotation of the bombs in Japan, when seemingly uninjured or conventionally-burned patients began to show up at the Hiroshima hospital. Their fever, nausea, and bleeding puzzled Japanese doctors who were unable to cure them. When the doctors and nurses began to sicken, the medical establishment realized that there was something else going on. The death toll estimates vary widely depending on the source reporting them. Modern American sources generally agree that over 120,000 Japanese civilians were killed in the initial blasts of the two atomic bombs, and another 120,000, or more, died in the weeks, months, and years following from injuries, radiation sickness, and cancers.

A few weeks after the successful nuclear detonation at Trinity, General Leslie R. Groves and J. Robert Oppenheimer, joint leaders of the Manhattan Project, posed for a photograph on the remnants of the test tower at Trinity. They wore only paper shoe covers. This image, more than any other document of the time, illustrates the prevailing scientific ignorance of the effects of radiation generated by atomic weapons.

General Groves eventually died of a heart attack, but Oppenheimer lived for another twenty-two years in both infamy and legend, as he struggled with the credit for, and implications of, atomic weapons. Oppenheimer became a leading proponent of the United Nations as a world-governing instrument of control over nuclear weapons, and carried the burden of his involvement in atomic bomb development for the rest of his life. He died of throat cancer in February 1967, at age sixty-three.

Tip's reaction to the use of the atomic bomb was similar to widespread sentiment at the time. He didn't write about it directly, but commented to friends and family that he felt "it saved a lot of American lives." In the years immediately following the end of the war, the bombing of Dresden became as controversial as Hiroshima and Nagasaki, despite the significant differences in the weapons involved. Part of the reason for this was the continued secrecy that shrouded all aspects of the atomic bomb. The public had no idea that this was a new, different, and profoundly dangerous technology that had just changed the face of world politics. In fact, scientists and political leaders at the time had only a small sense of what they had unleashed. The amount they didn't know about their new bomb was astonishing.

Many years later, a minor aspect of the role that aviation played in the dropping of the atomic bomb would come to affect Tip personally. He would plan a trip to Japan more than a decade in the future, but because of the close similarity of his name to Paul Tibbets, Jr., the pilot of the plane that dropped the first atomic bomb, he would be denied a visa and have to forgo his visit to Japan.

World War II was over and the heat of battle would subside, but the Cold War had already begun. The alliance of the US and the Soviet Union split apart with the uranium atoms over Japan. The aftermath of WWII was marked by reorganization and rebuilding. The Nuremberg Trials began in November 1945, and would continue for more than a year as responsibility for the Holocaust was investigated and assigned. Aviation technology had been advanced so rapidly by the war effort that standardization of civil practices was even more urgent. War surplus aircraft now supplied almost every country in the world with the equipment to start their own airlines. When President Truman stopped the lend-lease agreements that enabled private US companies to supply weapons to other friendly nations, Tip's program in Brazil was directly affected.

Tip's civil aviation agreements were founded on wartime equipment supply chains. American interests in Brazil were certain to change, but for the present time the civil aviation mission remained a well-funded and securely supplied activity due to Ambassador Berle's interest in civil aviation policies. Additionally, one of Ambassador Berle's main preoccupations was securing supplies that Brazil produced and America needed. There was now a sudden surplus of war machines and a shortage of everything else. Ambassador Berle reiterated Tip's orders to do everything he could to secure rubber production and export.

Tip was busier than ever with the mission to extend standard civil aviation practices in Brazil, and the end of the war did not immediately change his everyday life. Louise was occupied with the family's move from the Ipanema Beach apartment to a large house in the Copacabana neighborhood. She supervised the household staff and now had several spare bedrooms for Tip's visitors or their many friends. But in the meantime, Ambassador Berle needed rubber and he ordered Tip and the Beechcraft into the air.

The embassy was receiving more and more calls from Washington urging the Brazilians to increase their rubber output. An organization called the Rubber Development Corporation had been authorized by the US and Brazilian governments to fly raw rubber out of the Amazon basin to Belem, and then on to the US. This operation was costly and not very efficient. The main problem seemed to be finding the rubber trees. Unfortunately, the trees were scattered in the jungle instead of growing together in groves.

Ambassador Berle called me to his office following the Asuncion flight and advised me that the Minister of the Interior of Brazil had requested assistance in making a flight into the unexplored central jungle in search of rubber trees. The area to be scouted was approximately 900 miles west of Sao Paulo and 900 miles south of Manaus. No flights had been made over this area principally due to the fact that there had been no aircraft capable of making the flight. I was advised that a landing strip had been carved out of the jungle about 400 miles west of Sao Paulo, and several drums of aviation fuel deposited there by field troops. As my special twin Beechcraft could carry fuel for 1,000 miles, the jungle strip made the flight feasible.

My good friend, Brazilian Colonel Paulo Sampaio, who was close to the air minister and a renowned jungle pilot, was assigned to the flight along with Jean Manzon, a French photographer, and the air minister himself. We made a daylight departure in bright, sparkling weather with light winds and unrestricted visibility. Very careful navigation located the jungle strip after a flight of approximately four hours. The area was scrub jungle and our altitude was three thousand feet, read off the aircraft's altimeter. The aircraft was refueled using a chamois-covered bucket to insure no water or other contaminates entered the fuel system. The minister, wanting to appear useful, insisted on manning the hand pump, pumping from the drums into the bucket. We noticed the old boy was tiring after about twenty minutes of pumping, so we replaced him with Manzon, the photographer. Sampaio did the pouring into the tanks while I pretended to be busy checking the aircraft. It was times like this when leadership came into play.

We decided to spend the night using our sleeping bags and sharing tents with the few ground troops assigned to the landing area. Colonel Sampaio skillfully prepared a gourmet meal of canned rice and black beans along with some hearts of palm, which he had thoughtfully brought with him. The next morning was clear, following a heavy rain through the night. Although we had no particular spot or area in mind, we were heading for the Xingu River headwaters and the legendary Rio das Mortes area.

The sketchy information on our maps did not describe the type of land awaiting us. We cruised at 5,000 feet over fairly thick jungle with bush vegetation and very large rivers. Colonel Sampaio was busily correcting errors shown on the maps, such as the direction and flow of some of the larger rivers encountered. Manzon was photographing the area from the camera mounted in the belly of the aircraft, just aft of the pilot's compartment. The minister was looking out the window, viewing for the first time a part of his country as yet unexplored. Looking ahead and scanning the area, I suddenly spotted a large clearing in the jungle. It was a circular enclosure of very large palm frond huts. I immediately called the minister's attention to this obvious village of unknown inhabitants. As this aircraft would have been the first the inhabitants had ever seen, I suggested that I retrace our course and let down to a minimum altitude so that Manzon could photograph them before they could hide or run into their huts. Setting my directional gyro on a reciprocal heading, I descended from 5,000 feet to about 300 feet, then down to treetop level.

Jean Mazon captured these photos using a camera mounted on the belly of the plane as Tip flew over the jungle clearing in August 1945.

The first pass over the huts, which appeared to be about thirty-five feet tall, was made at a minimum air speed, flaps down, gear down, practically hanging on the props. Flying the aircraft in this slow configuration consumed all my attention, so I had no opportunity to view the results of the fly-over. I heard Colonel Sampaio shout "Pull up! They're shooting at us!" but as I was about fifty feet over the village huts, I could do little but continue across the village clearing and apply power to clear the area. I continued the flight over the village for about a mile further on course and made a procedure turn to come back on track for another look. When we were safely out of range of the Indian's spears and arrows, I asked Sampaio and the minister what had happened. The minister was pleased and amazed to learn of this new settlement. Sampaio announced that the Indians had hit the plane with arrows. Manzon reported that he thought he had taken some good photographs of the action and of the Indians.

Photo by Jean Mazon.

Tip could not pull up fast enough to avoid the arrows.

I had to navigate carefully on the return trip to our jungle field because our fuel supply, although adequate, was not ample enough for us to have to search for the strip. Upon landing, we were astounded to see that three arrows had penetrated the tail surfaces of the aircraft. These arrows were over six feet long, made of bamboo strips with a tiger tooth as the tip and parrot feathers on the stabilizing ends. The arrow points were smeared with a dark substance, which the minister warned us not to touch. We later found it to be curare, a dangerous poison. Had these arrows hit the wing of the aircraft, they would have penetrated the thin aluminum skin and we would have lost our fuel over the Amazon jungle. Not a pleasant thought!

The Beechcraft's shadow is visible in the lower left corner of this photograph by Jean Mazon.

Rumors had circulated for years along the Amazon and Xingu Rivers of a ferocious tribe of Indians called the Chavante who lived in the interior of Brazil and killed any Indian or tribe that ventured into their territory. We believed we had found them. Upon returning to Rio, we made a full report on the trip, indicating that if any rubber trees existed in the area we had explored, the extraction of rubber sap would prove most difficult and hazardous.

Jean Mazon's photographs provided new information about the Chavante Indian's lifestyle. These images, and pictures he took on a second trip without Tip, were featured in magazine articles that announced the discovery of the Chavante Indians of the Mato Grosso.

Tip was engaged in Brazil's second "rubber boom," which lasted from 1942 to 1945. The war effort had consumed so much of the world's easy rubber supply that there was a significant shortage. Government and private industry provided ample money and pressure to get more because rubber was a critical commodity. It was so important that it may have been one of the main reasons such a significant politician as Adolf Berle was appointed ambassador to Brazil at that time. While Tip was writing of his concern about the difficulty of bringing rubber out of the Amazon jungle in sufficient quantity, the US government was close to finding another solution. By the end of 1945, the US Synthetic Rubber Program had begun to successfully produce enough synthetic rubber to meet the need and the ambassador would soon be able to turn his attention to other issues.

The flight with the Brazilian Air Minister, Colonel Sampaio, and Jean Manzon was made in pursuit of rubber, but resulted instead in the long sought after discovery of the actual location of the Chavante Indians. Brazil's government had been trying to approach the Chavante for a very long time, but had not known exactly where they were. They had only stories, rumors, and travelers who had disappeared to point the way. The Chavante Indians were a prized target for anthropological study, but were also a significant travel hazard to anyone trying to explore or develop this remote area. Finding the tribe, and establishing safe communication, was important enough that a well-funded Brazilian expedition was already in the Amazon at the time of Tip's flight, trying to find the Indians and begin a new program of pacification. The expedition had experienced several brief encounters, but no significant success. In the previous decade, the Brazilian Indian Bureau had mounted at least two expeditions intended to peacefully approach the Chavante. Each had met with tragedy, either swallowed by the rainforest or killed by the Indians.

Tip and his passengers had been flying over the rainforest portion of the Brazilian state of Mato Grosso, which was characterized by wide-open plains, Amazon rainforest, and flooded flatlands known as the Pantanal. It was deep in the heart of the South American continent, one of the most inaccessible places on earth. The Chavante had counted on it for their isolation, but aviation had changed their situation completely. They were now exposed. With the coordinates supplied by Tip's flight in the Beechcraft, a program was launched to approach and protect the Chavante.

Following the August 1945, flight, the Brazilian Indian Bureau began a campaign of airdrops. Parcels made up of goods, medicine, and images of western culture were pushed out of the backs of cargo planes into the Chavante compound. It took two years, but eventually a peaceful delegation from the Brazilian government was

WHEN NO ONE ELSE WOULD FLY

able to meet with Chavante Indian leaders without bloodshed. Jean Manzon photographed that historic visit, reaching the area again by air without Tip, and published an article about it in O Cruzeiro magazine. In the late 1950s, this area became Brazil's first national park and was set up primarily to protect the Indian's culture and lifestyle. In 1961, a larger area of the same region was designated as the Xingu National Park and encompassed fourteen more Indian tribes.

Jean Manzon was already an accomplished photojournalist when he went to Brazil from his native Paris in the early years of World War II. Manzon was thirty-one at the time of the flight with Tip and a logical choice of photographer on the part of the Brazilian government. He was already heavily involved in documentary filmmaking. Manzon's photographs from the Beechcraft's fuselage were published worldwide. They became classic images representing the first modern approach to the Chavante Indians of the Amazon. Tip stayed in touch with Manzon after the flight and kept a file of prints from the photographs Manzon had taken on the flight, as well as the spear pulled out of the plane's fuselage. For Tip, the entertainment value of the story of finding hostile Indians in the Amazon was always tempered by his memories of how close they came to a punctured fuel tank over the rainforest canopy.

Ambassador Berle had requested permission from the Foreign Ministry to take a trip to Belem to explore the Amazon basin and tour the headwaters of the Amazon River. The trip was to be made in a variety of aircraft. I was to be the pilot for the entire trip and fly the Ambassador and his wife to Belem through the interior route, land to refuel, and then fly on to Belem. From Belem to Manaus, we would go by the Rubber Development Corporation's amphibian planes, and on from there by Grumman amphibian. A side trip to the Madeira-Mamore railroad was also scheduled.

The trip to Belem was uneventful. We were met in Belem

by the US consul and the Brazilian military governor of the
province. The local hotel was comfortable and the dinner given
by the governor was most pleasant. The following morning, we
departed Belem in a specially equipped PBY (a patrol bomber flying
boat built by Consolidated Aircraft) headed for Manaus. The flight
distance was approximately 1,200 miles. During the low altitude
flight, Mrs. Berle insisted on landing at one of the Indian villages
along the Amazon, which was a pickup point for the raw rubber
extracted by the Indians. Mrs. Berle, a doctor in her own right,
inspected the village thoroughly and interviewed the Indian chief
through an interpreter as to health care and food needs. She was
surprised to learn that the Indians were completely self-sufficient,
insofar as food was concerned, and that medical supplies were
available but that many of their cures for fever, dysentery, and
infections were supplied by the jungle itself.

   Flying over the river, in and out of rain showers, can be
pretty boring. Almost no life is visible other than an occasional
toucan or flight of brightly colored parrots. The picture is entirely
different inside the jungle. The jungle is a maze of insect, animal,
and bird life. One must know and respect the dangers to live with
them peacefully. Following a two-day stay in Belem, taking in all
the many sights and visiting the famous opera house, we picked
up a Brazilian aide and departed by German amphibious truck for
the ride to the Madeira-Mamore railroad. This railroad was built
by Chinese laborers, and the story has it that for every mile of the
railroad completed, one thousand Chinese died. Yellow fever and
malaria were rampant.

Tip returned Ambassador Berle and his wife safely to Rio
after their tour of the Amazon. He turned his attention back to his
work, but by the end of 1945, the CAA mission in Brazil had begun
to change. Civil aviation in the US had always included a strong
independent component that set it apart from the military. The Civil

Aviation Administration (CAA) would one day become the Federal Aviation Administration (FAA) in the US. But in Brazil, aviation had been in the hands of the military from the very beginning. Now that World War II was over, the Brazilian military and civil aviation establishments were looking for as many surplus aircraft as they could get. Tip summarized the situation in a January 1946 memo to CAA headquarters, advising that the best way to create a strong civil aviation program in post-war Brazil was to first set it up through the military. He recommended that a civil branch be supported within the Brazilian Air Force (Forca Aerea Brasileira, FAB), which would later split off and become strictly civilian.

Washington responded by appointing Tip to the temporarily vacant position of Civil Air Attaché for the American Embassy, putting him in exactly the right position for following through on his recommendation. In addition to continuing his CAA mission in Brazil and defending his funding as post war politics went through budget realignment, Tip was now the main contact for US interaction with the Brazilian Air Force.

Following the visit to Belem with Ambassador Berle and his wife, the Ambassador called me to his office one morning and informed me that Brazil had been given a lease program for twenty DC-3 / C-47s and that they were to be delivered to Belem by the US Proxy Command. Once delivered, they would be officially handed over to the Brazilian Air Ministry. From Belem, they were to be flown to Rio to be integrated into Brazil's airline systems. Mr. Tom Park, head of the US-funded Paraguay Supply Corporation, was empowered to find the pilots to fly these aircraft. I had worked with Tom Park in Argentina and he requested that I lead this program in Brazil and use our training facilities and instructors at the flight school to move the planes. The C-47 ships were flown directly from the Douglas factory to Brazil, complete with a camouflage paint scheme. Upon arrival in Rio, we had to

remove the paint, which was a difficult and costly operation. I sent
a message through the embassy requesting that the aircraft not be
painted at the factory and I was informed that the aircraft must be
painted as per contract requirements, but as they were rolled onto
the production line, the aircraft would have the paint removed prior
to delivery.

Some time during the summer of 1945, before Tip made
his rubber flight over the Amazon, Louise had shared the delightful
news that she was once again pregnant. Michael had started school.
He spoke as much Portuguese as he did English, and now had a line-
up of Brazilian school photos to display on the family wall. Louise
and Tip had been living in Rio for almost three years and very much
enjoyed the city, parties, and their embassy friendships. Tip was flying
as much as ever and had recently been away for long periods of time
while he evaluated the civil aviation needs of Peru and Paraguay for
the CAA, but Louise had plenty of domestic help. She was living the
Latin lifestyle she had so admired in the households of the people
they had met on the flight down from Washington D.C. in the
Cessna.

Early in the morning on March 16, 1946, the family
welcomed baby Susan Tippett. Tip was now thirty-three years old,
Michael almost seven, and thirty-two-year-old Louise felt the family
was complete. Susan was a golden-blonde bundle, born during a visit
to the nearby city of Sao Paulo, and Louise had both a maid and a
nanny to help the household run smoothly.

Louise was on the look out for orders from Washington.
The end of the war changed things for most of the embassy staff
and Louise felt that Tip would be no exception. She watched the
scouting trips to Peru and Paraguay closely, knowing that these could
be indications of her future residence.

In October of 1946, when baby Susan was seven months
old, Tip flew the Beechcraft back to Washington on a short trip to

the States to complete a course that would certify him as an Airline Transport Pilot for the embassy in Rio. Multi-engine aircraft were now routinely setting new speed and distance records, and Tip wanted access to these larger ships. Tip backtracked his previous route to get back to the US through Cuba. This was the fourth time Tip had flown between the North and South American continents, but the first time going north.

Shortly after his arrival in Washington, Louise used her own embassy connections to get urgent word to Tip that the embassy rumor mill was circulating word of Tip's permanent reassignment to the US. The Brazilian civil aviation department was so distressed that Percy de F. Warner, Tip's main State Department contact, advised him to formally apprise the Brazilian government of his plans. Tip was even more valuable to Brazil now that he was the acting air attaché and the Brazilian government was invested in having him stay in Rio. Ambassador Berle had returned to the United States and his replacement, William D. Pawley, had not yet arrived. Tip immediately communicated with his staff and contacts in the Brazilian government, reassuring them that he and the Beechcraft would return in a matter of months, but the rumors held elements of truth and Louise quietly prepared to move without knowing if her destination would be the North or South American continent.

Tip's return flight would be his fifth air traverse, but this time he picked up a more attractive passenger than the US Ferry Command officer who had accompanied him in the Beechcraft's maiden voyage. Mary Jane Tuttle (soon to become Mary Jane McBarnet) was Louise's cousin from Hawaii. She was in Washington D.C. with her parents. Mary Jane's mother was Love's sister, and Mary Jane's father, Howard Tuttle, was the aviation enthusiast Tip had first met in Hawaii in 1935. Howard Tuttle was the reason Tip had met Louise in the first place. Mary Jane, now in her early twenties, wrote about the circumstances leading to her flight with Tip.

Mary Jane Tuttle McBarnet

Mary Jane: It was in Honolulu in 1935 that I first met C. J. Tippett, universally known by all, then and forever more, as Tip. My cousin, Louise, who was as close to me as a sister, had met Tip in Honolulu and they were later married in California. I saw them again in December 1941, when I had driven with Louise, and Michael, their small son, to Houston where Tip was stationed. There he took me up in a two-seat open cockpit plane and did the most fantastic aerial acrobatics with a finale of flying upside down all the way back to the airfield. It was marvelous!

In the summer of 1946, after having spent World War II in Honolulu, my mother, father, and I took a long delayed trip across the United States. My father picked up a very sporty maroon Mercury convertible in Seattle, and we headed east. I was relegated routinely to the back seat with the luggage piled on either side of me. Needless to say, my view of the entire US was of the sides of suitcases and the canvas interior of the convertible roof, which was never put down.

The trip was not all pleasure. For one thing, it was partly business for my father, who was looking at shopping centers then being developed in various cities across the country. My job was to attend meetings with him with city planners, shopping center developers, and realtors, and take notes. In Washington D.C., we met Tip who was up from our embassy in Rio de Janeiro where he was air advisor to our ambassador. He was in the US to do some advanced training in four engine planes in Oklahoma, and Louise was still in Rio with Michael, and baby Sue. As my father, Tip, and I were talking, Tip suddenly turned to me and asked if I would like to fly back down to Rio with him in the embassy's plane, a Beechcraft. Without a second's hesitation, I immediately said, "Of course!" and thereby embarked on an adventure that was to forever change the course of my life. I was thrilled and excited, eager to see the world and all it had to offer.

As Tip's assignment in the US was going to take about two months to complete, I was lucky that my good friend, June, was living in Washington D.C. at the time on an old houseboat permanently tied up at a wharf on Main Avenue Southwest, on the Potomac River. Also fortunately (or not) for me, there was an empty cabin, which I rented on the wharf side of the boat. June's cabin had a beautiful view of the water across the river, and my cabin had a more murky view of the underside of the pier with banana peels and other assorted flotsam floating on the water or stuck in the mud. There were some very interesting, rather unconventional people also living on the boat, and we all hung our laundry together in the old, gutted boiler room. Tip had gone to Oklahoma, and June got me a job with the American Association for the Advancement of Science where she worked. I typed mailing labels eight hours a day in the basement.

In the meantime, I was busily getting my passport and visa for Brazil, and all the shots I needed. Tip had gotten permission for me to fly from our ambassador to Brazil, Bill Pawley, who was in Washington at the time. My father was there to vouch for me and to get the passport and other documents that were needed. After Tip returned from Oklahoma to Washington D.C., we were ready to go. We made one abortive trip to the airport and had to cancel due to weather. I think it was late October or early November 1946 that we actually started our flight to Rio. Because it was before Christmas, the plane had been packed full of Christmas gifts bought for embassy people in Rio who had asked Tip to bring things back for them. The whole plane, a not-too-large-twin-engine Beechcraft, was packed full except for one passenger seat in the cabin and the co-pilot's seat. There were bicycle wheels in the lavatory, so that was unusable, and boxes were piled high on the seats. We were taking with us a State Department man from the embassy in Rio who was very stiff and proper, always wore seersucker suits, and carried a black umbrella. Whenever we stopped anywhere, he seemed to disappear and I never saw him again after that trip. I was lucky enough to always sit in the co-pilot's seat, and this time he sat back with the luggage.

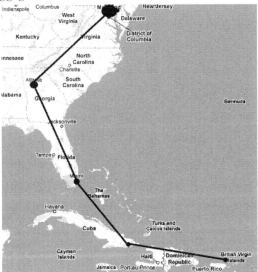

We stopped in Atlanta to refuel. I remember looking at the people around the plane, pitying them for being so unlucky as to not be flying down to Rio. How could they help but envy me? Our plane had some minor problem with the brakes. I believe it was a leak in the hydraulic fluid requiring us to stop relatively frequently before it all leaked out. Miami was our next stop. It was here that I had a most embarrassing experience.

Tip and I had been invited to dinner with Ambassador Pawley, now temporarily back home in Florida, and Mrs. Pawley. The only other guests were an elegant Brazilian couple who spoke no English. So in deference to them, the entire conversation at the table was in Portuguese, of which I knew not one word. I sat on the ambassador's left in rigid, self-conscious silence, trying to pretend an ease that I certainly did not feel. We were served pheasant, which the ambassador had shot in Montana. I did not have the presence of mind to observe how the Brazilian woman across from me removed it from the platter, which was being passed by a very stiff, unsmiling butler. When it was my turn to serve myself, I felt all eyes on me as I stared absolutely blankly at the pheasant on the platter, still seemingly attached to the carcass in some way, I think even with feathers. I didn't know what to do and finally the ambassador leaned across me and removed a portion of one of the cleverly sliced pheasants and put it on my plate. The embarrassment I suffered was agony.

After a dreadful silence, fortunately these very polite people resumed their incomprehensible conversation and I was left to try to tackle the pheasant now on my plate. I did the best I could to eat, but to my horror started grating on hard, little pellets getting stuck in my teeth. I just sat there, once again not knowing what to do. The Ambassador must have seen my stricken face, as he leaned over me once again and said in a loud whisper, audible to all, "Spit the buckshot out." Later, Tip and I did go to the Club Bali for a little resuscitation for me and we laughed about the hazards of formal dining.

Next, we headed for St. Thomas in the Virgin Islands, after a refueling stop at Guantanamo Bay in Cuba. The sky was beautifully clear over the island of Hispaniola, and we got a good view of Haiti and the Dominican Republic. On St. Thomas, we

stayed at a charming small hotel owned by a friend of Tip's. As
I recall, it was an old Danish building up in the hills with a sugar
boiler on the patio. The owner was from the US east coast and had
escaped to the lovely life of the Virgin Islands, restoring this old
building with warmth and affection. One morning, another friend
took us on in his speedboat around the island to the beautiful bay
on the other side. I straddled the bow the whole way. We also visited
other friends who had a beautiful house high up on the spine of the
island with gorgeous views on both sides. I remember feeling guilty
about my disloyalty to Hawaii, thinking how beautifully clear and
blue the Caribbean waters were and how lovely the islands.

Trinidad was our next refueling stop. Weather predictions
for our projected route were not good, but we took off anyway
and had an uneventful trip to Dutch Guiana, now Surinam, where
we spent the night. We always flew during the day. There was
some excitement on our flight from Surinam to Belem. I had
never crossed the Equator before so over the many mouths of the
Amazon, very muddy and uninhabited, Tip dipped his wings in my
honor. Immediately after that, one engine sputtered and conked
out. I looked down at the many channels of the river, at the water,
the mud, and no sign of life, wondering what was going to happen
next. But I had absolutely no anxiety, just curiosity. Tip immediately
began pumping fuel into the tank for the dead engine with the
pump between our seats and once again we were flying on two
engines. What had happened was that the mechanism on the fuel
gauge for that engine had become stuck and didn't register that it
was time to switch tanks. We had auxiliary tanks on the plane for
the long trip. This was my time to be the heroine as I found some
eyebrow tweezers in my purse and Tip neatly fixed the gauge. I
had total and unreserved confidence in Tip as a pilot, even though
he occasionally read magazines as we flew along. I felt no fear
whatsoever. It was grand fun.

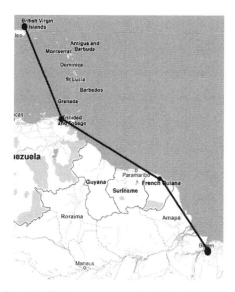

The hotel in Belem was wonderful and was my first taste of Portuguese colonial buildings. My bedroom had a very high ceiling with heavy dark furniture, an armoire, a ceiling fan, and a huge four-poster bed. I loved it. The people, however, looked very poor, miserable, and undernourished. From Belem, we struck off across the interior of Brazil, stopping en route at a Brazilian air force field right in the middle of the wild vegetation with very primitive facilities. Our landing in Rio was spectacular as the runway was on an island with finite length and our brakes were either non-existent or barely operable at that point. We sped down the runway, which was quickly ending. The water was abruptly ahead of us when Tip did a fantastic 180-degree turn and we tied triumphantly up to the terminal where Louise was waiting. The trip was the most exciting and thrilling thing I had ever done in my life.

And from there begins another story, a pivotal turning point for my life thereafter. I stayed with Louise, Tip, Mike, and Sue for a few months and got a job at the American Embassy with the agricultural attaché. I was nominally a secretary, but did mostly agricultural reporting. I moved into an apartment with three other American girls near Copacabana Beach when Louise, Tip and family moved away from Brazil to their next assignment. Nightlife in Rio started at about midnight and ended about five a.m., which was hard on us Americans who had to go to work at eight a.m. while the Brazilians slept until noon. In June 1947, I was traveling again, having been transferred by the State Department to Madras, India. There I met my husband, Alex, and so it is easy to see how that marvelous trip to Rio changed my life. How exciting it was!

Tip closed out 1946 by continuing his work with the embassy in Brazil and used his new multi-engine certification to continue his civil aviation mission. In March of 1947, the rumored changes to Tip's assignment became official as Ambassador Pawley formally notified the Brazilian government that US assistance to the civil aviation program was being withdrawn. Louise was ready and had help packing up the house. Her return to the United States was welcome, but it also meant the end of her luxurious South American lifestyle. There would be no maid or nanny in the US.

Louise had stayed as fashionably dressed as she could given the availability of modern wear in Rio's upscale shops. 1947 heralded a new style in clothing that had been severely demure throughout the war due to both rationing and a sense of propriety. In England, there had been actual laws against the use of excessive fabric, buttons, or thread, which made pleats and complex patterns illegal. Now fashion designers in Europe and America rebelled with voluminous folds, double-breasted panels, and long draping lines. Louise's slim height suited these changes and although her clothes were likely several months behind the mode, she got ready to return in style.

Louise, with one-year-old Susan in her arms, and eight-year-old Michael, joined Tip on a commercial flight to New York. The CAA had assured them that a job would be waiting for them in the family's favorite city, San Francisco, on their return from Brazil. Louise was elated, and Tip was very well satisfied. He had been hoping to secure a home-based civil aviation leadership position and had finally succeeded. Brazil was sorry to see Tip go. By the time he was finished, Tip had completed certification and regulation of commercial airline pilots, established flight test procedures and training of inspectors, developed and reorganized the general inspections, trained inspection personnel to check and certify private pilots, aircraft, and engine mechanics, established accident investigation divisions, organized airport management divisions, and standardized the courses of aero club inspectors throughout Brazil.

In return, the Brazilian government made an extraordinary gesture by awarding him the Brazilian Order of Merit; Grade Cavalheiro, an honor that was rarely bestowed on a civilian, let alone a foreigner. The award caught the attention of many of the highest-ranking officers the State Department and in the civil aviation world, including the founders of the United Nations.

The Civil Aeronautics Administration was delighted with the attention Tip was receiving from the State Department. On May 22, 1947, Theodore P. Wright, CAA Administrator at the time, wrote his own letter of congratulations to Tip. He enclosed copies of State Department letters and dispatches that had circulated in response to news of the award. Tip had been working with the State Department for years. Harry Hossack was still active with the Reconstruction Finance Corporation, which also had ties to the State Department. Up to this time, Tip had found his way through civil aviation channels primarily as a result of his own work and Harry's influence. But the work he had just completed in Brazil, and the under-currents of the cold war, had brought Tip to a new kind of attention from the US Department of State.

Information was as valuable as currency to the State Department. Diplomacy was always a two-way process, and Tip had already been a reliable source of information regarding Argentina. When the Brazilian government awarded Tip the Brazilian Order of Merit, ripples ran through the State Department and under the closed doors of some of the highest-ranking leadership concerned with foreign affairs. Tip's success was about to interfere with his plans for his own future.

During some of my trips to northern Argentina in my usual work with the Brazilian CAA, I had heard increasing rumors of swarms of locusts coming out of the jungle areas of northern Bolivia, Brazil, and northern Argentina. The Department of Agriculture had provided funds and supplies of kill-dust for conventional aircraft to combat these swarms with no success. Sixteen aircraft were lost flying into the swarms. Apparently, Bell Helicopter's attention was drawn to this problem and these areas were seized upon as a place to market their first B and D model helicopters.

I was first alerted to these negotiations when I was still

working in Brazil. I got a call from Dr. Bosch, back in power in Argentina's civil aviation administration, in which he advised me that President Peron was insisting that helicopters be used against the locust swarms. Dr. Bosch wanted my advice. Having no knowledge of helicopters, I said I wasn't aware of their potential. I had never even seen one fly. The matter was dropped until about a month later when I received a call from the State Department in Washington D.C. asking me to consider setting up a helicopter program for Argentina. The operating company was to be working directly under the control of the Department of Agriculture and was to be well financed by Argentine capital funds. I advised the State Department that I would not be interested in becoming involved in a helicopter operation and would be soon departing for San Francisco to assume the position of Chief of the Air Carrier Inspection Office for the South Pacific.

Brazil and Argentina, as the largest South American countries, were still key to US foreign policy. Tip's popularity within both those governments, and his past willingness to report information that he had charmed out of the officials he met, was a valuable asset to US foreign relations. John E. Peurifoy was a State Department diplomat who had been involved with the conference that led to the founding of the United Nations. From there, he went on to work on State Department security policy and became known for his stand against communism. He would soon enter the Foreign Service and eventually became the US ambassador to Greece, Guatemala, and Thailand. But in 1947, Peurifoy was the Assistant Secretary to the Secretary of State. On May 12, 1947, Peurifoy wrote a letter to W. Averell Harriman, the Secretary of Commerce, alerting Harriman to the fact that the president of Brazil was preparing to award Mr. C. J. Tippett the Order of Merit. Peurifoy brought to Harriman's attention a summary of Tip's accomplishments that had led to the award.

Harriman and Peurifoy reported directly to President Truman. Tip's name on these letters hinted at closed door discussions that were taking a whole new direction from the one Tip had planned for himself.

Tip left Louise and the children in New York City when he returned to Rio for the Brazilian Order of Merit medal. The ceremony took place in July 1947, in the office of the Brazilian Air Minister Armando Trompowsky. An unclassified State Department dispatch noted that Mr. Cloyce J. Tippett was decorated with the Aeronautical Medal of Merit, Grade Cavalheiro, with an accompanying citation stating that the medal was given as a reward for Mr. Tippett's extremely valuable services and cooperation with Brazilian authorities in developing a civil aviation program in Brazil. The dispatch also contained the comment: "it is believed that this is the first instance of such a medal being given to a civilian in Brazil."

Chapter Fourteen

1947 to 1948

Trabajos Aereos Y Representaciones, Buenos Aires, Argentina

Louise enjoyed being back in the United States and toured the sights and shops of New York City. She prepared for their triumphant return to California and looked forward to reconnecting with friends they had left behind. Tip came back from Rio on time, but as he began to make travel arrangements for San Francisco, he was ordered to temporarily remain in New York City pending discussions with the State Department. The family stayed with him.

World War II had lifted aviation into the jet age and helicopter technology was rising with it. The first helicopter flight was credited to the French in 1907, but it wasn't until 1924 that another successful helicopter flight made the record books. The advantages of taking off vertically and being able to hover in place were obvious to every pilot, but vertical flight was harder to achieve. In 1946, while Louise was in the last stages of her pregnancy with baby Susan, a Sikorsky helicopter in Connecticut set an altitude record of over 18,000 feet making fixed-wing aviators pay attention. But Tip was more interested in the civil aviation applications of multi-engine aircraft than he was in helicopters.

Fixed-wing aviation reached a milestone in 1947 when Howard Hughes completed the largest flying boat ever built. Hughes named it after himself, the Hughes H-4 Hercules, but it would be forever known as the Spruce Goose. It flew only once, with Hughes at the controls, before it was retired. The US War Department had contracted for a heavy transport during the war, but Hughes Aircraft did not make the deadline and the war was over before the airplane was ready. The Spruce Goose more than qualified as a multi-engine aircraft, with eight Pratt and Whitney radial engines and the longest wingspan in history. Tip's love of multi-engine craft encompassed the Spruce Goose and he celebrated it many years later by hosting one of his air attache parties in the aircraft's display hanger.

While Tip remained generally in touch with his Argentine connections, he had not maintained any official ties. Argentina had gone through paroxysms of change during the last years of the war. As the fortunes of the Axis powers waned, Axis support in Argentina collapsed, giving the US another opening for diplomacy with a new regime. Although Argentina had still not become as closely affiliated with the US as Brazil, the party of Juan Peron was at least in conversation with them again.

Peron was elected President of Argentina in 1946 by defeating his pro-communist running mates. Peron was not a proponent of capitalism, but he was also opposed to outright communism. He did not admire all aspects of socialism either. As he began to do what he could to improve Argentina's economic and social conditions from within, he created what would become a classic South-American-style dictatorship. Peron tried hard not to alienate other world powers, but neither would he engage in the various cold war alliances. In these early days of his power, Peron was making huge improvements in Argentina, often by nationalizing foreign interests.

Peron wanted a resumption of the US backed CAA program for Argentina's civil aviation business. The US wanted a bi-lateral air agreement that would streamline commercial aviation and become a model for other foreign nations. But Argentina had a problem. An unusual series of winter rains in the northern provinces had triggered a succession of locust plagues. The insect swarms were unmerciful, and Argentina was losing critical grasslands which fed the beef cattle that were the nations most important export. Mr. James McCauley Landis, chairman of the CAA in 1947, was in charge of the tricky negotiations. The chief negotiator of the Argentine delegation suggested Argentina might compromise on the strict restriction of foreign aircraft carrying passengers to Argentina if the US could assist them in obtaining helicopters and pilots to fly against the locusts.

At the same time that the locusts were swarming in Argentina and neighboring countries, Larry Bell of Bell Helicopter was looking for ways to expand his helicopter sales into commercial enterprises. Bell had been manufacturing the Bell Model 47 helicopter ahead of customer needs and was actively looking for uses that would drive sales. Bell's helicopter sales in 1946 had fallen short of their expectations. Larry Bell saw the Argentine locust plague as the perfect opportunity to prove what his helicopters could do.

Leaders in Argentina's civil aviation offices, watching American activities in South America as closely as they were watched in return, had learned that Tip was finishing his CAA mission to Brazil. Dr. Bosch had survived the Axis-influenced years and emerged inside the Peron government with his civil aviation program intact. Dr. Bosch was Tip's biggest fan, and many others in both the military and civil aviation leadership also trusted him. The Argentine government proposed that the US would get the long-desired bi-lateral air agreement if Tip came down to run the helicopter operation, but Tip had other plans. Locusts swarmed the Argentine president's home in Buenos Aires while the State Department got to work.

While I was in New York City, I was called to an office
in the State Department and advised that a phone call would
be coming through from Mr. Larry Bell, president of the Bell
Helicopter Corporation, who wished to speak to me personally.
Over the phone, Mr. Bell told me that the Argentine government
and the State Department wanted me to be the head of an
operation and that it was a most important assignment. The
helicopter was the only instrument that could combat the locusts
successfully. I advised Mr. Bell that I did not feel qualified to accept
the position, as I knew nothing about helicopters, having never seen
or flown one. Bell replied that if I would come back to Buffalo,
they would teach me all they knew about the machine in a matter of
weeks.

The Argentine project was fascinating as it was true
pioneering of the helicopter and its usefulness. The locust plague of
1947 was destroying millions of dollars worth of crops. Airplanes
were useless since the swarms were sometimes fifty miles deep, ten
miles wide, and extended up to 3000 feet in altitude. The dense
cloud of insects choked the air intake on the engines, causing engine
failure and fires, downing the aircraft and losing lives. Larry Bell of
Bell Helicopter had urged me to take on the project for two reasons.
He had not sold one helicopter yet outside the United States, and it
would really prove what the helicopter could do. It was a chance to
see where the limits of helicopter operations were. At the time he
first called me, I had only seen a helicopter in a photograph.

Lawrence Dale Bell was at the height of his aviation career
when he tried to convince Tip to take the job. He had worked with
fixed-wing aircraft manufacturing from an early age and was building
jet-powered fighter craft through his own company during World
War II. Bell Aircraft had built their first helicopter in 1941 based
on a design by Arthur Middleton Young. Young had taken on the

languishing invention as a mathematics project and approached Bell Aircraft with patents in hand. Now, six years later, Young's helicopter was perfected and moving down Bell's assembly line. Young moved on to other interests.

The Bell Model 47 helicopter, freshly certified for civilian use, was ready to enter the world of commercial aviation. These early models had open-top cockpits and bare tubular body structures. Four tires made up the landing gear, but Bell's pilots and engineers would soon propose a skid configuration that would become standard. The helicopters were light, maneuverable, and gave the pilot unprecedented views from aloft, but they were not for the faint hearted. The early rotors were made of balsa and fir woods with a steel reinforcing bar. The rotor noise was incredibly loud, and weight and balance limits were stringent. Bell wanted the opportunity for his helicopters as much as Argentina needed the help.

Larry Bell stepped forward with a solution designed to lure Tip to the project. After days of energetic calling, Mr. Bell was able to produce a letter from the CAA that had been approved by the State Department. It promised that, at the conclusion of the Argentine assignment, Tip could continue with his planned position with the CAA in San Francisco. Mr. Bell's enthusiasm masked the reality of the heavy hand of the State Department resting on Tip's shoulder. Argentina remained an elusive alliance and the Truman administration needed to forge a good relationship with Peron, while maintaining diplomatic neutrality. The demonstrable effectiveness of civil aviation missions and private enterprise in aiding diplomacy in South America once again offered the US government, and the US intelligence agencies, an ideal opportunity. The CAA, along with Tip, was expected to answer to a higher power. The chance to court Juan Peron's favorable attention was too valuable to pass up.

Tip left New York for Buffalo, but Louise and the children were finding their hotel on 60th Street expensive and stifling. Louise

accepted an offer from the Starkloff family; the doctor that Tip had
flown to Paraguay that stormy night in Rio. Dr. Gene Starkloff was
now living in Little Rock, Arkansas and invited Louise and baby
Susan for an extended stay. Michael, and the family dog acquired in
Rio, went to Grandmother Verna in Ohio. Both Tip and Louise were
determined not to suffer any more long family separations. Tip was
under family orders to find a house immediately upon arrival in
Buenos Aires. He spent six weeks at the Bell factory and emerged
with his helicopter rating in hand.

*Tip and Joe Mashman, along with C. W. Wes Moore, set
first-in-flight helicopter records almost every time they took to
the air.*

We gathered what was probably the most experienced
group of helicopter pilots and mechanics available for the project.
Among them was Joe Mashman, who later became Vice President
at Bell Helicopter, and C. W. Wes Moore, later Director of
Commercial Programs for Boeing-Vertol Company. The Argentine
company, named Trabajos Aereos Y Representaciones (TAYR)
bought eleven helicopters and they were flown down to Argentina
in a C-54 aircraft. Crews flown in from the Bell factory in Buffalo,
New York, assembled the helicopters at the airport upon arrival in
Buenos Aires. The assembled helicopters were then flown directly

to their various bases, some 500 miles away. Many of the ships went straight to the jungle. Neither the pilots nor mechanics spoke Spanish, which led to considerable confusion as the program went on.

We started a very successful pilot and mechanic training program and eventually replaced the American pilots with Argentines. Joe Mashman and Wes Moore stayed on for almost two years. I ended up with the first helicopter license in Argentina. Mashman and Moore were probably the first American pilots to have their US licenses validated in Argentina. We had our share of maintenance problems with the early Bell B and D models. Our maintenance chief was Pete Rivas, an Argentine magician with the helicopter, who had been employed by Bell in Buffalo. Some of the problems were overcome in unique ways. We found the starters were faulty and without them, it was virtually impossible to start the engines manually. We discovered that a 1926 Chevrolet starter could be used with very minor modifications so we retrofitted the helicopters with the Chevrolet starters. Likewise, bearings had to be replaced every few hours and it was impossible to import them from Bell without weeks of delay getting them all the way to South America. We found that SKF Swedish bearings were available in unlimited quantities in the area at a fraction of the cost and, in fact, were the exact same bearing we were using.

But the spraying project was successful and our helicopters proved their worth. The whole Argentine operation proved to Bell that the helicopter was a much more rugged and versatile machine than anyone had suspected at the time.

Equipped with side-mounted sprayers, the open cockpit Bell Model 47B-3 helicopters made progress against the Argentine locust plague of 1947.

Joe Mashman wrote a book about his lifetime of helicopter experiences titled *"To Fly Like a Bird,"* with R. Randall Padfield. He described his experiences with Tip and the locust plague in great detail. Joe had also brought his family to Buenos Aires, so when Louise arrived with Michael and Susan, she had a built-in social life. Tip had rented an apartment in the Acassuso neighborhood of Buenos Aires. Louise could once again have household help and Michael started school at St. Andrews, where classes were conducted in both Spanish and English. Together, the family enjoyed the metropolitan sights of the city that never sleeps.

Mashman, Tip, and Moore were pilots, not agricultural experts. For Tip, the flying was as much an adventure as the job of killing a locust swarm of biblical proportions. In addition to logging two to three helicopter hours every day, Tip was running the business side of the operation. It was a combination of commercial business and helicopter-centered civil aviation infrastructure. Joe had been piloting and engineering helicopters for most of his career already, and he knew exactly how much weight they could, or could not, carry. Joe observed that the system used to carry the toxic dinitro-ortho-cresol that their operation was dumping on the locust swarms was breaking frequently, and sent home for help to fix it. Two new spraying assemblies were given priority by Bell's engineering department and shipped south with top speed. None of the pilots wore any protective gear in the open cockpit helicopters. Perhaps the downward wash of the air currents helped, or perhaps they were simply lucky, but none of them suffered later complications from exposure to the chemicals. The technicians who loaded the insecticide wore protective suits.

The pilot's plan was to approach the swarms by helicopter in the early morning, when the insects were still on the ground after the cool evening. They would try to disperse most of their poison load at that time, hovering only twenty feet above the ground. They usually had to go back in for another attack as the day progressed. When the swarm took flight, the spraying continued, at 150 feet in the air. Locusts would obscure the bubble cover of the cockpit and Joe wrote that his left shoulder would be coated with smashed insects because it was exposed to the open air.

These early model Bell 47B-3 helicopters had a shape similar to the insect they were battling. The four landing legs with small round tires supported a cockpit that could hold only two people, and the spray mechanism was bolted to the outside edge. Directly over the pilot's and passenger's heads was open space and the whirling rotors. The clear bubble front, open sides, and open top gave extraordinary views to anyone daring enough to fly them.

The locust plague was controlled, or subsided enough to enable the Argentine government to claim victory. LIFE magazine did an article on the effort in early October 1947, complete with a photograph of the Bell 47B being loaded up with dust. Bell Helicopter used the story in a full-page ad for American Helicopter Magazine in the fall of 1947. The Peron government was very satisfied.

Joe Mashman began to do more pilot and mechanic training than he did dusting, and Tip began to fly farther afield with the helicopter well stocked with parts. The helicopters would not fly far enough or high enough to clear the Andes Mountains, so the TAYR team enlisted the help of DC-3 cargo aircraft. Joe would load up a helicopter on the DC-3, be flown over the Andes, unload and fly the helicopter up and down the coast. When his demonstration or mission was complete, he would disassemble the helicopter, load it back up, and be flown back to Buenos Aires. Once over the Andes, Tip and Joe did fly from country to country with little regard for international boundaries. In this way, they set almost every first helicopter flight record in South America. Tip was once again sitting in a cockpit with unlimited permission to fly. Anywhere that Tip wanted to go would be a first-in-flight record.

He and Joe Mashman made the first helicopter flight from Buenos Aires to Rio de Janeiro in a Bell 47D, mainly to pick up helicopter parts in Rio where the import restrictions were much easier to manage than in Argentina. They went in and out of Uruguay and Paraguay, decorating their passports with colorful and exotic visa stamps. Parts and mechanics often had to be floated in by boat through the extensive Amazon tributaries to reach stranded helicopters working in remote areas.

Bell 47B-3 Helicopter with Tip at the controls.

It was often more practical to take the helicopter to a region, and then fly in engine parts and materials using other craft. Tip used an amphibious Seabee to take off on the rivers, lakes, and coastal areas where there were no airstrips. The Republic RC-3 Seabee had a cabin uniquely suited for transport and cargo operations, and Tip used the pontoons and water capabilities to full advantage.

Although Tip was slowly falling in love with the complicated machine, he did not hesitate to protest the high maintenance requirements of helicopters. TAYR operated wherever there was a need. Tip, Mashman, and Moore knew that they were pioneering rotary wing technology simply by doing their daily business, and Tip was particularly enjoying his freedom from fixed-wing limitations.

The helicopters operated under the most hostile conditions imaginable. Monsoon rains, or desert heat, often hovering at treetop level in jungle areas over solid foliage for extended periods. The operation, although plagued with engine failures and damaged tail rotor blades, operated without a major injury to either pilots or mechanics for the whole two years. However, TAYR hosted the first mid-air collision of two helicopters. One helicopter was attempting to land when another went right through him. The lead ship fluttered to the ground while the colliding ship made a circuit of the field with over two feet of his rotor blade tips missing. The pilots escaped uninjured, but the helicopters were completely destroyed.

Both Tip and Joe Mashman were focused on the technical aspects of TAYR, like keeping the helicopters safely flying and piloting the craft into new frontiers. There was no marketing team promoting the business. Opportunities came through coincidence or through social connections, and it was up to Tip to pursue any advantages that came to him in this way.

While the Tippett and Mashman families explored South

America's most elegant city, Joe Mashman was delighted when Tip offered him the opportunity to meet Bob and Dolores Hope. The Hopes were visiting a prominent Argentine landowner and Bob knew that Tip was in Buenos Aires due to their continued letter correspondence. In what would today be called "networking", but was probably simply a conversation over cocktails, Bob spread the word about Tip's access to helicopters in Buenos Aires.

In September 1947, Tip received a request from the Dominican Republic's ambassador to Argentina, Porfirio Rubirosa, to accommodate his new wife on an aerial tour of certain real estate prospects that she was interested in buying. Ambassador Rubirosa had married American heiress Doris Duke, and she collected houses. TAYR was able to add aerial real estate shopping to the list of commercial uses for Bell helicopters. Over cocktails, Tip discovered that Doris had gifted Rubirosa with a B-25 bomber and Tip delightedly borrowed it on regular occasions to ferry helicopter parts from Brazil to Argentina, avoiding red tape and trade bureaucracies.

Larry Bell's vision of the Argentine effort showcasing his helicopters was a success. TAYR was the first and largest helicopter operation in the world at the time. In 1947, Bell Aircraft Company, and the world, saw a new advancement in aviation technology as Chuck Yeager broke the sound barrier in a Bell X-1 rocket plane. With that success, Bell Aircraft contracted with the newly named United States Air Force and the National Advisory Committee for Aeronautics to build the XS-1. The X designated "experimental" and the S referred to "supersonic." It was the first plane to achieve supersonic speed. The flight and aircraft were in military hands, but it was a proud breakthrough for Bell Aircraft. Larry Bell was invited to the White House for the honoring ceremonies. Speed, altitude, and duration were the new frontiers in aviation. The National Advisory Committee for Aeronautics would become the National Aeronautics and Space Administration (NASA) in 1958 as the United States turned government aviation resources toward space.

After the locust plague was controlled, Tip was flooded by requests for further agricultural help. The "flutter wagons" were in high demand. Representatives from the Brazilian government contacted Tip directly, pleading for help with a broca plague infecting their coffee trees. Helicopter spraying was able to save over eleven million coffee trees from the borer worm causing the plague, in terrain impossible to access by fixed-wing aircraft. The planes could not safely get close enough to the trees to make an effective pass, but the helicopters could hover within feet of the target. After the coffee trees were protected, Tip managed the next application of the TAYR helicopters, which was to spray areas infested with mosquitoes carrying malaria and yellow fever. These spray missions were carried out over Brazil, Uruguay, and Northern Argentina.

But once the primary locust mission was complete, TAYR began to change. Joe Mashman returned to Bell Helicopter and continued his rotary wing career by flying senatorial candidate Lyndon B. Johnson to all of his campaign stops throughout 1948. Mashman remained instrumental in the development of the helicopter for the rest of his career. His contribution to helicopter safety and operation was recognized in 1994 when the Helicopter Association International renamed one of their top safety awards in his honor.

Tip once again turned his attention toward San Francisco and the post he had been aiming for since he joined the CAA: Civil Transport Chief. He had completed the helicopter assignment with dignity and professionalism and was certain that a summons would come soon. He was right about the summons, but the source was not the CAA.

Several years earlier in 1945, ten weeks after the Hiroshima and Nagasaki mushroom clouds dissipated, the United Nations was formed. The organization's immediate focus was control of atomic weapons and the aircraft technology that had delivered them. Wealthy member nations worked publicly on the military applications of aviation, and secretly on nuclear energy. The rest of the world scrambled for war surplus aircraft which made civil aviation possible, and provided weapons delivery systems. While Louise and Tip had been living in Buenos Aires and fighting the locust plague with Bell Helicopters, the need to standardize worldwide civil aviation practices had become gruesomely apparent as crashes and fatalities mounted worldwide.

By April 1947, the United Nations had responded to the crisis by forming the International Civil Aviation Organization (ICAO). ICAO was expected to take control of worldwide civil aviation by applying uniform standards, training, and practices. Tip had the exact kind of civil aviation experience ICAO leadership was looking for, and he had the respect of South American aviation community. In early 1948, just as Tip was expecting to be reassigned to California, he was called to Washington D.C. for an important meeting. This time, he took a commercial flight.

I was asked by Edward Warner (Professor at MIT and former head of the Air Transport Board) who was now the elected Secretary General of ICAO, if I would be interested in accepting the position of Director of ICAO's South American Office, which would include all the countries in South America, Central America, and the Caribbean. I accepted the position with the understanding that I would remain for two years, after which I would be named Civil Aviation Association Senior Air Carrier Inspector in charge of the South Pacific Operations, based in San Francisco, California. The CAA and the State Department knew that it was important for me to be in charge of the office in its formative years, and that another director could be selected after the initial two years.

Tip had expected a very different interview to the one that took place in the State Department on his return from Buenos Aires.

The closed-door conversations and negotiations must have been delicate. Tip's superiors could not afford to lose his commitment, as it was both his personality and connections that made him the perfect candidate for this particular ICAO post. But Tip was ready to return to a life inside the US. The post he had been working toward most of his career was within reach, and this would be the second time it was postponed. Tip was well respected and admired by South American governments. From the State Department's perspective, Tip was a proven, reliable conduit of information on sensitive subjects. His observations from the cockpit, flying into every valley and harbor of the countries he navigated, had informed State Department reports for years. Tip's cheerful communiqués of confidences shared over gin and canapés were some of the best that Washington had received on South American aviation. In these first years of the Cold War, the battleground was information and Tip had become an irresistible asset. The Directorship of the South American Office was prestigious and important, but it would be headquartered in Lima, Peru. Tip accepted the post after negotiating the two-year commitment and postponed his phone call to Louise.

While Tip had traveled back to the United States in late-1948 Pan-American Airline luxury, Louise and the children remained grounded in their Buenos Aires apartment, luxurious by Argentine standards. The nanny and maid supported Louise, but she spent restless nights rechecking locks on the doors and windows. President Juan Peron and his beloved First Lady, Eva, were enjoying outstanding economic success for Argentina by implementing socialist policies and nationalizing foreign-held resources, such as railroads, mines and banks. Louise, at age thirty-three, was a slender and elegant example of the modern expatriate wife, but as an American, she felt a direct threat from increasing Argentine nationalism. Susan, now two, was producing her long anticipated first words - in Spanish. Michael was nine and now often played alone, as his playmates and their families had joined the exodus, driven by the changing political climate. Louise reached her limit. She packed up the children and boarded a plane to New York City.

Tip had secured a lifestyle for himself and Louise that easily surpassed any they could have achieved in California. Louise and the children would remain in New York City for several months until Tip could assemble a household and executive office staff in Peru. His salary was extraordinary for his age at the time, and even more so considering the spending power it would have in South America. It was just two years, and it would be a life of luxury. Louise prepared herself to assume the role of diplomatic hostess and Tip returned his attention to his most basic focus, the flying itself.

Among the benefits he had negotiated for Louise, he retained a significant victory for himself. The CAA had promised to get the Beechcraft C-45 from Brazil for his official use in Lima, Peru. He would have his favorite long-range dual-engine passenger craft in his hands and a series of governments paying his fuel bill. However professionally reluctant Tip may have been, he got ready for his new assignment with characteristic charm and enthusiasm.

Four offices were to carry out the standardization of policies and procedures set up by ICAO throughout the world. The South American office in Lima, the European office in Paris, the Far East office in Bangkok, and the Middle East office in Cairo. Our assignment as directors was to set up standard-practice procedures covering every phase of international civil aviation: pilot training, language, communications, weather, airports, landing systems, landing rights, and passenger-carrying safety practices.

I was the first director appointed by ICAO to head their South American office based in Lima, Peru, in 1948. The three other offices were established at the same time, but I was the only American heading a region. My particular region covered some of the most hostile areas in the world to overfly, thousands of square miles of rain forests, 21,000 foot mountains, and some of the highest altitude airports in the world. During this period, I made the first flight across South America from Rio de Janeiro, Brazil, to Lima, Peru, landing at La Paz, Bolivia - airport altitude 14,000 feet. I might add that flying through the Andes, not over them, is an exhilarating experience. Getting a Beechcraft off the ground at high altitude after a long run on a dirt runway was a real thrill. I made many such flights after that first one throughout South America to Mexico City, Bogotá, Montevideo, Buenos Aires, Asuncion, Paraguay, and Caracas. Dueling airport landing systems, airport and tower communication language barriers, (the official language is English at all designated international airports, but it had to be enforced) as well as weather reporting and weather systems made the job both interesting and challenging. The commercial airlines were flying DC-2s, DC-3s, a couple of Boeing 247-Ds, Junkers Ju-52s, Ford Tri-motors, an assortment of French Dewontine fighters, German Focke-Wulfs, and a few British Sunderland flying boats. I applied ICAO's training and philosophy to them all.

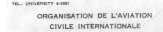

The International Civil Aviation Organization is often referred to as ICAO. It was established by the United Nations in 1947 to guide the development and safe practices of international aviation.

Chapter Fifteen

1949 to 1952

Director of the South American Office
International Civil Aviation Organization

Lima, Peru

In January 1949, Tip entered the social and political life of Lima, Peru. At age thirty-five, he was given the authority to expand on the type of work he had begun in Argentina and continued in Brazil. His territory included the countries of Argentina, Bolivia, Brazil, Chile, Colombia, Panama, Paraguay, Peru, Uruguay, Venezuela, British and French Guiana, and Surinam. As Director of the South American Office of the International Civil Aviation Organization (ICAO), he would be leading an agency that was part of the United Nations. He would report to ICAO headquarters in Montreal, Canada and his paychecks were subject to Canadian tax. He was still an American citizen, and answered to the American Embassy. He was also a military reserve officer with the military rank of Major, and was assigned to the Caribbean Air Command, headquartered at the Canal Zone, in Panama. Tip started looking for a plane to fly.

The job was both more, and less, than he expected. Despite promises made at headquarters, he had no aircraft assigned to his office for his own use. In addition to finding a house for his family, he had to set up his own office and staff it within the budget ICAO had allotted him. The work had already started with immediate and alarming safety issues that he rapidly brought to the attention of everyone within his reach. He was not yet set up, but the meetings would not wait. Within a week of his arrival, Pan American Airways brought an issue to Tip's attention Military aircraft on the heavily trafficked New York to San Juan route were using the wrong altimeter setting, based on civil commercial aircraft standards. Pan American pilots were having to unexpectedly deviate from ICAO standards in mid-flight. It was ICAO's mission to set and implement standards in cases like this, but it was Tip's challenge to get all the different flying organizations to follow them. Out of all the immediate tasks on Tip's mind, getting access to a plane was top of his personal list. He had located his beloved Beechcraft C-45 in Rio, where it was sitting outside in grass grown up to the wings but the ICAO wheels of administration could not free it for him. Tip wrote to the Department of the Air Force:

"...I have no aircraft here to fly at present but hope to work out something whereby I can fly the Air Force Mission planes or the attaché ship enough to keep my hands in. You don't have a spare Beechcraft or Cessna laying around for sale cheap to the ICAO Rep. do you?..."

It was inconceivable that Tip would remain isolated from the cockpit for long. He set out to introduce himself to both the Peruvian president and the US ambassador to Peru. The new ambassador, Harold Tittman Jr., had arrived in Lima only months before and Tip was well suited to get along with him. Ambassador Tittman was himself a WWI flying ace. He had joined the Foreign Service after suffering a serious battle injury and was assigned as Chargé d' Affaires to the Vatican City, attending Pope Pius XII during

WWII. Tip found that aviation and Catholicism were excellent things to have in common with an ambassador.

Major C. J. Tippett, Director of the South American office of the International Civil Aviation Organization, headquartered in Lima, Peru in 1949.

General Manual A. Odria was the Peruvian president in Tip's time, and Tip carried General Odria's business card in his wallet. President Odria had come into power through a military coup, then stepped down until elected. He was the only candidate running in the subsequent election and served as president until 1956. His elected dictatorship rode on top of a good economic time for Peru, with a typical amount of corruption and restriction.

Tip's plan to use the aircraft assigned to the US air force mission to Peru and the embassy air attaché offices was successful and he soon had regular flight time in both a new Beechcraft C-45 and Douglas DC-3, as well as connections to the commercial aircraft flying in to the main airport, Limatambo.

The airport was the logical place for the directorship and

Tip's second floor office there was equipped with everything he needed in true 1950s style. His wooden swivel chair pulled up to a broad desk, where he could lay out his papers, day calendar, and fat address book. The inkwell held fountain pens, a miniature Peruvian flag, and two navigation instruments from an aircraft cockpit. A four-drawer upright file cabinet and a large electric heater completed the décor. Every windowsill was stacked with papers and booklets. Tip now routinely wore a narrow tie, white collared shirt, and tailored suit in keeping with current style. With his fashionable raincoat and leather briefcase, he looked like a movie star.

Tip arranged to rent a house on Los Laureles Street, in Lima's San Isidro district. It was a nice neighborhood, close to the airport, and the street ended at the Los Inkas Golf Club, styled in the British fashion. The house would not be ready in time for the family's arrival, so he arranged a short stay at the golf club guesthouse, then flew back to the United States to bring Louise and the children to their new home. On July 27 1949, the family arrived by steamship. They had started out from New York City using a combination of rail and steamship and found it a very pleasant way to travel. The ship traversed the Panama Canal, and Mike, almost ten years old, had stayed on board at the invitation of the captain during the passage through the locks. Through ICAO diplomatic connections, Tip, Louise, and three-year-old Sue, joined Minister John Dee Greenway, His Majesty's Envoy Extraordinary and Minister Plenipotentiary at Panama, for dinner and a tour of Panama City. Greenway had been the British Ambassador to Panama for three years and was one year away from the end of his assignment.

The happy summer introduction to their new Lima home was slightly marred when Louise immediately came down with a case of jaundice. Doctors treating her advised no alcohol consumption for a full two months, and she was sentenced to bed rest for ten days. By the time she was well again, the Los Laureles house was ready. She relieved Tip of his unexpected childcare duties and he took the opportunity to tease her about the improvement in both his schedule and his bar bill.

Louise's first mission was to set the house in order. The family once again was able to staff the household with hired help. Nannies at the time were mostly educated Peruvian middle-class women, but the maids and cleaning staff were likely of Amerindian descent, Quechua or Aymara. Louise hired two Peruvians, who quickly became part of the family. Leonor, who was both maid and cook, and Clemente, who was a combination of butler, handyman and manager when the household had to deal with local merchants. Leonor and Clemente spoke only Spanish, and so Spanish became the household's language. Louise was fluent enough in Spanish, and thankful to no longer have to struggle with Portuguese, as she had done in Brazil for many years. Michael was fluent in Portuguese, and spoke Spanish more often than English. Little Susan was beginning to put together sentences in a mix of all three languages, to her mother's exasperation.

Lima was a Spanish-style metropolis. It was both the capital and the largest city in Peru. After more than 400 years of Spanish influence, Lima's architecture reflected Spanish colonial styles, and the social life was based on that of Spain's aristocracy. The city's many Catholic churches, cathedrals, and palaces were in constant use for ceremonies and cultural events. Hanging balconies were an outstanding element of Lima's architecture. There were so many clinging to the brilliant white stone building façades that they became a signature element of the city.

The desert location of Lima led Louise to expect climatic extremes, but the weather was mild. The Pacific Ocean was less than a mile from their house, although the accessible beaches were to the north and south of their neighborhood. The ocean moderated the temperature, Lima was neither very cold in winter, nor hot in summer. Summers occasionally had a morning fog reminiscent of San Francisco. Their hacienda-style house was two-level with a whitewashed walled garden. It had curved doorways with lightly ornate wrought-iron bars. An interior walled garden with louvered doors to the outside enabled the family to enjoy the outdoors in privacy, another piece of Spanish colonial influence. The tile work was heavily Peruvian, almost Moorish, and dark wooden overhead beams finished the effect. Tip described the house in a letter to family:

> "…We've finally gotten settled in Lima. We've taken a house in the San Isidro section and have bedrooms all over the place. We have a bathroom about two acres square, with a sunken tub all in black and green. All I need is an olive branch and some bubble bath to set it off. The house is in the San Isidro section (near the golf course) and is also only a few minutes from the airport where our offices are located. Of course, being just around the corner from the golf course makes it imperative that I improve my game, which incidentally can stand some improving as you know…"

With the family secure, Tip rolled up his sleeves and got to work. He joined the Pan American Bowling Club, bought a share in the Lima golf club from an American businessman returning to the States, and ordered up ten cases of Old Grand-Dad bourbon from New York using his new diplomatic status. He also sent a letter to the CAA publications office ordering a copy of every document in their catalog, and began to arrange for their translation into Spanish.

The chief of the Air Force mission to Peru was Colonel Samuel Galbreath. Colonel Galbreath was organizing a meeting of the air mission chiefs at Albrook Air Force Base in Panama to acquaint them with the ICAO mission and needed Tip's help drafting a memo of introduction. Military aviation for all the member nations was exempted from ICAO control, but part of Tip's mission was to coordinate with military leadership on aviation issues. In countries like Peru, there was almost no civil aviation infrastructure outside

of the military. There was a single commercial airline that had
been founded by an American, Elmer J. Faucett, but there were few
aero clubs and fewer non-military aerodromes. Faucett, who had
emigrated to Peru in the 1920s, was responsible for most of the
commercial flight development in Peru. There was an overwhelming
amount of civil aviation work for Tip to do to implement ICAO's
regional plan. He would need all the support he could get.

Through the years of Tip's work in Peru for ICAO, he
would rely on Albrook Air Force Base in Panama. The base was
Tip's headquarters for his military service, and the source of many
of his supplies. Albrook was headquarters to the US Caribbean
Air Command, known as CAirC. It was located outside of Balboa,
Panama, on the Pacific entrance to the Panama Canal. Balboa was a
town created by the United States in order to build the canal, so it
was not a typical Panamanian city. It was stocked with Canal Zone
government services such as schools, post offices, a commissary, and
places where US servicemen could relax. In the 1950s, it was a piece
of America set in Panama's extreme climate.

The US military controlled the canal, which had opened in
1914, after a ten-year building effort primarily executed and funded
by the US government. An earlier French effort had been both
absorbed and abandoned as the Americans took over. Control of
such a valuable shipping shortcut between the Atlantic and Pacific
oceans was firmly in US hands for the duration of both world wars,
and only transferred to Panama in 1999, in accordance with a much-
contested and re-written treaty.

In the early period of his directorship, Tip was more often
explaining his mission than working toward implementing aviation
standards. He had been an aviation diplomat before, in Brazil, as
acting air attaché and much of his work in Peru would be similar. He
began his draft for Colonel Galbreath by including the preamble of
the International Civil Aviation Organization's convention, which had
been signed and accepted at the 1944 Chicago meeting:

*Tip worked with both military and civil aviation leadership
throughout his region. In Peru, Faucett was the first commercial
airline and pioneered most of Peru's air routes.*

WHEREAS the future development of international
civil aviation can greatly help to create and preserve friendship
and understanding among the nations and peoples of the world,
yet its abuse can become a threat to the general security; and
WHEREAS it is desirable to avoid friction and to promote that
cooperation between nations and peoples upon which the peace of
the world depends; THEREFORE, the undersigned governments
having agreed on certain principles and arrangements in order
that international civil aviation may be developed in a safe and
orderly manner and that international air transport services may be
established on the basis of equality of opportunity and operated
soundly and economically; have accordingly concluded this

Convention to that end.

ICAO provided a centralized, standardized plan for worldwide aviation, referred to as the "Regional Plan." Regional plans covered personnel licensing, Visual and Instrument Flight Rules (VFR and IFR), meteorological codes, aeronautical charts and the unification of methods for preparing charts, dimensional units to be used in air and ground measurements, operation of aircraft including international commercial air transport, aircraft nationality and registration marks for identification and registry, airworthiness of aircraft certification and inspection, facilitation dealing with documentation required to allow passage of aircraft, passengers, and cargo through national boundaries, aeronautical telecommunications, air traffic establishment and maintenance of air traffic control, flight information and alerting services, search and rescue (SAR) organization establishment, aircraft accident procedures to secure uniformity regarding notification, investigation, and inquiries, the physical characteristics of aerodromes, aeronautical information services, and uniformity in methods of collection and dissemination of information, including using English as the global language for aviation.

Directors of the regional offices were expected to implement ICAO recommendations by establishing personal contact with civil aviation administrations in the member states of their regions. They were instructed to do this through correspondence and travel missions. Tip was ordered to "encourage, assist, expedite, and follow up actions by member states to implement regional plans." He complied by commandeering a DC-3 and travelling to Paraguay, Argentina, and Panama, within weeks of settling the family.

Tip worked closely with Walter Binaghi, who became Council President of ICAO in 1957. Binaghi is second from the left in the photo above.

In between flights, Tip had his hands full with visiting aviation dignitaries. In 1949, Eddie Rickenbacker, aviation ace and president of Eastern Airlines, was looking to expand his business interests toward South America by working out a business arrangement with Pan American. Rickenbacker organized an air tour of South America and brought along Arthur Godfrey, who was already well established as a radio and television broadcaster. Godfrey was also a licensed pilot and aviation enthusiast, proving useful to Rickenbacker in more ways than filming and publicity. As Rickenbacker's tour required diplomatic and embassy assistance, it was natural that the group would connect with Tip. Rickenbacker's visit was the first official aviation event Tip participated in as director. Godfrey asked Tip to help get twenty-four undeveloped rolls of film back to the US safely and quickly. Tip loaded up a returning US diplomat with the box of film and sent him off by boat. In Tip's letter to Godfrey, apprising him of the film's disposition, he proposed a different set of guidelines for Godfrey's next visit. Tip stated that he preferred rules where the loser of the various drinking games didn't end up with such a serious headache and bill.

Louise and Tip quickly became a beacon for every kind of visiting American, and Tip collected stacks of thank-you notes from people throughout their time in Lima. Lloyd Welch Pogue wrote him on Pogue & Neal letterhead thanking him for the alligator handbag and wishing him well in his new post. Pogue was considered an aviation law pioneer and was credited with busting the monopoly threat of a single world airline, a short-lived idea that would have hurt the progress of commercial aviation. Another visitor in 1949 was Emmett Evan Van Heflin. He was an American movie actor who was busy filming in the early 1950s when Tip met him and his wife, Frances, in Peru. Keeping up his movie star collection, Tip responded to a letter from Bob Hope congratulating him on his directorship. Writing to Bob, Tip described Michael's recent enrollment in a Jesuit school and the fact that Susie was threatening to run away if Louise didn't send her to kindergarten soon. Tip had taken Mike to see Bob Hope's latest film "The Paleface" and Tip reported that they had both enjoyed it.

The visitors were usually invited for a game of golf down the street. By 1950, Tip had won both the Apertura and Apertura Mixto trophy cups from the Los Inkas Country Club located there. With the household successfully established, Louise used visits by business associates and personal friends to tour the sights of Peru. They visited Machu Picchu and some of the lesser-known Inca cities, never using supplemental oxygen as some visitors did, despite some of the extremely high altitude locations.

While Tip was working, flying, or winning golf trophies, Louise wrestled with Peruvian governmental rejection of her birth certificate and driver's license when she applied for the Peruvian version of both. She launched a barrage of paperwork that was returned decorated with incomprehensible stamps. In the middle of this domestic bureaucratic frustration, North Korea invaded South Korea, taking the US by surprise and triggering the Korean War. North and South Korea had been established by the Allies at the end of WWII because defeated Japan had ruled the Korean peninsula and as part of Japan's territories, it was therefore considered Allied property. Soviet troops occupied the North, and North Korea had developed a communist government. South Korea, occupied by US troops, established a capitalist government. Korea had become a hot zone in the Cold War and erupted into armed conflict when North Korea invaded the South. As the US forces pushed the North Koreans back, China joined the fight with the Soviet Union's support and after a period of see-saw attacks and retreats, neither side ended up making much progress, despite heavy losses. The Korean War ended when an armistice was signed on July 27, 1953

Tip was temporarily loaned to the US Caribbean Air Command and given training specific to his special intelligence activities. Louise remained at home in Lima, once again an expatriate American homemaker alone in a foreign city at a time when the US was at war. But as had been the case in Rio de Janeiro, Louise had an active community of American, European, and wealthy Peruvian friends to keep her busy. Tip's Peruvian driver's license was completely in order, and he had procured a car for his personal use. The car, a 1920's era Rolls-Royce Phantom, was Tip's delight. For Louise, it was less practical as she needed Clemente both to drive it, and to manage the hand-crank starter.

The aviation world in early 1950s Peru was small, and anyone who was also connected to the United States was sure to pass through Tip's office. Tip had staffed his office with a capable secretary who was also born to a prestigious Peruvian family. Pilar Pallette came into Tip's office on her journey from being a Pan

American stewardess to becoming a movie star. She was fluent in English and knew Peruvian aviation from the inside, so she was a logical resource for Tip's office. Sue remembered her well as a gracious, attractive, and highly competent woman who kept Tip on track in his frequent travels and duties. Tip could not keep her for long, but as was Tip's habit, he remained in contact with her, and she was the reason Tip met John Wayne.

John Wayne, the movie star, came to Peru in 1952 to look into some investments, scout some locations, and take a vacation. He had been told to contact a man named Richard Weldy for a possible hunting trip while he was in Peru. Richard Weldy was an American pilot working for Pan American who guided hunting safaris on the side. He had married Pilar Palette but they were now estranged. By the time Wayne was visiting Weldy, Pilar was on location in the Peruvian jungle, filming her second movie, "Green Hell." Weldy took Wayne to visit Pilar thinking that the trip would be a combination of interests for Wayne, and Weldy would have the chance to win Pilar back.

John Wayne went to the set with Richard simply for enjoyment, but stayed for Pilar. Richard Weldy's plan to reconcile with his beautiful wife while showing a client a good time had seriously backfired. Wayne was fascinated with Pilar and when he returned to the US, he began to take an active interest in the divorce proceeding which his second wife, Chata, had already initiated before Wayne's trip to Peru. That same year, Pilar travelled up to the US and began to quietly date John Wayne. By 1953, Pilar was staying in the US and seeing the Duke so regularly that the secret romance became public. The couple was in for some heartbreak before John Wayne was legally able to marry, but they made it through and wed in 1954. Pilar was John Wayne's third and final wife. Tip would see more of the Waynes when he returned to live in the United States, but for his Peruvian tenure, he stayed in touch by letters and dinners during visits.

The notes that Tip accumulated show a bureaucracy of the highest order, in which vast amounts of time were spent organizing, managing implementation, and determining the actions required by the orders. The work Tip had done so directly in Argentina and Brazil was very different in Peru under the auspices of the United Nations. In this much bigger role, he was not able to do things as quickly or effectively when he came across them. There were layers of diplomatic red tape, and obstacles of protocol, even in something as simple as putting together a civilian training center. The initial two-year posting period passed quickly. The family enjoyed Lima and their lifestyle, and Tip made tremendous progress despite the difficulties. Based on the honors, medals, and awards that Tip earned during this portion of his life, it was the height of his career, but he chose this time in his written memoir to end his account.

In Tip's opinion, the directorship of ICAO was the final posting of his aviation career, but he was only thirty-seven and it was by no means the end of his life. He and Louise stayed in Lima at the heart of a vibrant social and political circle until 1959. There was more aviation work to accomplish, more aircraft to fly, and more people to meet. His story continues even though his manuscript had ended.

I remained in charge of the South American Region for eleven years. My involvement in constructing three new airports, landing systems, pilot training, future construction networks, and weather stations, made it impossible for me to leave the area.

In 1960, Tip completed his work as director for ICAO and his life took an unexpected new direction. The change was so profound that he mentally divided his life into before and after, which is one way to explain the end of his manuscript with his directorship in Lima. The next eleven years of his story is told here through materials from his archive of letters, telegrams, passports, flight logs, photographs, memos, articles, copies of official documents, and independent research. Because of his extraordinary record keeping, his direct voice is not entirely silenced with his final paragraph.

The first hints of change came in 1952, as Tip's documents begin to show his interest in a new direction. Tip remained uncompromisingly strong as an aviation leader, but his increasing disenchantment with a stifling bureaucracy was giving him motivation to bring more outside activities to his working days. As 1952 began, it was almost as if he had hung a sign on his cockpit door that said "Gone Fishing."

Chapter Sixteen

1952 to 1953

The Club at Cabo Blanco, Peru

At the time that Tip started his ICAO directorship, the countries in his region represented one of the largest collections of political philosophies in modern history. The only system lacking was a monarchy, but most of the South American dictators lived like kings. High-class South American families behaved like aristocracy, and wealthy or influential American businessmen were automatically welcomed to their ranks. Peru was a fashionable destination for celebrities, either on business missions or looking for vacation spots. 1952 was a good time to be rich or powerful in South America.

Tip's work was primarily social. The only way to implement ICAO's mission was to talk directly to everyone in the offices of commercial, private, government, and organizational authority in his region. The American Embassy provided most of his introductions, and there was always his military connection if the embassy came up short. Once he had an introduction, Tip's own charisma, expertise, and aviation experience took over.

South American dictators loved Tip. Presidents wanted him to tour their capitals. Brazilian generals invited him out to dine. Colonels from Uruguay encouraged him to stay for the weekend on their lavish estancias. One Peruvian businessman took an immediate liking to Tip. Enrique Pardo was a genial man, older than Tip, and very wealthy. Enrique was the first in his family to break the long line of Pardos who had run for president of Peru. He was the distinguished-looking son of a family which embodied the heritage of Peruvian aristocracy. The Pardo family had founded the Civilista Party in the 1880s. Their mildly-socialist ideology was still popular with the people of Peru. But it was not popular with the military juntas that were seizing, and losing, power in a succession of coups that would last the decade. After Enrique Pardo's grandfather and uncle were assassinated, Enrique could not be persuaded to run for president and he turned his attention, wealth, and popularity, to business. Tip and Enrique had many interests in common and quickly became genuine friends. Tip had uses for Enrique's introductions to Peruvian business and society. Enrique had plans for Tip's access to a fleet of passenger aircraft, which now included a Douglas C-47 Skytrain, Cessna T-50, and Douglas B-23 Dragon. There was a special place off the western coast of Peru that Enrique was interested in, and it was much more pleasant to go there by air.

Peru is on the Pacific coast of South America, between Ecuador to the north, and Bolivia and Chile to the south. Enrique's destination was close to the northern border in a desert area devoid of large cities. Deep ocean trenches parallel the Peruvian coastline and sheer cliffs border isolated beaches. The land climbs rapidly from the coast, through utterly dry desert, to the high mountains of the Andes. The extreme arid emptiness of the coastal desert contrasts with the rich sapphire ocean, bountiful in all kinds of sea life. In the 1950s, the small fishing villages that subsisted on the coast had new competition from a big commercial fishery. They were also neighbors to a couple of large oil companies that prospected in the interior.

An airstrip at Talara, 600 miles north of Lima, had been built by the Lobitos Oil Company and also served a new commercial anchovy fishery based in the small town of Mancora. Neither of these towns was Enrique's destination, but they provided the means for him to get where he wanted to go. It was a place he was about to put on the map, with Tip as his witness and right-hand man. Enrique was headed for the village of Cabo Blanco, which was not much more than a couple of shacks and a boat jetty built and maintained by the oil company.

Enrique Pardo was a sport fisherman and had toured the usual places that attracted millionaire fishermen, such as Bimini, Cuba, and the Australian coast. He was on friendly terms with other sport fisherman of the era, and in particular had entered a conversation, perhaps a bet, with S. Kip Farrington Jr. And Alfred C. Glassell Jr. who were each world record holders with rod and reel. They speculated about the kinds of oceanic conditions that would attract the big fish that sport fisherman dreamed about. On the shores of Cabo Blanco, Tip and Enrique looked out over exactly the unique conditions the fishermen had been talking about.

Cabo Blanco was at the confluence of two ocean currents. The northbound Humboldt was cold, deep, and murky because of an upwelling of dense nutrients. It collided with the clear, blue, warmer waters of the Pacific Current, right offshore from Cabo Blanco, within reach of a sport fishing boat. In 1948, Enrique had taken an 824-pound black marlin on rod and reel, which was evidence enough for Farrington and Glassell. Over the intervening five years, Cabo Blanco had proven to be an extraordinary fishing site. It offered a rare combination of being the only place in the world where broadbill swordfish, striped marlin, and black marlin could be found all in the same place, along with sailfish, , bigeye and bluefin tuna, among other species. The desolate spot was a sport fisherman's paradise. It only needed a few amenities to make it perfect.

Enrique took Tip to the site where he was overseeing the construction of a building to house the exclusive fishing club that Farrington had founded in 1951. The Cabo Blanco Fishing Club

was comprised of handpicked wealthy men, and membership was
by invitation only. Pardo, Farrington, and Glassell hadn't waited for
a clubhouse to begin fishing the astonishing grounds. They already
had their fish stories; complete with proof in the form of a series of
record setting "granders," 1,000 pound, or more, black marlin caught
on rod and reel within months of each other, and shipped to Florida
by air for taxidermy, at great expense and to the delight of Panagra
Airlines.

Enrique had secured a long-term lease to the land on the
bluff from the Lobitos Oil Company by adding both F. L. Bates of the
International Petroleum Company, and C. N. Carroll of the Lobitos
Oil Company to the membership roster. Farrington's membership
requirements were a personal invitation from himself or Enrique,
plus a $10,000 fee ($83,000 today). Even before the Clubhouse was
built, word of the world-record catches had spread and Farrington
had scandalized the world's elite by turning down membership
requests from millionaires without reason or explanation. The
original membership list was short, only twenty men (eighteen
of them Americans) and despite lacking the membership fee, or
the particular social, family, or industry-giant standing common to
the list, Tip was on it in an honorary capacity. His organizational
skills were much in demand. The South American Director of the
International Civil Aviation Organization had just joined the Cabo
Blanco Fishing Club Board of Directors as club manager.

The majority of the original members were from the east
coast American social elite, all well known to Farrington or Pardo.
Some were businessmen with financial empires so vast, their names
are still well known today. Roger Firestone of Pennsylvania had not
yet created his well-known Firestone Tire franchise when he became
a founding member. James Hutton of Ohio, whose family was in the
process of founding the brokerage firm today known as E F Hutton,
made the list. John M. Olin, of the ammunition industry Olin Group,
was a huntsman and sport fisherman, and would become a champion

of game bird conservation. Tony Hulman, of the Indiana Hulmans and Clabber Girl Baking Powder ascendancy, was bringing the Indianapolis 500 motor-racing industry back to full profitability at the time that he joined the Club. William Carpenter, a sport fishing fanatic best known for his big bluefin tuna catches, was on the roster and was already well connected with the International Game Fish Association. The IGFA was the registry where world-record catches would be recognized. Julian T. Crandall and his brother, L. R. Crandall of Ashaway, Rhode Island were founding members, and their Ashaway linen fishing line was the standard of the day. The brothers were already working on a new product and envisioned a day when their invention, nylon line, would be in every fisherman's reel.

Enrique selected the two South American members. Jaime Llavallol was an Argentine businessman who traced his family heritage back to the Spanish Conquistadors. Raymundo D. Castro Maya was Brazilian, and as much known for business as for his patronage of the arts. Guests had to procure an invitation through a member, and it was a highly sought-after prize.

The exposed rock of the cliffs at Cabo Blanco shone white in the glaring sun and gave the village its name. Cool offshore breezes, sometimes strong enough to fling sand, contrasted with the beating noonday sun. There was nothing on the desert coast to compete with the ocean and draw the eye. Cabo Blanco was all about the ocean, the colliding currents, and the fish.

Overhead, Tip saw petrels, gannets, and terns in great numbers. In time, he would record seeing albatross and Andean condors, all attracted by the same thing that attracted the sport fishermen, an abundance of sea life outstanding in both variety and numbers. Colliding currents and upwelling occurred in other places in the ocean, but here they supported one of the richest ocean life food pyramids ever found within sight of land. The nutrients attracted plankton, which were consumed by incredible numbers of anchovy, which were in turn eaten by mid-sized bonito and pompano. The gigantic bony fish, like the black marlin, hunted the bonito. The top predatory fish were sight hunters, and cruised the clear Pacific Current. The murky Humboldt Current held the food source for the smaller fish, which were the food source for the larger fish, and so it was at the line where the currents met that the billfish could be found. It was there that they hunted, either waiting at the current confluence, or venturing into the cold dense murk. Fishermen knew to look for the places where the ocean waters changed colors. Cabo Blanco crews rarely trolled for fish. They waited until they saw a fish large enough for sport, then dropped a baitfish on a line and played it out within sight of the game.

Sharks were rare, which was another unique condition of Cabo Blanco, and an attractive one to the fishermen because their catches were not stripped bare on the journey back to the jetty. But occasionally a mako would itself be the catch of the day. While heading out for the billfish, Tip could sometimes see pilot, sperm, and humpback whales, manta rays, pelicans, booby birds, cormorants, frigate or man-of-war birds, Inca terns, and gulls. Night fishing for Humboldt squid was another feature of club life. The six-foot-long squid fought ferociously, jetting the boat and crew with ink and seawater until subdued. In addition to providing an exciting evening of fishing, the squid were valuable as bait, and for lunchtime ceviche.

Selwyn Kip Farrington Jr. was a stockbroker from New Jersey who scandalized his family by quitting his day job and devoting himself to full time, big game fishing. He was a square jawed, dark browed, weather beaten man totally dedicated to the sport and pursuit of oceanic big game. He was proving to be a pioneer and champion of the sport and his vision for the Club at Cabo Blanco was that it be a place devoted to the uncontestable establishment of world records. This meant building an infrastructure that could witness, weigh, and follow the stringent rules of sport fishing regulations.

The clubhouse, designed by Peruvian architect Pepe Alvarez

Calderon, was finished in January 1953. Farrington's dream of a club where undisputed record breaking fish could be caught was realized. It was a simple, spartan structure built at the top of a hill accessed by a long dirt driveway.

Huge marlin tails nailed to posts lined the drive from bottom to top and became a distinctive feature of the Club.

The bedrooms had windows overlooking the pool and ocean, and each had a private bath and shower. The floor-to-ceiling glass walls of the main room framed the ocean horizon. The room included a bar and featured a fireplace with mantel, where the first record-setting black marlin was mounted.

The club rooms were spartan but stylish and comfortable.

The marlin on the mantel was not the biggest catch, since Alfred C. Glassell Jr. had beaten that record soon after the fish was hooked, but it was a centerpiece for the Club. Sue remembered tossing coins into its open mouth for luck before fishing trips. White jacketed servers brought whiskey on ice to guests relaxing in 1950s style wooden chairs on rattan matts, where they watched through telescopes for the boat's return. Success was communicated through a system of flags. Red for black marlin, blue for striped marlin, yellow for tuna, green for broadbill, white for sailfish, and black for mako.

Tip with his record setting eighty pound roosterfish, caught on a fifty pound line in 1956. Tip lost the roosterfish record first when the International Game Fish Association stopped segregating world records between men and women, and then again when someone caught a bigger fish in 1960.

      Member accommodations were included as part of their dues, excluding only the bar tab. Invited guests could pay for rooms and meals at a rate of $25 a day ($209 today) and transport to the Club from Talara cost $10 ($83 in modern rates). Boats were $100 a day ($837 currently) and big-game tackle was available for $10 a day. Fishing from the beach where records could be set was also an attraction. Surf casting tackle was $5 a day ($41 today).

      More money had been invested down in the wood paneled

tackle room, where huge tables were laid out for working with the long fishing rods and heavy reels. Each member had a fishing locker ready for his use, and great care was taken with the linen line and barbed hooks. Tip's own locker housed gear identical to the kings of industry he fished alongside - gloves, fighting harness, lucky rod, regulation hooks, and a change of clothes. The fishing gear was meticulously checked so that it was in compliance with sport fishing regulations.

The Club had a four boat fleet, custom built in Nova Scotia specifically for this purpose. All cleats and railings were purposefully missing, so that nothing would catch the line during a fight. The rear transom was significantly lower than normal. The fleet was designed for sport fishing success, and comfort was distinctly lacking. There were no stoves or cooking facilities on board. The boats put out for one purpose only: to catch record setting game fish. The gaff poles were all exactly fourteen feet long, to aid in measuring the fish, and the fighting chair was bolted deep into the hull.

The flying bridges were built tall enough so that record catches could be hauled up completely out of the water for the trip to shore, protecting the fish from shark attack. Too many catches had been lost on the tow back to weigh in to neglect this detail, even though it had never happened at Cabo Blanco.

Tip fished from each of the boats in turn. The Pesacodos Dos was forty feet long with a twelve foot beam and enclosed cabin. The Petrel, the Miss Texas, and the Miss Peru, were all slightly smaller at thirty eight feet with eleven foot beams, and had up top controls. The dual Chrysler engines on all four boats were specially geared for the backing and maneuvering required in a long sport-fishing fight. There were hoists and booms for taking the fish on either side of the boat. However, all of these custom specifications made the boats vulnerable to rough seas and bad weather, and these fishermen were totally dependent on clear skies for safety and success.

Everyone on the boat worked together as soon as the fish was hooked. The mate stayed with the angler strapped into the fighting chair and the captain handled the boat from the flying bridge.

The captains and crew were full blooded Peruvian Indians from the local fishing community and were already familiar with the fishing grounds and big catches. But the Club's insistence on rod-and-reel fishing was a new challenge for them, and they had been personally instructed by world class sport fishing captains paid for by Farrington and Glassell. They were proud, skilled, and devoted to successful catches. Days of no fish made them more depressed than the unlucky fisherman. The boat had to move with precision to help fight the fish without breaking the line. The marlin would leap and dive, and the linen line would sometimes play out so fast that the crew had to dump buckets of seawater into the fisherman's lap to prevent the reel from catching fire.

The fight went on for hours. If it was a success, the exhausted fish would be gradually reeled closer to the boat where the crew would pull it in with gaffing poles.

The crew looped a rope around the black marlin's tail, hoisted it up, and then grabbed the bill to bring it into the boat. Those times when the fish was not large enough to challenge a record, it might be released, but most of the time the catch was brought home. The real trophy, regardless of an entry in a record book, was the photograph with the fish. Black marlin was not considered good eating by North Americans. If the fish was not going to be transported to Miami for taxidermy, it was given to the local village who consumed it with enthusiasm. Tuna and swordfish were included in the Club menu and many of the big tuna caught at Cabo Blanco in the 1950s would now sell for tens of thousands of dollars each in Pacific fish markets.

The jetty at Cabo Blanco was as utilitarian as the Clubhouse, but less comfortable. The thick, weathered wood beams and planks, rope hawsers, wood and iron pulleys, and great steel hooks existed for the single purpose of hoisting fish for weighing and photographs. It was a stage set for a performance, and the fish were the stars.

Tip stands with S. Kip Farrington, Jr. and Enrique Pardo on the dock at Cabo Blanco with their 800 pound black marlin caught with rod and reel on October 5, 1954.

It was customary to write the weight, date, and location on the fish, hung head down by a thick rope looped around the tail. The proud fisherman, occasionally a woman, posed full length next to the fish. These black and white photographs captured the glamour and excitement that took place in this desolate looking place. Nature's monochromatic landscape gave a neutral background for these proud portraits. The fish were so big and fought so fiercely, that it was considered an honorable battle, one in which the fisherman did not always prevail.

Tom Bates gave Tip a signed photograph of himself with a
record setting black marlin, and challenged Tip to top him.

Enrique, as Honorary President, oversaw the finance
and policy decisions. Tip was in charge of the organization, daily
maintenance, and oversight of the Club. He began to rack up his
own impressive list of fish tales. But it was Alfred Glassell who broke
Tom Bates' record with a 1,090 pound black marlin caught two
weeks later. Glassell's fish held the world record until Tom Bates
broke it again on July 29, 1953.

One of Tip's duties in managing the Club was scheduling
charters involving Club boats, or visits by guests who arrived in

their own yachts. These guest and charter visits were revenue for
the Club, which was expected to meet its own expenses regardless
of the wealth of its members. He also managed the membership
schedule, Club functions, and along with Pardo, Farrington, and
Glassell, was the Club spokesman to media and other entities. Cabo
Blanco didn't need to generate publicity, as public interest matched
the amazing fishing conditions, but the Club did like to manage it.
The Ashaway brothers business ran its own publication devoted
to the sport fishing industry, and in 1953 the Ashaway Sportsman
ran an article about Inez Alavarez Calderon of Lima, Peru, who was
the first Peruvian woman to land a marlin off the coast of her own
country. Her 202-pound fish was eclipsed even in the same article by
member Tony Hulman's achievement of boating three black marlin
in four consecutive days. The magazine noted that black marlin
were reeled in, photographed, and listed on the Club wall in record
numbers, and to the highest standards of sport fishing conduct.

The biggest catches were still to come, but Tip's day job back
in Lima frequently demanded that his attention be focused on the
cockpit. Tip's ICAO directorship pulled him away from the fishing
in September of 1953 when he flew to Columbia, Brazil, Uruguay,
and Panama in succession. Immediately upon his return to Lima, he
reported to ICAO headquarters in Montreal flying a deHavilland
Comet, the first jet-powered commercial passenger liner and one of
the largest multi-engine aircraft he had yet flown. His multi-engine
license and his instructor ratings required him to log flight hours,
and he wanted to be in the cockpits of the latest planes. While flying
a jet-propelled commercial aircraft was not the same as flying a jet
fighter, piloting or co-piloting commercial flights travelling the routes
of his region was a fine way to accomplish both travel and ICAO
standardization.

In 1953, Tip was one of very few foreigners to be awarded the Peruvian Flying Cross, First Class, by the Peruvian military.

Tip was away only for a few weeks, and returned in time for an important ceremony. Louise was on his arm, her hair upswept in a severe chignon, when the Peruvian military awarded him the Peruvian Flying Cross First Class for "distinguished services in the field of international civil aviation." Tip had notified ICAO headquarters of the award and received a telegram saying:

"...YOUR SECRETARY GENERAL APPRECIATES COURTESY YOUR COMMUNICATION AND HAS NO OBJECTION ACCEPTANCE STOP. PLEASE CONVEY TO AIR MINISTER THE SECRETARY GENERAL'S GRATITUDE FOR THE IMPLIED APPRECIATION OF ICAO AS WELL AS PERSONAL HONOR TO YOURSELF..."

The awards ceremony made the Port Clinton newspaper back in Ohio with a half-inch headline reading "Former Port Clintonite receives high award from Peruvian government." Verna proudly clipped the newspaper story and added it to her scrapbook

of Tip's career. The newspaper story mentioned her and Adolf
Eyth as Tip's Port Clinton parents. The commanding general of the
Peruvian air force, General Octavio Rios, pinned the medal on Tip's
coat in an event attended by a multitude of Peruvian air force and
diplomatic men. The New York Times cabled from Lima to New York
with the story, expanding their reporting to acknowledge that the
only other civilian who had been awarded the Peruvian Flying Cross
was Elmer J. Faucett, civil aviation pioneer, who had flown the first
flight over the Andes in 1922. Tip was in good company wearing the
gold cross on his lapel.

*Many years later, in 1966, the Peruvian government went
even further in honoring Tip by awarding him the Jorge Chavez
Medal. Jorge Chavez Dartnell was a Peruvian aviator who made
the first flight across the Alps in 1910. The record setting flight
was a success, but the landing was a disaster and Chavez later
died of his injuries. The Jorge Chavez medal and the Peruvian
Distinguished Flying Cross were both prestigious awards in*

Peruvian aviation and Tip appreciated them.

In June 1953, Tip was working with an aero club that had formed on the outskirts of Lima by the tiny airstrip of Collique. This kind of direct contact with civil pilots was what he had been expecting to establish right away, but it had taken years to organize. He felt that it was his work as an instructor, inspector, and certifier at the most basic level of private aviation that set solid foundations for safe and sustainable aviation. The Collique club was flying many of the basic aircraft Tip had started out in, like a PT-17 Stearman Kaydet, as well as an older PT-13 which was the same model, but an earlier build. There was the old and familiar Fairchild PT-19. Student check flights were interspersed with trips in and out of Talara in the larger C-47 Skytrain or the B-23 Dragon. Although the B-23 Dragon was originally designed as a bomber replacement for the Bolos that Tip flew in Oakland, the model had been retired as a bomber and Tip was flying a reconfigured executive style passenger craft on the trips to Talara.

The ICAO work was often as social and enjoyable as it was grindingly administrative. Tip spent weekdays flying around Ecuador, Panama, Venezuela, Colombia, Chile, and Argentina. In November 1953, he flew the DC-3 on a series of meetings throughout Brazil, first to Sao Paolo, a city he knew well from past visits, to the fabulous gardens of Curitiba, and on to Foz de Iguacu, with its legendary waterfalls three times bigger than Niagara and location of the Triple Frontier where Brazil, Argentina, and Paraguay meet. From there he went on to Asuncion, Paraguay, site of his emergency flight with Dr. Starkloff. He flew into Uruguayana, a city in Brazil, and Montevideo, a city in Uruguay. He was back in Lima at the Collique Aero Club in time to check fourteen year old Mike out in a PT-19. The Fairchild flying tradition had been passed on.

The flights to North America frequently went through New

York City, and Tip was often carrying courier pouches for diplomatic and military recipients. Some of his errands were just as important, but somewhat less official. Tip's communications with Enrique Pardo had pertained mainly to fishing issues, but in 1953 Enrique had a new problem and he needed Tip's help. Enrique, Peru's most eligible businessman, had met a beautiful Icelandic woman while he was visiting his family's estate in Paris. Her name was Rita, and she was a fashion model who lived in New York City when she was not travelling the world. Enrique had fallen in love, but he still needed to convince Rita to spend her life with him. Tip became a cupid on metal wings carrying gifts and letters in a high class courtship. While acting on Enrique's behalf, he set the foundation for a life long friendship with Rita, who remembered the time well.

> "Tip was very dashing," Rita said, reminiscing. "We would meet under the clock tower at the Biltmore and go to lunch at the Wings Club. Tip had just been elected to membership there. I told him how I met Enrique, which was in Paris during a fashion show my agency put on for a government meeting. Enrique was in the front row and he came back afterwards to find me and ask me to dine with him. I liked him, but I said no, of course. It wasn't done. I usually ate in the automat in Paris anyway. I was always on a diet. Grace Kelly and I were there together; she was my rival you know. Anytime somebody wanted a square-jawed model, it was me or her, but we were great friends."

Rita often commandeered Tip to help her shop for an appropriate gift to send on Tip's return flight. Enrique was a man who had everything, and Rita needed to send just the right message. But the day Rita chose a wheel of Stilton cheese to send to Enrique, she had not consulted Tip.

> "The package was gift wrapped when I gave it to Tip," Rita

pointed out. "He said he was going straight back to Lima, I made sure of that. But he had engine trouble in Panama and was held over at the airport for several days. And Panama is so hot, don't you know. It was a terrible thing. The airplane was stinking so badly he searched it from end to end, but he never suspected my package. He had to fly all the way with that Stilton cheese in his nose. When he finally gave it to Enrique, it was rotten all through. Can you imagine? We laughed about it for years."

Rita Tennant de Pardo (left) and Louise Hossack Tippett (right) enjoy oriental food in Lima, Peru.

Enrique's long distance courtship of Rita was ultimately successful and they married in 1957. Mr. And Mrs. Enrique Pardo would, after their wedding, live down the street from Tip and Louise and come over every night for french champagne with cognac. Before then, Rita visited as often as her busy modeling schedule would allow.

Louise and Rita came to the Club at Cabo Blanco as often as the men could convince them to brave the sun and surf. Louise came for the pool, and Rita went out on the boats as often as she pleased. Rita's New York crowd of friends mirrored Enrique's and she was often present as hostess for a pageant of American and European social elite.

Jimmy Stewart, already a well established movie star by 1953, was a frequent guest at the Club. Stewart, now age forty five, had an distinguished wartime flying history, and was a colonel in the Air Force Reserve alongside Tip. Stewart was considering a career in aviation, if his re-entry into film did not succeed, and was already a major investor in an American airline. He and his wife, Gloria, came down to Cabo Blanco for the fishing and talked aviation for hours with Tip. Jimmy Stewart's name does not appear on any of the big fish lists at the Club, but he enjoyed the facilities even if he didn't land a record. Tip and Louise enjoyed his company, and Tip would stay in touch with him through his lifetime.

In 1954, baseball legend Ted Williams took a break from the Boston Red Sox to fish Cabo Blanco, and triumphantly joined the granders list with a 1,235 pound black marlin. Ted's visit was world news, and some footage of his catch became widely viewed in a film called "Ted Williams at Cabo Blanco." The footage was also used for other purposes, like a public service announcement, and Williams' fish trophy photo was immortalized on a 1959 version of his baseball card. A Cabo Blanco black marlin catch was tops in everyone's book, not just elite sport fishermen.

CABO BLANCO FISHING CLUB
Casilla 89, Talara
PERU

Cable:
CABLANCO, PERU

New York Address:
247 Park Ave.
New York 17, N. Y.

Big game fishing was in the news already with the record catches happening so frequently at Cabo Blanco, but the sport had also captured the world's imagination with the 1952 publication of Ernest Hemingway's book, "The Old Man and the Sea." The story was set in Cuba, and centered on a battle between an old fisherman and the black marlin he had hooked while alone in a small boat far from shore. Hemingway had used fishing to illustrate his concept of the value of a fight to the death in honoring and appreciating life. Hemingway was already well advanced in his career by that time and the book was an immediate best seller. The book won a Pulitzer Prize and was cited when Hemingway was awarded the Nobel Prize in Literature in 1954. It took Hemingway to a level of celebrity he had not achieved before, even with his colorful lifestyle, and interest in the sport of black marlin fishing rose with him.

Warner Brothers Studio's bought the movie rights to the book and needed to film a black marlin fishing sequence. A logical place to capture such footage was Cabo Blanco. Executives from the studio went through Farrington to secure access. Tip suddenly had a request to house an entire film crew at the Cabo Blanco Fishing Club. He got out his calendar and made it work.

On August 4, 1953, Alfred C. Glassell Jr. was rolling up his sleeves to take back the Club record from Tom Bates in their continuing black marlin rivalry. The clubhouse was filled with the men from the Warner Brothers Studio, and Tip was exhausted from all the fishing trips he was taking them on. Glassell suggested that the film crew join him and they all piled into the boat. Glassell's tall frame and wide shoulders would have taken up most of the space on the transom of the fishing boat, but once he was strapped into the fighting chair, he left plenty of room. The film crew worked around him with tripods and film magazines piled on every surface. Tip wrote his own version of the events in his usual laconic style.

> "I spent a couple of days at Cabo Blanco a short time ago and fished for the studio group who were filming "The Old Man and the Sea." Glassell hooked into a new world's record fish that we estimate at over 1,500 pounds. The Warner Bro's boys tell me it looks real pretty in cinemascope. It jumped several times about forty

feet from the boat."

Glassell had indeed hooked into a world record black marlin, weighing in at 1,560 pounds and measuring over fourteen feet long. The film footage of that fight did appear in the movie, although the credits incorrectly identified the filming location. The fish itself hangs in the Hall of Sea Life at the Smithsonian Institution in Washington D.C. Glassell's catch remains the largest certified world-record black marlin caught on rod and reel. The film, starring Spencer Tracy, won an Oscar.

Chapter Seventeen

1954 to 1956

Flying and Fishing in Lima, Peru

1954 brought Tip several prize experiences of his own, in a world that revolved around his flying, fishing, and family. He was promoted to lieutenant colonel in the Air Force Reserve, bagged a very large fish, and earned another pilot certification that raised him to a new level of the pilot elite.

During one of his regular tours of active duty in the Canal Zone, Tip made the leap from soloing in propeller craft to jet engines by certifying in the Lockheed T-33 Shooting Star. The T-33 was a two-seat jet trainer based on the P-80 jet fighter, and with it, forty one year old Tip had entered the jet age. Tip's first jet solo was a very different flight than the solo he made in his Curtiss-powered JN4 biplane when he was sixteen. There was little glide in the jet trainer. It was a heavy, sleek, metal bullet propelled by the extraordinary power of its single jet engine. The T-33, also known as the T-bird, had distinctive tip tanks on each wing that held the additional fuel required to feed the engine housed in the fuselage. Pilots in T-33 training were already qualified and experienced in propeller aircraft, so all of the training was specific to jet conditions, such as the vast differences between bailing out and ejecting.

Albrook Air Force Base had prepared for the training transition to jet aircraft carefully. As a pilot of the 5700th Operations Squadron, Tip received a memo detailing T-33 indoctrination and proficiency flying. The memo declared that pilots requesting checkout in the T-33 would be scheduled for three days a week of training until checkout was completed. Flight training would take place at nearby Howard Air Force base, as Albrook's runways and hangars were not well suited for the jet-powered T-33. Proficiency checkout in the T-33 was a long-term commitment. It wasn't going to work to simply take the course, checkout solo, and fly into the sunset.

Lieutenant Colonel C. J. Tippett in the cockpit of the Lockheed T-33 in Panama, 1954.

The T-33 was a very different plane and the process required dedication. After that, the pilot would be required to fly at least once a week until he had racked up twenty five hours of solo pilot time. Tip was going to have to be routinely present in the Canal Zone in order to maintain his T-33 certification.

Even the pilot attire was different. Instead of the metal rimmed goggles and sheepskin lined leather jacket, Tip was fitted for the P-4 helmet. This hard shell helmet completely covered his head and had a built in darkened visor. The total coverage was necessary because of the higher noise of the jet engine, but also because of the possibility of ejection. Bailing out of propeller craft at lower altitudes and speeds was quite different from high energy ejections from jet aircraft. The P-series helmets featured built in microphones, visors which raised and lowered on metal tracks, and a fitted oxygen mask.

After Tip completed his check-out training in 1954, he regularly flew the T-33 out of Albrook Air Force Base until the early 1960s.

Training preparation began with a visit to the flight surgeon's office for oxygen and altitude indoctrination; helmet and oxygen mask fitting. On prior flights, Tip had oxygen available and knew that use was required above 12,500 feet, as well as recommended at night at 5,000 feet, but the use of the oxygen mask for a jet aircraft was very different. The jet aircraft pilot would wear the oxygen mask continually. Both the expected altitudes and the rapid changes in g-forces were going to require a steady and reliable supply of oxygen. Often, the jet cabins were not be pressurized.

Tip received a memo detailed the training he was expected to complete before climbing in the T-33 cockpit. After successfully completing the physiological training, he was directed to make a thorough study of the pilot's operating handbook, study the T-33 procedures and cruise control booklet, as well as the CAirC T-33 training manual. He had to complete the T-33 aircraft questionnaire, and the emergency procedures certificate, as well as read and comply with all the requirements of the T-33 information file. He was also to read the AFR 55-19, 55-42, and supplements, and take a blindfold cockpit check.

Tip was instructed to have the proper equipment prior to his first flight. The fitting department supplied the mask, helmet, flying suit, gloves, and parachute. He would have to visit the base equipment room for the one-man dingy, Mae West (flotation device), survival kit, bailout bottle (small oxygen bottle sometimes attached to the parachute), and emergency radio. Tip was expected to supply his own jack knife and screwdriver. After that preparation, Tip was ready for his one-hour parked cockpit orientation, his five hours of acrobatics, emergency procedures, and landings, and a course of day and night procedures, transitions, and training. With all of this training and aircraft handling done, Tip was additionally expected to pass and maintain the proficiency training regarding navigation, pre-flight inspection, and aerodrome regulations, which now included planning and identifying aerodromes that were adequate for jet aircraft landing, take off, and servicing operations, communication and planning requirements, itinerary planning, route and position reporting, radio range orientation, and fuel planning.

Weather flying was an entire additional instruction course, as the instrument flying regulations for jet aircraft were as different as were jet aircraft themselves. Tip passed them all and began to fly the jet craft on his ICAO assignments. At over 500 miles per hour, the T-33 transformed Tip's commute time between meetings. A mandate from ICAO headquarters had been to prepare for jet penetrations throughout his regional air space, and so he did it from the cockpit of a jet.

In January 1954, Tip greeted the USAF jet wing of the "Wings for America" goodwill tour as it landed in Lima. The tour was intended to introduce jet aircraft, in the hands of the United States military, to countries in South America. Many of the jet landings performed on the tour were the first ever in the countries they visited. Tip took the controls for the T-33 flight from Lima, Peru to Antofagasta, Chile to participate in the tour, and met Major General Claire Lee Chennault. Chennault was now retired and famous for his successful career as the head of the Flying Tigers in China. He was accompanying the goodwill tour of Central and South America as both pilot and aviation ambassador. Since leaving his work in China, Chennault had seen that country fall to the communists, a blow to both his own work and the US government's hopes for China's future. Tip made a special note of the meeting in his flight log as he flew the two-hour Lima to Antofagasta flight. Tip had stayed interested in the Flying Tigers' progress because he had trained some of the earliest members himself in San Francisco for Mr. Won Goon Dick. Chennault was sixty-one at the time of this meeting and would be promoted to lieutenant general just before his death in 1958 at age sixty-five.

Tip's military promotion to lieutenant colonel was not linked to his employment by ICAO, but as Tip's two-year directorship posting entered a fifth year, ICAO's Secretary General, Carl Ljungberg, wrote to Tip expressing "appreciation of his

continued valuable services to the Organization and best wishes
for the future." He also gave Tip a raise to P-5 Senior Officer level,
which boosted his pay and his travel, home leave, and benefits. Tip's
salary would now be $11,310 a year ($95,720 today). To top off a
banner year, in addition to a raise, a rank promotion, and jet pilot
wings, Tip triumphantly entered the Thousand Pound Club at Cabo
Blanco with the 1,010-pound black marlin he caught in May, 1954.

*Tip and his boat crew were delighted with the prize
grander.*

Tip's trips to the Canal Zone were often spontaneous.

Susan kept a small bag ready for any invitation to go with her father, taking nothing more than a toothbrush and pair of pajamas. She remembered that the cabin of the aircraft frequently held things brought back from Panama. Sometimes it was luxury foodstuffs from the American commissary, or equipment in unrecognizable boxes, and, sometimes, it was weapons.

Albrook Air Force Base, and the nearby town of Balboa, were American territory in Panama and well stocked with American goods. Tip's shopping list would have been augmented by requests from other department staff and embassy families. The equipment could have been official, or things like a replacement for Louise's broken Magnavox radio, which the Magnavox Company was refusing to ship, citing export regulations. The weapons could have been the result of a mission Tip was participating in, but were more likely destined for a quieter purpose, such as Tip's own collection.

Later, in 1979, Tip would reluctantly comply with a request from the Bureau of Alcohol, Tobacco, and Firearms and surrender items he had been keeping for "gopher control." The bureau felt that one French 8mm M1914 Hotchkiss machine-gun with tripod, one German MG34 7.92mm machine gun with bipod, one Czechoslovakian V226 7.92mm machine gun, and one Yugoslavian mortar with bipod were not appropriate for private ownership. Tip sadly stood by as the ATF took them away.

Tip met the Panamanian President, General Jose Remón Cantera, aboard one of the larger commercial airliners, perhaps for an inaugural flight, or to introduce a new airliner to Panama's fleet. Cantera wore a classic Panamanian light colored suit, and Tip topped him by several inches in height. General Cantera had successfully amended the Panama Canal Treaty with the Eisenhower administration, securing a much higher annuity for Panama. These negotiations earned him the respect of the Panamanian people.

Colonel José Antonio Remón Cantera, President of Panama, met with Tip in 1955 and discussed civil aviation, among other things.

Tip and General Cantera talked enthusiastically of planes, racehorses, and Panamanian politics. Tip was sad to hear the news in 1955 when President Cantera was machine-gunned to death at the Panama City racetrack, either in a coup by his own administration, or in an American gangster retaliation for a heroin shipment Cantera had recently confiscated. Cantera's murder was never solved, and Tip continued his work with Cantera's successor, Jose Ramon Guizado until Guizado was implicated in Cantera's demise. As with many of the governments in Tip's region, the leadership changed hands, but Tip's interaction with the offices remained the same.

In the same way that Tip collected exotic equipment, he collected interesting people. In May 1955, Tip corresponded with Roscoe Turner, who had formed the Roscoe Turner Aeronautical Corporation in Indianapolis. Roscoe Turner had set his first-in-flight records in the 1930s with transcontinental flights and National Air Race wins. He was best known for being a Hollywood stunt pilot who worked closely with Howard Hughes, and for flying with a lion cub named Gilmore. The lion cub was a publicity stunt that worked very well. Turner needed sponsorship for his races and the Gilmore Oil Company needed publicity. Their trademark pictured a lion's head, and so Gilmore arrived and joined Turner in the cockpit for several of his record-setting flights. When the cub grew into a lion, Turner stopped bringing him into the cockpit, but kept him safe. When the lion died of old age, he was stuffed and joined Alfred C. Glassell's black marlin at the Smithsonian Institution.

Turner hinted that he was working on an executive aircraft that would give Pan Am some competition in speed and comfort. Turner wrote to Tip asking for some background information, as he was not pleased with the rumors he was hearing. He did not disclose what the rumors were, but whatever clarification Tip provided, Turner was satisfied and wrote again to thank Tip and congratulate him on the T-33 pilot wings. Roscoe Turner lamented that he was too old to try for jets. Jet aircraft proficiency was the new measure of the old pilots, and the division between those who were certified for jets, and those who were not, was growing.

In October 1955, Tip stretched his new jet wings on a trip back to ICAO headquarters via London, where he flew the deHavilland Vampire, a British jet fighter comparable to the Lockheed T-33. If anyone had the influence and connections to make the leap from the T-33 to the Vampire, it was Tip. The opportunity to fly another jet fighter, particularly the Vampire, was irresistible. The de Havilland Vampire had just missed being active in WWII but had set several aviation firsts just afterward. It was the first jet aircraft to take off from an aircraft carrier. It was also the first jet aircraft to fly across the Atlantic Ocean, beating out a competing squadron of T-33 Shooting Stars, to the great delight of the winning pilots. The Vampire was a visually unusual design. The engine was in the main body of the plane, but the tail extended farther out on twin parallel booms. The engine shared the cockpit in a single sleek nacelle between unswept wings. It had a very modern look for the time, and Tip was in his element as he streaked through the sky in a Vampire.

Later that year, Tip made a round-trip flight from Panama to Miami at the controls of a Boeing B-17G Flying Fortress, one of the most famous aircraft of all time. The Flying Fortress had achieved fame in WWII during the strategic bombing campaigns against Germany by the Eighth Air Force based in England. It was called a Flying Fortress because it was heavily armed and designed to defend itself in the air while conducting bombing and attack missions against the enemy. The aircraft and crews sustained incredible damage, injury, and attrition, but the B-17's ability to absorb battle damage yet bring its crews home brought it iconic status among aircraft. Stories of torn and twisted B-17s landing safely were supported by films and photographs. By 1955, the B-17 Flying Fortress had an aviation following that only grew as time went on.

The one that Tip flew was not armed, and not on a bombing mission. Post-war use of the Flying Fortress included patrol and rescue work, as well as long-range transport and observation. The machine gun turrets were often replaced with a radar dome, and camera installations. The B-17G that Tip was flying was the final version of the Flying Fortress and in wartime it had carried thirteen machine guns in addition to, typically, a four thousand pound bomb load.

1955 was a year of record airline traffic growth worldwide. In contrast, progress by the International Civil Aviation Organization seemed slow. But Tip was getting things done, and conditions were improving. At the ICAO Staff Association meeting in April 1955, Secretary General Carl Ljungberg expressed his belief that aviation business worldwide had still not completed its trend of rapid development, and that more growth would demand more airport planning and traffic separation. At the same time, the

UN was pressuring ICAO headquarters to cut staff and increase operational efficiency. ICAO was trying to comply and suffering under the scrutiny of investigations of their offices. The constant oversight and calls for budget cuts pinched the regional offices. Congratulatory recognition was rare and celebrated when it came. In an uncharacteristically laudatory comment, Brigadier Steven Booth applauded the work being done by the Lima office, and particularly Mr. Tippett. As Booth was chairman of the Finance Committee, and this was a time of budget debate, the praise was even more noteworthy. Secretary Ljungberg sent Tip a copy of the council minutes which recorded Booth's comment and added his own personal note drawing Tip's attention to the tribute.

Most of the time, Tip worked around ICAO politics and made progress in the areas he knew would derive the most benefit. He could not ignore the requirements of the administrative load, but he could often use one action to accomplish many directives. His letters to his chain of command became less formal and more informative as the relationships matured. Tip wrote to Colonel Samuel Galbreath of CAirC soon after the ICAO meeting:

> I had expected to be up to see you before this but we've been overwhelmed by work. We've just completed drafting plans for the new communications system for Peru as well as a search and rescue unit and the air traffic control procedures. Everyone got the fright of their lives here a week or so ago with a couple of near air collisions between jets and the commercial carriers. Anyway, I've been working for CAirC through the mission whether you were aware of it or not.

The family was now rooted in Lima, Peru, and the Los Laureles house was full of activity as each member pursued his own interests. Like his mother, Tip was a magnet for all sorts of animals. Two Scottish Terrier puppies had entered the household. Gallagher and Sheen joined a Siamese cat, a basset hound, and a bird given to the family by Dr. Cesar Grillo, Tip's old friend from the Civil Aeronautics Department for Brazil.

Louise had just passed her fortieth birthday, and had resumed her watercolor painting with a passion. One of the upstairs bedrooms had been converted into an art studio, and she painted daily and with great skill. Sue remembered her mother trying to share her passion for painting and art, but at ten years old, Sue was interested only in horses.

The household staff, Leonor and Clemente, essentially raised Sue, who had the run of the house. Although her teachers at the Franklin D. Roosevelt School were doing a decent job educating her, Sue was clearly happier outdoors. When she wasn't in the garden making a tent out of Tip's parachute, which greatly annoyed him, she was down at the Club riding her pony, Tor de Llino. Sue had been delighted when an Argentine polo player gave her his losing polo pony, and Tip could not say no. The horse's upkeep at the polo club was not expensive, and kept Sue busy as she took him through the paces of dressage and as much jumping as she could get away with.

If Louise had objected to the gift pony, she was overruled, for Tip had a horse of his own. Sue and Tip went regularly to the racecourse to follow the progress of Peruvian Flyer, a thoroughbred mare that Tip had a share in. Tip's horse won some and lost some, but the race was always exciting for the father daughter cheering squad. Tip wrote to Adolf Berle, former US ambassador to Brazil and now a family friend, describing Mike's plans:

"…Michael is very busy in Lima studying primary flying and attending ground school classes on theory of flights and mechanics. He feels, and I agree, that if he's going to be a good aeronautical engineer he should at least know how to fly an airplane…"

Sue Tippett was almost ten years old when she finally got the horse she had always wanted. Tor de Llino had failed as a polo pony, but Sue didn't care. Together they learned jumping and dressage. This picture shows Sue and a mare named "Lady."

It was time for Mike to consider high school. Tip and Louise wanted him to go to Phillips Academy in Andover, a prestigious boarding school on the east coast of the United States, but a childhood of South American education, and interests outside the classroom, had resulted in an educational gap for Mike. Mike would need some tutoring. He went, alone, to the Searing Tutoring School in New York state, a boarding institution with focused tutors on staff. Mike worked diligently and successfully caught up enough for entrance to Andover in time to become the forward for the soccer team and letter in the JV track team. The entire family was relieved, and Mike felt that scoring goals was nothing in comparison to the Searing school curriculum. Mike was able to spend holidays with family friends, like the Berle's, in the New York area.

Before Mike left, the family took a last Peruvian trip together, joining a group of embassy families. Tip described it in a letter to Archbishop Francesco Lardone, who was the Papal Nuncio to Peru in 1956 and Tip's occasional martini partner.

Tip finally had a chance to try the trout fishing on the Fortaleza River, north of Lima, in 1956.

We whirled off to Monterrey for a few days of fishing. We went in a bunch, complete with kids. Everyone else went to Chimbote and up by train, but not the Tippetts. We did it the hard way, through Pativiloca. Actually, it wasn't too tough as we remained overnight at Paramonga and were shown around the place. I've wanted to fish the trout stream along the valley road for years and I didn't want to miss it this time. It's really a lovely spot in spite of the altitude and we must go there on your next visit to Peru. You will be interested to know that one of the glacier lakes is full of trout. We saw three little Indian boys, aged eleven, with twenty-five rainbow trout, the largest of which would weigh at least four pounds. They had caught them by hand. They have a tricky system of damming up a little stream out of the lake and then when two or three trout come down the little stream, they scoop them up on shore. Frankly this system appears to me much cheaper and more successful than using flies and spinners.

Mike's departure for high school was a transition for Louise, although part of normal family life for the American families of Lima. Many of the high-school aged children of the embassy families returned to the United States for education. Although Tip's official directions came to him through Montreal, he held diplomatic status in Peru and identified closely with the embassy staff and culture. It was a main source of information and supply that could not be found otherwise in Lima. Around the same time that Mike left for New York, Louise was tremendously relieved to hear that Tip had received word that the Salk vaccine for polio immunizations would be made available to American citizens through the embassy. The American Society of Peru had been working with the embassy to obtain the vaccine and administer it to eligible American citizens, as it was almost impossible to get elsewhere in Lima. Polio was the terror of the 1950s and the availability of the vaccine was eagerly awaited.

The extended family back in the States had also made a transition. Verna and Adolf Eyth left Ohio for retirement to New Smyrna Beach, Florida. Tip was always in close communication with Verna, sending her telegrams for Mother's Day and visiting her when his trips north permitted. Now most of the family was on the east coast of the United States, which made visiting easier. Only Harry

Hossack remained on the west coast, after retiring from Washington D.C. and returning to his favorite city of San Francisco. In January 1956, Harry Hossack died at age 70, and was buried in the Presidio in San Francisco. He had suffered declining health for more than a year, and had been blinded by diabetes. His death was not a surprise, but Louise retreated into herself with the news. Harry was the last of her immediate family, as she had no siblings. Tip was the one to notify friends. He wrote to Rats Burholt, who knew Harry from the days of Tip's California courtship of Louise:

> "…Sorry you didn't know of Pop's death. Louise didn't write to anyone. I saw him just a short time before he died. He was in a terrible condition physically, but mentally very alert and seemingly happy. A very great guy in my book…"

Louise gathered Sue and her painting easel and joined Tip on a Cabo Blanco excursion. Tip kept his Club management notes and correspondence in meticulous order and faithfully recorded fishing catches, even the ones that got away. On February 9 1956, a black marlin estimated at over 1,500 pounds was lost at gaff after an hour and a half fight on a thirty nine pound line. The ten striped marlin sighted on the same trip were an afterthought. The next day another black marlin, estimated over 1,000 pounds, was again lost at gaff, but the 115 pound sailfish caught on a twenty fou pound line made it back to the jetty. Once again, the five striped marlin sighted were a side note next to the emphasis on the clear water and light southwest winds in the record.

The Club was a tonic for all sorts for work frustrations and family burdens. In the bright sun and simple comforts, Louise and Sue were as happy as Tip to spend long weekends watching the ocean. Sue's job was catching bonito as baitfish. They were always caught with hand lines or rod and reel, never netted, and some of the twenty pound fish fought so hard they almost dragged her overboard.

By March 1956, the Club began to prepare for one of the highest profile visitors it had ever received. Tip was notified that Ernest Hemingway was ready to come down and spend a couple of weeks in April at the Club. Enrique Pardo had intended to accompany Hemingway and take him out to catch a black marlin of his own, but Enrique's business interests made his schedule impossible to change. Enrique turned to Tip to show Hemingway a good time.

Ernest Hemingway was now a mega star, four years after the publication of "*The Old Man and the Sea*." The movie was still in production, and Hemingway recently had been recovering from injuries he suffered in a plane crash while on safari. He planned to arrive with his wife Mary, and needed a quiet place to recuperate. Tip was in charge of all the arrangements.

Despite security and discretion, Hemingway's visit to Peru was a major media event. A crowd appeared from nowhere at the village in Cabo Blanco to see him. A stowaway was found and expelled from one of the boats before he boarded. Tip took Hemingway out in person in an effort to inaugurate him into the Thousand Pound Club. This was Tip's second close encounter with Hemingway, and he may have been reluctant to remind him of their past encounter in Chicago, when Tip was a youthful contender in the YMCA Golden Gloves boxing championship and Hemingway had been his coach. Tip wrote to him after Hemingway left Peru:

"Dear Ernest, You will be happy to learn that my eye is almost normal and no permanent damage is expected outside of a small bit more of scar tissue to add to my rather old collection. I trust your hand is undamaged even if it was a pretty sneaky left hook. It was very nice meeting Mary, yourself, and the gang, good luck on your fishing, I hope everything works out OK on the pictures."

In 1956, Ernest Hemingway visited Cabo Blanco to fish for black marlin. Enrique Pardo welcomed Hemingway at the airport, but business obligations prevented Enrique from taking Hemingway out in person. He asked Tip to step in and show Hemingway a good time on Marlin Boulevard.

Ernest didn't catch a grander, but over the two weeks of fishing, he did catch a 720 pound black marlin. Tip caught one weighing 792 pounds, another at 900 pounds, and his own personal best of 1,020 pounds. Despite his host's behavior, Ernest enjoyed his Cabo Blanco visit, both for the fishing and the hard-to-find privacy. He and Mary were at ease there. He wore his safari shirt, khaki shorts and loafers.

Hemingway was fifty-seven when he fished with Tip in Peru. Mary was his fourth wife and they had homes in Cuba, Key West, and Idaho. By this time in his life, he had suffered many serious injuries, and Cabo Blanco was a comfortable refuge, at least inside the Club.

Ernest and Mary Hemingway at Cabo Blanco, Peru, 1956.

Within four years, Hemingway's health would deteriorate to the point where he became unable to write, but he lived long enough to see the 1958 release of the movie, "The Old Man and the Sea," and Spencer Tracy's Oscar win for portraying the fisherman.

Modern analysis of his medical records revealed numerous serious health conditions that may have contributed to his increasing battle with depression. At the time, it was blamed on his well publicized hard drinking lifestyle.

In 1961, five years after his trip to Cabo Blanco, Hemingway took his own life at his home in Idaho. Tip, and the rest of the world, would receive this news with shock and sadness.

"To Tip,
Best always to him and all his projects,
Honest Ernie Hemingway"

After Hemingway's visit to Cabo Blanco, the Club suffered
some misfortune of its own. On August 14, 1956, Tip wrote to
Enrique, who was abroad with Rita in Europe. There had been an
accidental drowning at the Club. The temporary night watchman,
replacing an employee on vacation, drowned when checking on the
boats. The watchman's family was filing a lawsuit against the Club.
Adding to the stress and repercussions of that event, an article in
the March 1956, edition of *Sports Illustrated* had not turned out the

way the Club expected.

Kip Farrington was a regular writer for *Sports Illustrated*, and Alfred Glassell had also been frequently published in the magazine, so when the editors of *Sports Illustrated* asked to send down a reporter for an anchor piece on Cabo Blanco, the Club happily complied. Tip made the arrangements and opened the facilities, tackle, and boats to a journalist named George Weller. Nobody thought to ask for an advance copy of the article.

On March 19, 1956, the headline "The Fabulous Cabo Blanco Club - In Color" blazed from the cover of *Sports Illustrated*. It pictured Alfred C. Glassell Jr. with one of his many black marlin catches on the dock at Cabo Blanco. Tip's happy anticipation in reading the article, mailed to him from New York City, quickly turned to unease as the author began to systematically bash the Club's exclusive policies. Weller sincerely praised the Club's dedicated staff, but he was highly critical, even sarcastic, about the membership roster and guest requirements. Weller suggested that most guests never even saw a marlin, and declared that most of the custom-built boats spent more time in dry dock than at sea. He went into great detail on the fishing techniques, which were the sporting aspect of the article, but toward his conclusion he mentioned the unsportsmanlike practice of harpooning. While Weller never claimed that Cabo Blanco fishing crews used harpoons on marlin during club activities, the inference was enough.

Weller called it murder, referring to the practice of harpooning, and the Club's membership called it slander, referring to the article itself. In the sport fishing world, harpooning was anathema. For a fishing club that was built exclusively for the purpose of certifying world record catches by the most stringent sport fishing standards, the accusation was utterly damning. Harpooning violated every code of sport fishing, but the inference was inaccurate, and club members were incensed.

Tip may have hoped that the article's critical undertone

would pass unremarked and for several months he thought it had, but six months after publication, several key club members finally read the article and were enraged. By September 1956, Tip was elbow deep in damage control. He sent a telegram to Farrington and to John Henry, the director of Lobitos Oil, and followed up with a letter.

> KIP FARRINGTON. EAST HAMPTON, N.Y.
> I HAVE WRITTEN HENRY AND YOURSELF A LETTER
> AIRMAILED YESTERDAY STOP.
> SITUATION SERIOUS BUT CAN HANDLE STOP.
> REGARDS TIPPETT

Dear Kip,

I am enclosing a copy of a letter I wrote to John Henry apologizing for the "Sports Illustrated" article. I have indicated, as you can see, that I have only just seen the article thinking that it would be better rather than for him to know that I had seen it long ago. I understand from Plater that John is really up in arms and threatens to withdraw all assistance to the Club. Just how upset he is, I don't know, hence my immediate letter to him. I strongly advise you write him a letter of apology on the part of the NY directors and perhaps even enclose a copy of a letter blasting the magazine. As a matter of fact, you're welcome to send a copy of my letter to the Knox's if you like. If John is as mad as Plater says he is, we may not even get winch or pier service until a retraction is forthcoming. Last Monday, I spent the night at the Club following an inspection trip of all the airports in northern Peru. The inspection party included a close personal friend of Pardo and the present Minister of Agriculture. I brought them to the Club as my guests and we had a most pleasant evening with the Owens and Capt. Stewart. The outcome of the whole business was that Hilbeck and I are going to the minister tomorrow, then to the president to request a

law outlawing the harpooning of black marlin anywhere in Peru.
Hilbeck tells me there is no question but that the president will
approve. We had a long talk while at the Club about releasing fish.
I think that should be encouraged - perhaps we can suggest it to
members and guests unless it's their first black marlin or it's a really
big one.

By the end of 1956, the Club had begun to struggle
financially. Tip was trying to book charters to maintain solvency,
but the bad publicity was not helping. He and Enrique Pardo were
called to court to answer charges over the drowning lawsuit. It was
an overwhelming time to be juggling both managing the Club and
his day job establishing and maintaining South America's aviation
infrastructure. Tip's letter was the first whisper about conservation
regarding the record-setting fish that were being pulled out of
Cabo Blanco waters. Although many of the Club members would
become renowned wildlife conservationists later in their lives, it
was not something that seemed to concern fishermen in the Club's
early days. Modern research has revealed that the truly big fish were
mostly females of reproductive age. These enormous fish were
notoriously easy to hook, as they hunted at the edge of the colliding
currents. But they were not easy to land, and few members or
guests were willing to give up on the trophy shot, posing with their
kill on the dock, in favor of catch-and-release fishing methods. It was
also not common practice in the 1950s.

The Club's slow decline had begun, although there were
two more years of good fishing ahead for Tip. High society had a
notoriously short attention span, and the bad publicity hurt Club
pride more than it actually deterred visitors. The giant fish at Cabo
Blanco would disappear by the early 1960s, but not due exclusively
to the predations of the millionaire enthusiasts. While members
and guests of the Club were discussing rod and reel, eschewing
harpoons, and posing with their catches, the commercial anchovy

fishery several miles north of Cabo Blanco was pulling unsustainable numbers of anchovy from the same productive waters.

The real cause behind Cabo Blanco's downward slide was the decline of the anchovy. The commercial fishery established just before the Club was built had been logging record catches every year. More anchovy had been netted and processed at the Mancora facility that anywhere else in the world at the time. A collapse in the American fishery industry at the beginning of the 1950s had spurred American interest in the Peruvian coast. They were attracted by the same conditions that attracted the granders. Despite stern warnings and evidence offered by biologists and political activists against the establishment of a large-scale fishing enterprise, the Peruvian government had allowed them. When the anchovy shoals collapsed due to over-fishing, the entire food chain collapsed. Without the anchovy, the bonito went away. Without the bonito, the black marlin went away.

But that cascade of events was still two years in Tip's future. 1956 had been a tough year for the Club, and Tip took the opportunity to log some hours in a different kind of captain's chair.

Chapter Eighteen

1957 to 1961

Change comes for the Director,
Lima, Peru

In January 1957, three Boeing B52 Stratofortresses set the first round the world non stop flight by turbojet-powered aircraft. They were refueled in flight and followed a northern hemisphere route. Jet aircraft were in ascendancy, although propeller craft merely moved over, instead of going away. Jets were faster and more powerful, thus could fly farther and higher. An ICAO memorandum at the time noted that the need to adjust civil aviation regional plans to accommodate jet aircraft was compelling. Jets required that the air navigation services and meteorological reports cover altitudes up to 45,000 feet, much higher than previously planned. Traffic patterns had to be adjusted to fit faster, more agile aircraft. Jets changed many of the basic elements factored into facilities and services.

Tip added a Powerplant and Airframe License to his collection of aviation certifications. The new license demonstrated his familiarity with the engines, structure, and operations of the aircraft he was piloting. This underlying knowledge was one of the reasons behind his success in setting the infrastructure and training systems that remain in place today. Tip thoroughly understood what was needed for aircraft, pilots, and passengers. With his T-33 wings, he had the personal experience required to anticipate the needs of jet aircraft. In February, Tip wrapped up his Club and ICAO duties in anticipation of scheduled active duty and headed for the Canal Zone for a 500 mile an hour experience that he would remember for the rest of his life.

I was in Panama on my two week active duty tour in February 1957, and had a cross country set up in a T-33 from Panama to Los Angeles via Miami. Unfortunately, due to a great deal of maintenance trouble, I was forced to spend three of my precious five days at the air depot in Mobile, Alabama. Even at that, on my return trip across the Caribbean, I damn near didn't make it.

I was flying at 41,000 feet on top of a heavy overcast condition when I lost my ADF (automatic direction finder) and my slave gyrocompass. Although I did not know it at the time, my gyrocompass was in error. I later found that I was flying thirty degrees off-course helped along by a seventy-five mph crosswind. This put me somewhere over Barranquilla, Colombia, at my estimated time of arrival instead of San Blas Island, Panama. I was still on top of a solid overcast.

Some inner sense told me that all was not well insofar as position was concerned – also, I had a problem of how and where to let down without an ADF. I called for a DF steer and fortunately, for once, the Panama DF station was working. They gave me a steer of 278 degrees, which confirmed my theory that I was not where I expected to be. To complicate matters, my left main-wing fuel pump had left sixty gallons of fuel in the tank, which I could not recover. At this time I had approximately one hundred gallons of fuel aboard. I put the engine in idling position and started letting down at 150 knots, which gave me my maximum glide.

At 18,000 feet, I saw a break in the clouds for a moment and recognized the isthmus near Turbo, Columbia before I went back on instruments. I was finally in the clear at 8,000 feet and established my position as abeam of Rey Island, on the Pacific side of Panama. I had sixty gallons of fuel left, which in a jet is about ten minutes if it is used conservatively. All this time, Panama radio was inquiring for my position, as well as what my bail out time would be. I finally told them that I would leave the ship in five minutes and that I would try to land my parachute on the beach, not caring much for either the jungle, or the sharks in the bay. At this time, I could see Tocumen, Panama, in the distance but decided that with the fuel I had aboard, it would be impossible to make the airport there. The best thing that I could do was to use the few remaining minutes of fuel I had aboard to gain enough altitude to safely eject.

Making one last effort to salvage the trapped fuel, I gang-loaded all the fuel switches even though doing that was a fire hazard, and regained another forty gallons. With this fuel in the main tank, I calculated that I could arrive over Tocumen with 2,000 feet of altitude but no fuel, and I decided to do it. Fortunately, everything worked out as planned and I was able to make a dead stick landing at Tocumen with no problem. I must admit that it is a little bit embarrassing being towed off a runway, but by that stage I was happy to be on the ground with a whole airplane.

Tip's close call didn't keep him on the ground for very long. He flew the propeller driven Douglas B-23 Dragon to Chile, Argentina, Brazil, and Uruguay in the fall of 1957. He also flew a Curtiss Wright C-46 Commando on some of these routes, not because it was an exceptional ship, but because it was on the flying line. The C-46 was known in military circles as "the flying coffin" due to fuel system design flaws, but Tip was not a picky pilot regarding available aircraft.

Knowing that there was no classroom preparation that could replace physical flight experience, Tip contacted the Curtiss-Wright Corporation to look into the purchase of a Model 501A

Instrument Flight Duplicator, with associated radio navigation aide
equipment. This massive machine was a flight simulator and enabled
a student pilot to go through every in flight action safely bolted to
the ground. The Model 501 was adjustable to simulate any aircraft
and was electrically powered. Tip received a quote from Curtis-
Wright for $63,000 for the simulator and an additional $29,000
for the radio unit, which today would be almost three quarters
of a million dollars. There's no evidence whether ICAO bought
the flight simulator, but it was so desirable as an enhancement to
the flight training and certification programs that Tip had to try.
He was also pricing the more established "Link" training systems
and corresponded with Glen A. Gilbert regarding an order. The
budgetary considerations between buying a flight simulator, or losing
aircraft, and often lives, must have been a constant tension.

At the same time, Tip was coordinating the establishment of
a joint ICAO-Peruvian government civil aviation school at Collique.
He had already been working with the small aero club active there,
and wanted to make the Club official. Peru had no formal civil
aviation training program at all, and Tip was interested in getting it
started with ICAO involved at the beginning. He was negotiating
with the USAF to get several North American T-28 primary trainers,
which were being phased out of the training command and were
available for good prices. ICAO planned to furnish the school
director, ground instructors, and some of the ground training
equipment. Peru was expected to provide the basic and primary
training aircraft, local staff, the building, and fix up the runway and
hangars.

Tip was anticipating Mike's June 1958, graduation from
Phillips Academy in Andover, and encouraged him to apply at
Stanford University for a major in aeronautical engineering. Tip
reached out to influential San Francisco businessman Albert E.
Schwabacher for help boosting Mike's chances of acceptance. This

was not only how Tip's own career got started, with help from
Harry Hossack's connections, but it was also advisable considering
the level of competition for entry into Stanford University. If Mike's
success at sports could have been considered, his acceptance would
have been assured. Louise went to Andover to visit Mike in October
1957, hoping to see his last game of varsity soccer. On his final high
school birthday, the family sent Mike a cable, addressed to Bishop
Hall, Phillips Academy, Andover, Massachusetts. It was signed Dad,
Mom, Susie, and Menagerie. The family was already planning a trip
for the 1958 graduation summer. They would start on the east coast
and drive across the United States to San Francisco. There, they
would take a house for about two months, then go to Los Angeles
for a couple of weeks, and cruise the west coast. Everyone, especially
Louise, was looking forward to some extended time back in their
home country. While the lifestyle of Lima was comfortable, Louise
was beginning to wonder when the Peruvian posting would end.

Elsewhere in the world, while Tip was working hard in Lima,
Peru, Russia had shocked the United States by being the first nation
to put an artificial satellite in earth orbit. Sputnik 1 was launched
on October 4, 1957, and is credited with starting the Space Race.
America was already looking at space as the new frontier and in July
1958, established the National Aeronautics and Space Administration,
which would be forever known as NASA. It was responsible for the
civilian space program and for aeronautics and aerospace research.
Civil aviation, which had only recently entered the jet age, was now
aiming for the space age. Tip's own aspirations were no less grand.
He joked in a letter to a friend " I'm flying T-Birds now – I think they
are getting me ready for outer space!"

At the Club at Cabo Blanco, and in the halls of the American
Embassy, Tip worked routinely with the world's wealthy and political
elite. In any conversation, he was only one or two acquaintances
away from presidents, royalty, or figures of global influence. And yet

his personal wealth and professional development were beginning
to stall. By 1958, Tip felt that his directorship had reached its peak
of accomplishment. He had established the infrastructure and
department organization he had been asked to create. The major
advancements had been accomplished, and further work was slow
and administrative. Tip's connections in the Peruvian government and
business told him that the economic boom times were coming to
an end, and South America in general had already palled for Louise.
He had a realistic view of where US influences would bring him if
the Peruvian government continued on its current course toward
a more military regime. His letter archive shows the beginnings of
inquiries into other lines of work. He briefly considered a push for
a secretary-level post in Washington, but instead began to collect
his military flight and service records for promotion to colonel in
the Air Force Reserve. Back in the States, Tip's salary would not give
them the high society luxurious lifestyle they had enjoyed for so
many years. Tip was forty-five and evaluating his options.

At the same time, Rita Pardo had invited a longtime friend
from her life before Enrique to join her at Cabo Blanco. When Rita
was working full time as a runway model, she had often visited the
California movie studios either on the arm of a dashing movie star,
or at the request of an agency. Among the many beautiful women
stalking the studio grounds in the 1930s, Rita had taken a liking to
one in particular.

Liz Altemus Whitney was present at that time in Los Angeles
because her husband, John Hay Whitney, was in partnership with
David Selznick and they were making a movie called "Gone with the
Wind." The beautiful and elegant Liz had screen-tested for the film
and lost the part, but stayed on to enjoy the social scene. She met
Rita through their mutual friend, the young actor Ronald Reagan.

Mary Elizabeth Altemus was born to Pennsylvania high
society and spent her youth on horseback. By her early twenties, she

was already well known for her beauty, spirit, and strong personality. She rode bareback to scandalize, and pulled it off with such skill that she earned respect in equestrian circles. Her oval face and high cheekbones caught society's prize bachelor and in 1930, she married John Hay Whitney, known as Jock. He was the multimillionaire son of the immensely influential Whitney family that traced itself back to Plymouth Rock. He was mesmerized, she was proud, and their wedding made national news.

Jock Whitney gave his young bride a farm in Upperville, Virginia, called Llangollen. He dabbled in race horses and other women. She took the farm and turned it into a formidable thoroughbred breeding and training establishment. Liz Whitney made herself well known on the racetrack as her horses began to win big purses. Llangollen became her home and her source of success after she divorced Jock Whitney and started her own string of marriages. By the late 1950s, she was wealthy, impatient, and headed to Cabo Blanco at Rita's invitation with her third husband, Richard D. Lunn, handling the bags.

Liz was not particularly interested in big game fishing, but she was interested in horses, parties, people, and new places. She was now in her early fifties, and regal rather than beautiful. She was imperious, striking, and charismatic when she wanted to be. Liz was not accustomed to a merely decorative role in any activity. She arrived at the Club and announced her intention to go out on the boats, regardless of their size or lack of comfortable accommodation. If fishing was the focus of the boat trip, Liz intended to fish and she would have rejected any protestation to the contrary. For the women willing to step this far into the man's world of the Club, it was their challenge to be both attractive and capable. The boats had no luxury cabin space for comfortable retreat underway. The dock had no viewing lounge or shaded benches. Only the Club itself had amenities, and they were also stylishly spartan. Women fished at Cabo Blanco for big game and for respect.

Mary Elizabeth Altemus Whitney Person Lunn in 1958 at
Cabo Blanco with her 275-pound tuna, caught on rod and reel.

In March 1958, Liz joined Rita and Enrique on their boat
and caught a 275 pound tuna. The Club piqued her interest, and
she stayed long enough to watch the First Annual North American
Big Four Match. There were teams representing the Atlantic Coast,
the Gulf Coast, the Pacific Coast, and the Cabo Blanco Fishing
Club. The Cabo Blanco team was comprised of Alfred C. Glassell,
Kip Farrington, and C. J. Tippett. The Cabo Blanco team won the
tournament and Liz's attention. As Tip posed with the other
fishermen and boat crews with his trophies, he was completely
unaware that he was about to hook the biggest catch of his life,

although some of his friends felt it was better described as the other way around.

The winning Cabo Blanco Fishing Club team posed with the boat captains, crews, and their families in 1958, along with their winning catches.

It was a sunny weekday after the tournament at Cabo Blanco when Rita and Liz, accompanied by Enrique, climbed aboard Enrique's boat and motored out to Marlin Boulevard. That was the name of the visible line in the ocean where the two massive currents met, but did not mingle. It was there, several miles offshore, where the biggest fish would be found either hunting in the ocean trench or resting at the surface, warming after deep dives. The boat would motor for hours, crew aloft on the flying bridge searching by naked eye and binoculars, for dorsal fins or tail splash.

The boat crews were as fanatical about the fishing as the millionaires. The captains were highly skilled in spotting and conducting the battle for record catches. It was often the crew's expertise and enthusiasm that landed the trophy, encouraging passengers to pass up fish that weren't big enough, or weren't likely to make the grade depending on the species. These men fished for their families and for pride. When they took out a boat, it was never to simply cruise around; they were serious about their work.

Liz was rarely serious about anything outside of thoroughbred horse racing. The boat was all the way out to the confluence of currents when, according to Rita, Liz suddenly remembered that she was due in Lima that evening for a society dinner being held in her honor. This was a problem, as it was at least an hour of hard motoring to get back to the Club, and the drive to Lima was more than ten hours after that. Enrique and Rita were expected to come up with a solution. Since there was no radio aboard the boat, Enrique had to wait until they got back to the Club to telephone Tip about the availability of one of his fleet of powerful passenger aircraft. Tip was on his way by the time Liz had finished showering.

It was a three hour, round trip flight from Lima to Talara and back. Tip may have met Liz before at social gatherings with the Pardos, but it was on this trip that he got to know her for the first time. Liz had nothing else to do on the flight but examine this most dashing pilot hero. They would have quickly discovered how many interests they had in common. Liz was already famous as a racehorse owner, and Tip had a passion for horse racing. They both loved dogs and Rolls Royce automobiles. Liz owned a sixty-five foot classic Trumpy motor yacht called "Adventurer." Tip loved motor yachts. They already had several celebrity friends and connections in common.

Rita believes that Liz was interested in Tip from that very first meeting. "Liz was a person who always got what she wanted,"

Rita said. "And what she wanted was Tip." After the dinner, Liz spent some time at the Pardo's house in Lima and joined the social circuit with ease. She sent her husband home, and languidly extended her Peruvian visit. Liz met Louise casually at the nightly cocktail parties, but both Louise and Tip were largely oblivious to Liz's intentions. Light flirting was part of the social scene, and as Rita remembered it, the Tippett marriage was already strained. Louise was not happy, and the undercurrents at the parties were too deep for her to see. Later, Rita said that Louise had asked why no one had told her that Liz was after Tip. Louise was not even aware of the extent of Liz's fortune and influence. The entire turn in Tip's life took Louise by surprise. There is some indication that it took Tip by surprise as well.

The fact that Tip and Liz both had spouses was an obstacle, but Liz was a capable woman with deep resources. Her own inconvenient husband, at home in New York, was a problem, but first she had to get Tip's attention. The planned driving trip in the summer of 1958 was a big event for the Tippett family, and much talked about at parties. When the subject of the car itself came up, it turned out that Liz had purchased a new station wagon at a dealership on one coast, and needed it transported across the United States to the other coast. It would be handy for everyone if Tip could combine the summer driving trip with this favor for Liz.

In June 1958, all four members of the Tippett family crossed the US in the new station wagon. It was a driving trip that none of them ever forgot, and reportedly an expansive experience of visiting almost every family member and friend at ranches, cities, and national landmarks. It was also considered the trip where Tip and Louise's relationship was heatedly discussed, then quietly decided. Neither Mike nor Sue were aware that the end of the trip was also the end of the marriage. Rita remembers that Liz had made sure she was present to surprise Tip when he arrived to deliver the station wagon.

Tip participated in a publicity photo shoot for Hiller Helicopter in the summer of 1958.

With the end of the summer trip, Tip took some time while in Alameda, California to pose for publicity shots for Hiller Helicopter and fly the Hiller Model E4. When Tip, Louise, and Sue returned to Peru and the house on Los Laureles, Mike stayed in California as he had secured a summer job at Douglas Aircraft Corporation in Long Beach. Liz began to arrange her calendar to make room for a stay at The Colony in Washoe County, Nevada. Nevada had become the fashionable place to go for an easy divorce because legal residents could file on nine different grounds with no burden of proof. There was no waiting period either, once residency had been established, and residency took only six weeks. People living in Reno and waiting for their residency term to pass became close acquaintances and often bunked together, which is why it was called The Colony. For the rich and famous, a 1950s Reno divorce was much like a modern Las Vegas vacation. The divorce ranches at the time had lurid reputations as divorce seekers spent their weeks shaking off their pasts and getting ready to be single again.

Back in Lima, Tip was away even more than usual as he flew to Chile, Argentina, Brazil, Uruguay, Colombia, Panama, Ecuador, Mexico, and Venezuela. The late 1950s in Argentina were a time when high-class Argentines could afford the latest models of private aircraft, and so Tip was climbing in and out of the cockpits of some of the sleekest private airplanes of the era as he made his airport and pilot certification checks. The Aero Commander 520 was a spacious two-engine craft with interior capacity for seven, if they were willing to squeeze, and it was fast. The Cessna 310 was more of a working plane with bush adaptations for short take-offs, more reasonable running costs, and excellent visibility from the cockpit.

Inspecting and reviewing certification procedures in the aero clubs of his regions was something Tip continued to do throughout his directorship regardless of whether it was specifically ordered in his ICAO mandate. From Tip's earliest days in civil aviation, he had insisted on pilot certification as the best foundation for flight safety. When Tip heard that the February 3rd, 1959, crash of a small Beechcraft passenger plane in Iowa was likely the result of an inexperienced young pilot flying on visual in instrument conditions, he was saddened. The plane crash took the lives of Buddy Holly, Richie Valens and J. P. Richardson, known as The Big Bopper. The three were cherished musicians with top rock and roll hits at the time, and the accident was considered a preventable civil aviation tragedy.

Tip now spent more time in the Canal Zone than he did at home. Each new plane that landed at the base turned up in his flight log. The North American T-28 Trojan was a modern version of the plane Tip had flown in San Francisco in 1938. The T-28 was a trainer, with tandem cockpits, but it was also an attack aircraft. The training was in flight, tactics, and targeting. The Douglas C-54 Skymaster was a big four-engine transport aircraft based on the design of the DC-4. This was the aircraft Tip would have been flying if he had stayed on track with his original goal of being a commercial pilot. The Skymaster was routinely used on transoceanic flights by most of the major carriers. It was the first plane to be designated Air Force One. Another commercial large multi-engine craft was the Douglas DC-6B. This was the plane that Pan American was using at the time. Tip was now current with all the aircraft that the major carriers were flying. The Convair C-131 Samaritan was not a big leap from the DC-3, Beechcraft or C-47 Skytrain. It was also a dual-engine large passenger plane, although it was designed with a pressurized cabin. This was also the standard type of plane for the commercial airlines, and so Tip was well qualified should he consider a career change.

On May 25th, 1959, Tip received a congratulatory letter from Lieutenant General Emmett "Rosie" O'Donnell, Jr., telling him that his promotion to colonel had been approved and that official word would follow soon. O'Donnell went on to mention that he had himself been nominated for a new job. O'Donnell was about to become a full general and Commander of the Pacific Air Forces, stationed in Hawaii. O'Donnell was a fellow Kelly Field flight graduate, but he had gone through the program well before Tip. At the time of his letter to Tip, almost-General Emmett Rosie O'Donnell Jr. had already earned some of the most prestigious flight and service awards possible, and in 1963, would be given the Distinguished Service Cross by President Kennedy for his piloting in the Pacific at the start of World War II.

Letters and telegrams from this time period illustrate Tip's quandary with respect to any plans to continue indefinitely as ICAO director. The Cold War and aviation developments in the space race were diverting focus and funding from civil aviation. Tip's world was changing, whether he took action regarding his directorship or not.

In July 1959, Louise left the Los Laureles house. She left Lima and she left Tip. Susan accompanied her to San Francisco on a trip that Sue thought was just a stateside visit. Louise and Tip had recently bought an old San Francisco house on Fillmore Street that needed renovation, and Louise surprised Sue by enrolling her in school at the end of the summer. The legal dissolution of the marriage was underway and this was the first step of the process. Friends were told about the separation, but Louise didn't mention it to Sue. Mike, at Stanford, was only thirty-six miles away from Louise and she was able to have both her children close by. Louise asked Tip how she was supposed to contact him in the event of an emergency, now that she was outside the diplomatic and society loop of Lima's close community. She wrote, much later in her life:

> Tip said, in that drawl of his that mostly drove me crazy, "Contact G-2. They always know where I am." So I did. I looked up how to contact G-2 and I found that they were Army Intelligence. This was really my only clue that he was doing more than his ICAO work in Lima. He didn't talk about it at all.

Now alone in the Los Laureles house, Tip began to consider other employment options. His underlying reason for considering a resignation from ICAO may have been well described by a paragraph Harry Hossack wrote to Louise years earlier when he heard of Tip's ICAO appointment back in 1949. Harry wrote:

> Dear Bobs,
>
> Your fine letter of the 16th brought interesting, if not startling, news. There is a rumbling undertone I don't like. There is, or may be, something ominous in the eagerness of the Armed Services to draw back into line good men they have lost and a hint of urgency in the need. But aside from all that, I quite agree that Tip might do as well financially, at once, to say nothing of the long run, getting back into either the Air Force or CAA. The endless chit-chat, memo-ing, red tape, confusion, international jealousies, all tri-lingually multiplied, in ICAO, which you have reported would be too much for me.

And that is exactly how it turned out to be, although Tip was satisfied and proud of the progress he'd made in advancing civilian aviation. Tip truly enjoyed this life of parties, dinners, cocktails, and the company of talented people who were top in their fields. If he left Lima, he left the life. His take-home pay was nowhere near enough to sustain this level of luxury anywhere else. Mike had made it into Stanford University and although Tip's ICAO benefits helped pay the tuition, it was still an expense to be considered.

Tip had topped out in salary. By May 1960, Tip's salary was $14,000 a year ($102,000 today) and he had been approached for jobs earning $18,000 ($132,000 now).

Tip had had enough of the slow progress and what he saw developing in the Peruvian governmental landscape gave him concern. The fishing and the Club had begun to decline, and the Peruvian economy was no longer attracting as many interesting and influential people has it had before. Rumors on his decision had begun to circulate. A secretary from headquarters added a postscript to a memo saying, "I understand via the grapevine that you will be the South American Representative for Lockheed." As Tip prepared to give formal notice to ICAO, he appeared to be considering more than one option.

> I shall be working with one of the large aircraft companies in South America, starting with them sometime in January. I have enjoyed my twelve years in ICAO even though some of it has been somewhat frustrating. I feel that we have, however, grown up with International Civil Aviation and we have contributed to its stature.

By October 1960, Tip had taken action. He wrote to Mr. K McAleavey, who was the Director of the North American and Caribbean Office of ICAO located in Mexico City:

Dear Mac,

As you probably have already heard, I have resigned from ICAO and will be leaving about December 15th. My future plans are not at the point where I can divulge any definite name but I will be representing one of the large aircraft companies in South America along with other commercial activities. I must say it was not an easy decision to make. I've enjoyed twelve years with ICAO during the formative years of International Civil Aviation as well as the contacts that have been made. It was with no little reluctance and sadness that I decided to leave the Organization. I appreciate especially the assistance you gave me during my first three months of indoctrination- at the "school house" in Montreal. As a matter of fact, you were the only person in Montreal that would take time to discuss ICAO matters with me. As I recall, everyone was so busy with their trying to get everyone else thrown out of the organization that there was no time for anything else. Fortunately the organization has survived this type of 'little people." Both Pat and yourself have been very kind to me during our association and I shall look forward to this continuing even though I will no longer be associated with ICAO. I certainly hope to see you both from time to time in Mexico. Best wishes to you both

ICAO Headquarters had a new leader, Ronald MacAlister Macdonnell, who had been in office for only a year. Secretary General Macdonnell wrote to Tip about his resignation.

Dear Mr. Tippett,

I acknowledge receipt of your letter of 10 October 1960 tendering your resignation from the service. I have noted that you gave first notice of your intention to resign to ASG/AN on 1 October 1960 and since the staff regulations provide normally for three months notice I have decided to accept your resignation with much regret with effect from 1 January 1961. However, I understand that for personal reasons you wish to be released from active duty from 15 December 1960. To meet this wish I am agreeable in the absence of any annual leave to your credit to your taking special leave without pay for the period from 15 December 1960 to 1 January 1961 inclusive. I take this opportunity to thank you for the good services rendered to the organization during the past twelve years and to extend to you every good wish for the future.

In November 1960, Tip had one last paperwork symphony to conduct. Louise had filed a motion for divorce on May 11, 1960, in San Francisco, but Tip needed it finalized quickly. Through his connections, he received assurances from Edward Hidalgo of Hidalgo & Barrera, a law firm in Mexico City, that the divorce decree legalized by the General Consul of Peru in Mexico was enclosed and should serve Tip's purpose. Edward Hidalgo had served during the war as an intelligence officer for the navy and been awarded a Bronze Star for his efforts. Nineteen years in the future, he would accept President Carter's nomination for Secretary of the Navy. Using Edward Hidalgo to secure his divorce decree may have been like shooting a bird with a cannon, but Tip could only draw on the resources he had access to. In 1960, Hidalgo was a lawyer in Mexico City, and Tip needed a quick divorce. There is no indication of the reason behind the rush, only the fact that on November 26, 1960, Mary Elizabeth Altemus Whitney Person Lunn became the second Mrs. C. J. Tippett.

Tip and Liz were married in Lima, Peru in 1960. They held another ceremony in the US in 1961 to clear up any marriage license discrepancies and to invite more of their friends and family.

Close friends, including Rita and Enrique, attended the ceremony, held in Lima. Tip wore an elegant dark suit and tie and Liz wore a fashionable and flattering dress. Rita signed as witness. Tip was forty-seven and Liz was fifty-four. The wedding made the newspapers back home:

Envoy's Ex-wife Marries Colonel

Lima, Peru. Nov 26, (AP) United States Air Force Col. Cloyce Joseph Tippett and Mrs. Mary Elizabeth Whitney Person Lunn, former wife of US Ambassador to Britain, John Hay

Whitney, were married here Saturday. Tippett, 47, announced earlier he will resign as head of the regional office here of the International Civil Aviation Organization and move with his bride to Washington. His bride, the former Mary Elizabeth Altemus, was married to Whitney in 1930. They were divorced in 1948 and she wed Dr. E. Cooper Person, who died a few years later. Her third marriage, to Richard Dwight Lunn, ended in divorce in May 1959.

Liz would be known as Liz Whitney Tippett after November 26th, 1960, and together, they were the Colonel and Mrs. Tippett. Rita Tennant Pardo, and her husband, Enrique, remained close to Tip and Liz for the rest of their lives.

Another newspaper clipping declared that the couple would spend the Christmas of 1960 at Liz's farm in Upperville, Virginia, and then divide their time between Peru, where the colonel had private interests, and California and Virginia. It generally wasn't clear to anyone what Tip would do next, but after the wedding, he did not take a position with Lockheed in South America. Tip packed up the Los Laureles house and left Lima. He would now call each of Liz's estates home, depending on the racing or social season. In one of the drafts of his manuscript, Tip had added a handwritten conclusion.

> In 1960, I resigned my ICAO position as I felt the original work was completed and successful. I returned to the US, purchased the first commercial Jet Ranger helicopter sold by Bell Air, and retired to Llangollen Farm in Upperville, VA, to raise thoroughbred race horses.

Tip at Llangollen Farm in Upperville, Virginia.

As 1961 settled around the newlyweds, Tip logged active duty hours as an intelligence staff officer reporting to HQ in Washington D.C. In leaving his official capacity in civil aviation, Tip had not left his air force reserve activities. He was assigned to the Foreign Liaison Division, Office of the Assistant Chief of Staff, Intelligence, Headquarters United States Air Force. His professional skill, knowledge of Latin American affairs, and dedication to the

USAF helped develop and maintain increasingly good relationships with the air attachés, representatives of foreign missions, and other representatives of foreign air forces in the D.C. area.

Liz was not a woman to leave her husband's interests alone. She maintained her own connections to power and authority, and became interested in the air attaché work Tip was doing. She suggested hosting some of the air attachés at her estates and over the next twenty years, Tip's air attaché parties would become some of the most exclusive and sought after invitations in diplomatic circles. For this, and other aviation diplomatic work, Tip was awarded the Air Force Commendation Medal in September of 1970.

For his part, Tip had no intention of acting disinterested in Liz's business activities. He was involved in the management of the ranches, estates, and farms from the start. He enthusiastically followed the horses to every track and training yard, accompanying Liz as she roamed the world in search of bloodlines. Tip was soon flying the first privately owned Bell Helicopter, painted in Liz's racing colors of purple and fuchsia, with Llangollen Farm blazoned on the side.

The Bell Textron 47J Ranger, better known by its military designation of H-13 Sioux, was Tip's delight.

Tip took Liz to racetracks and society parties, landing safely but scandalously in paddocks and parking lots to the envy of Liz's peers. Liz had previously been known for her shocking entrance into the ballroom of a society party bareback on a palomino horse and dressed as a squaw. She now made the papers and gossip columns for her fashionably late arrivals in her personal helicopter piloted by her colonel husband. The Bell 47J helicopter was a more developed version of the helicopter Tip had flown against the locusts in Argentina. It was the first helicopter model to carry an American president when President Dwight D. Eisenhower rode in the military version Bell UH-13J. Bell lost the presidential transport business to Sikorsky, but it remained a first-in-flight victory for Bell Helicopter. It was a first-in-ownership victory for Tip. After two or three years with the Bell 47J, Tip and Liz upgraded to the Bell JetRanger 206A helicopter, again painted with Llangollen's colors. By that time, one of their Bentley Continental T-series cars had been painted to match.

Liz travelled by helicopter or Rolls with a fur coat and toy poodle named Killer.

Tip's fishing days at Cabo Blanco would last until 1961, when he left Lima with Liz, returning infrequently. His enthusiasm for the sport, and for the Club, was evident in the lists and rosters of caught fish. Tip's name was listed under almost every species, most notably in the Thousand Pound Club. There are more photographs of him posing with bigeye or bluefin tuna than with any other fish. Fishing for tuna was either his sporting preference, or a result of his responsibilities toward supplying the Club's dinner menu. Marlin were not considered for the Club's menu, but tuna, once photographed, were hurried off to the Club's kitchens and were one reason for the Club's reputation for high quality cuisine.

Tip stands with his tuna catches in 1959.

Tip left his management duties at the Cabo Blanco Fishing Club when he left his ICAO Directorship, but the Club was already slowing down. The club declined with the economy and with the anchovy. By the time the Peruvian anchovy fishery catastrophically collapsed, the Club was already out of the news. The billfish were gone, and the Peruvian military government was not welcoming of American millionaire businessmen. Cabo Blanco returned to its origins as a tiny subsistence fishing village. The dilapidated clubhouse still remains today, rediscovered on occasion by lost tourists and overseen by a local caretaker. In modern times, the ocean currents have again proven uniquely attractive to the sporting elite in the form of a gnarly surf pipeline that attracts world-class surfers to the harsh shoreline. A point break at Cabo Blanco supports surf conditions rivaling Hawaii's best. Surfers who can get there set their own records, in the Cabo Blanco tradition.

Rita, Tip, Liz, and Enrique, ready to board one of Liz's ranch airplanes.

It had been an incredible time for Tip, in a unique place, populated by extraordinary people. He was in the center of a whirlwind of fame, fortune, and fantastic catches. When Tip looked around at the state of civil aviation at the beginning of the 1960s, he saw an immense body of completed work and he was satisfied. He felt he had done what he set out to do, and now it was time to do something else. In his mind, the life he led before 1961 was a separate story from the rest of his activities afterward. His life with Liz was not part of his own manuscript, and it was not part of his aviation pioneering life. While he continued to stay involved in aviation politics, he did it from a very different position in society. While he continued to fly, it was as a private pilot, at the controls of a private helicopter. The story of Tip and Liz is another book, for another time.

At the time that Tip left Lima, he had over 10,000 hours of flight time in his certified logs and had flown in over ninety-eight kinds of aircraft. He had started, in true aviation pioneer tradition, in a Curtiss Jenny, made the grade to jet aircraft, flown the largest multi-engine commercial craft available to him, and spent his retirement at the controls of a JetRanger helicopter. Everyone who was anyone in aviation history either met Tip or met someone who had met Tip. He was the most un-famous legendary aviation pioneer to fly during that time.

American aviation was ten years old when Tip was born. All of the longest, farthest, fastest, highest records were set during his lifetime. He watched the race for space with the same quality of attention he had paid to the Curtiss Jenny in Ohio, and although he could not join the new breed of pilots that were to become astronauts, he cheered every Apollo mission. Tip attended as many shuttle launches as he could.

American civil aviation has touched the world's civil aviation, and Tip had a hand in creating it. His name hangs in the OX-5 Aviation Hall of Fame among more well-known pilots for a reason.

Because aviation history was also His Story.

Chapter Nineteen

Epilogue

The Tippetts were the first private individuals to own a Bell JetRanger 206A helicopter. Liz had it painted to match her racing colors..

Tip remained by Liz's side for the rest of her life. During their twenty-seven years of marriage, Tip and Liz enjoyed the company of a range of diplomats, movie stars, musicians, politicians, society mavens, and working heroes. Some of them were close friends, with relationships that spanned decades. Rita and Enrique remained in touch with Tip and Liz and they saw each other frequently. The Pardos had property in Florida, and they continued their cocktail routines in the United States. Liz's friendship with Ronald Reagan continued as he entered the White House, and set the Tippetts on the path to a White House dinner invitation in 1988 honoring Egyptian President Hosni Mubarak. Tip had met Mubarak and several other members of the Egyptian government, at the air attaché parties, and he considered him a friend. Alejandro Orfila was now the Secretary General of the Organization of American States and stayed in touch with Tip. Tip had known him from their Argentine days. Former President Gerald Ford attended one of the annual air attaché parties that Liz and Tip hosted. Liz had a good time advising him on world politics.

John Wayne had remained Tip's friend after meeting him in Peru, and Tip took every opportunity to get together with him. Wayne's busy schedule gave them opportunities both to see each other, and to exchange negative RSVPs on invitations to parties and events throughout the years of their friendship. Tip had met Robert Mitchum through John Wayne and they remained good friends. Bob Mitchum signed his letters to Tip "Burning Stump." Jane Russell was a friend, through Bob Hope, and joined Tip and Liz whenever her schedule coincided with their presence on one of their farms. Bob Hope joined Tip and Anesia Pinheiro Machado in 1986 as Embry Riddle Honorees and commencement speakers.

Both Zsa Zsa and Eva Gabor where close friends of Liz, and they enjoyed dinners and parties at each other's houses, as well as stories about their mutual succession of husbands. Zsa Zsa was a gracious attendee at several of the air attaché parties, to the great delight of the attachés, who therefore had the opportunity to meet an American movie star in person. Joe Bushkin, a piano and jazz musician who played with many music greats such as Frank Sinatra, was a frequent guest at Liz and Tip's houses. Mary Lou Whitney had, like Liz, married into the Vanderbilt Whitney family.

She also became prominent in the horse racing industry through her own efforts as she built on what her second husband, Cornelius Vanderbuilt Whitney, had started. Liz and Tip were frequent visitors at Mary Lou's home and parties and Mary Lou was always invited to theirs. Mary Lou and Tip could usually be found on the dance floor whenever there was one.

Tip with Bob Hope and Joe Bushkin at one of the many parties that Tip and Liz either hosted or attended in the 1980s.

Johnny Meier had visited Lima with Liz when she first met Tip. Rita recounts meeting Johnny, who was a financial advisor to Howard Hughes, and said that Liz referred to him as "pick-up-the-check Johnny." Pearl Bailey and Linda Ronstadt came to Llangollen in Virginia for weekend visits that were supposed to be restful, although Liz always required them to sing. Tip was often the chef cooking the dinner and Ronstadt was always on a diet, to her great frustration as Tip served rounds of delicious gourmet temptations. Jimmy Durante joined Liz with warmth as they made noise at parties where their paths crossed. Elizabeth Taylor was a longtime friend of Mary Elizabeth, and the two Liz's rode the carriages kept at Llangollen. Liz Taylor held on while Liz Tippett took the reins, scaring their staff with their antics. Desi Arnaz was both friend and buyer of one of the Rolls Royce classic cars that Tip and Liz shared. The paint job was Liz's signature purple and fuchsia racing colors and so Arnaz was left with the re-painting tab, but apparently the friendship didn't suffer.

Llangollen Farm in Upperville, Virginia, was the headquarters of Liz's horseracing business. The main house at Llangollen was built in the 1770s. Liz received the farm as a wedding gift from her first husband, John Hay Whitney.

There were branches of Llangollen Farm in Temecula, California, and Saratoga, New York, as well as the main estate in Upperville, Virginia. Liz maintained a house in Palm Beach, Florida, and moved frequently between the properties to follow the racing season, or her own whims. Every time the household moved, the staff and dogs came along. Tip had contributed several black Alsatians to the large dog pack that flooded the rooms of each mansion and ranch with chaos, and they protected him with unnerving vigor. Liz had named a racehorse for Tip. They had travelled to Australia and Ireland with winning racehorses, and brought back from Australia a dog breed that Liz called a Dingo, but was actually the Australian Kelpie. The imports joined the matching Harlequin Great Danes and pedigreed Labradors and wreaked havoc on the furniture.

Liz died in 1988 at the age of eighty-two, succumbing to cancer after a long decade of poor health. Llangollen was sold, which was Liz's wish as well as a financial necessity. Her estate was bequeathed to a cancer research foundation in her name. By that time, the property was in deep disrepair, beyond Tip's resources to maintain or manage. He went to Fisher Island, Florida, a location they had chosen together as an ideal urban haven; a place to get away in the center of it all. Sue joined him there and began to help him manage his affairs, numerous awards, and the writing of his memoirs.

In the course of his life, because of his contribution to aviation, Colonel C. J. Tippett was awarded :
> The Brazilian Aeronautical Medal of Merit, Cavalheiro
> The Brazilian Aeronautical Medal of Merit, Commander
> The Santos Dumont Medal from Brazil,
> The Peruvian Distinguished Flying Cross
> The Jorge Chavez Medal from Peru
> The Aeronautical Wings from Ecuador
> The Medaille en Vermeil from the Societe
>   D'Encouragment du Progres from France
> The US Air Force Reserve medal
> The US Air Force Commendation Medal
> The American Campaign Medal
> The National Defense Service Medal
> The World War II Victory Medal.

He was inaugurated into the OX-5 Aviation Hall of Fame in 1984, and served on the Board of Trustees of Embry-Riddle Aeronautical University.

Four years after moving to Florida, Tip was enjoying an active social life. Rita Pardo, now a widow, was already living in Miami and the warm memories of their common past proved enjoyable. Rita became the third Mrs. Cloyce Joseph Tippett on May 25, 1991, and proceeded to beat Tip in every golf game within their reach. Tip was seventy-eight and Rita invited people to mind their own business regarding her age.

Tip and Rita were married for almost two years. They called Fisher Island, Florida home, when they were not out travelling the world.

In 1992, on a stop-over at home from one of their trips abroad, Tip got a cancer warning from his doctor. It was prostate cancer and he tried a variety of treatments, but on May 6, 1993, he died at his home on Fisher Island. His family followed express directions in his will and puzzled their way through a formal Jesuit mass at a cathedral in Miami. Friends staged a helicopter flyover at his grave during the funeral, blasting the hats off mourners in a thrillingly perfect epitaph.

At the time of this writing, Col. Cloyce Joseph Tippett has five great-grandchildren and civil aviation has entered both the safest, and the most active, time in aviation history.

Author's Note

This story describes a complicatedly fascinating time in history, when great change provoked extraordinary action by both people and governments. A time when technology and politics deeply affected the personal lives of people in every class and economic level.

The writing of this story has taken place across a twenty-year span of time that has seen an astonishingly similar combination of technological, economic, and political change that has likewise affected the process of researching and producing it.

Colonel C. J. Tippett finished his manuscript in 1990 and I immediately began researching. While I used as much of the Internet as I could, my main resources were libraries, archives, and other books. As the years passed, my web searches yielded more and more valuable and accurate information until, in 2012, I was able to actually sit - by YouTube - in the cockpits of the planes my grandfather flew. I was able to find out things about the people he flew with, and fill in the details surrounding his achievements in ways were impossible even ten years earlier.

I participated in a stunning change in information access and publishing technology that significantly improved the way I could present Tip's life story. And I've been living through an economic and political upheaval that bears some responsibilty for the fact that it took twenty years to produce a readable version.

Tip's museum-quality archive formed the factual basis for this book and I thank him for both protecting it over the course of his travels and for making it available to me. Thank you Michael C. Tippett, for organizing the archive and supporting the book project in every way. Thank you Susan Tippett, for even more documents and stories. Thank you Rita Pardo Tippett for documents, photographs, information, and factual resources.

For inexhaustibly reading and re-reading, and for spending an inordinate amount of time figuring out the correct editorial methods, thank you Margaret T. Tippett, Tom Berto, Blue Tippett-Hunt, Annette Shaked, Suellen Knopick, Faith Tippett, and Hope Hisey.

Special thanks to Andrew G. Hunt and Juno Tippett-Hunt for their encouragement and support.

For contributions describing their experiences and family knowledge, thank you Louise Hossack Tippett, Mary Jane McBarnet, Paul Krofft, Judy Krofft Nugent, and William C. Turkel.

Thank you Verna Tippett Eyth, Liz Whitney Tippett, Louise Lines Hossack, and Harry Hossack for unintentionally contributing documents and perspectives to the story.

The accuracy and detail of aviation history resides in the hands of experts who are supported only by their own interest and integrity. Without them, my descriptions and identification of the aircraft, flying conditions, and significance of the flights Tip made wouldn't have been possible. Thank you Tony C. A. Broadhurst, Christopher L. Hodgkinson, Bill Forstchen, and (for big game fishing information) Gail M. Morchower of the IGFA. For social history and timeline fact checking, thank you Pilar Wayne.

This book was made possible by people who researched, investigated, archived, organized, collated, posted, scanned, saved, studied, transcribed, listed, wrote, re-wrote, queried, answered posted, chatted, blogged, logged, snipped, photographed, conversed, read, re-read, memorialized, and preserved their knowledge and photographs. I am grateful to everyone who took that time, in every form.

Thank You

Bibliography

"AeroFiles!" Accessed March 10, 2013. http://www.aerofiles.com/.

Bach, Richard. *Biplane.* New York: Macmillan, 1983.

Barroso, Helio. *Tempos Da Pesca.* [Brazil: s.n.], 2002.

Berg, A. Scott. *Lindbergh.* New York: Berkley Books, 1999.

Cabo Blanco Fishing Club Book, Casilia 89, Talara Peru, June 10 1956.

"Can the Human Body Keep Pace With the Airplane?" Accessed March 10, 2013. http://www.ncbi.nlm.nih.gov/pmc/articles/PMC1634398/.

"Charles A. Lindbergh - Timeline." Accessed March 10, 2013. http://www.lindberghfoundation.org/docs/index.php/timeline-charles.

Colonel C. J. Tippett's archive, *letters, articles, notes, photographs, memos, orders, military records, flight logs.* Collected and archived in the course of this project, 1920s to 2013.

"Convention on International Civil Aviation - Doc 7300." Accessed March 10, 2013. http://www.icao.int/publications/pages/doc7300.aspx.

Culver, Edith Dodd. *Talespins: a Story of Early Aviation Days.* 1st ed. Santa Fe, NM: Sunstone Press, 1986.

Earhart, Amelia. *The Fun of It: Random Records of My Own Flying and of*

Women in Aviation. Chicago: Academy Press, 1977.

"Evergreen Aviation & Space Museum | Wings & Waves Waterpark | McMinnville Oregon." Accessed March 10, 2013. http://www. evergreenmuseum.org/.

"Fiddlersgreen.net." Accessed March 10, 2013. http://www. fiddlersgreen.net/.

Frank, Gary. *Struggle for Hegemony in South America.* Center for Advanced International studies, University of Miami, 1979.

"Great New Big Game Bonanza, Cabo Blanco Peru." *Ashaway Sportsman,* 1953.

"Home : Pima Air & Space Museum : Tucson, Arizona." Accessed March 10, 2013. http://www.pimaair.org/.

"Honolulu Star-Bulletin Local News." Accessed March 10, 2013. http://archives.starbulletin.com/97/10/20/news/story2.html.

"IGFA | Visit the Museum." Accessed March 10, 2013. http://www. igfa.org/Museum/Visit-the-Museum.aspx.

Jeffers, H. Paul. *Ace of Aces: The Life of Capt. Eddie Rickenbacker.* 1st ed. New York: Ballantine Books, 2003.

Kahn, E. J. *Jock, the Life and Times of John Hay Whitney.* 1st ed. Garden City, N.Y: Doubleday, 1981.

Lewis, W. David. *Eddie Rickenbacker: An American Hero In The Twentieth Century.* Baltimore: Johns Hopkins University Press, 2008.

Lindbergh, Anne Morrow. *Against Wind and Tide: Letters and Journals, 1947-1986*. New York: Pantheon Books, 2012.

Longyard, William H. *Who's Who in Aviation History: 500 Biographies*. Novato, CA: Presidio, 1994.

Lopez, Donald S. *Aviation: A Smithsonian Guide*. New York: Macmillan USA, 1995.

MacKenzie, David Clark. *ICAO: A History of the International Civil Aviation Organization*. Toronto ; Buffalo: University of Toronto Press, 2010.

Mansfield, Harold. *Vision: A Saga of the Sky - the Original Story of Boeing*. 2nd ed. Madison Publishing Associates, 1986.

Mashman, Joe, and R. Randall Padfield. *To Fly Like A Bird*. Potomac, MD: Phillips Pub., 1992.

Mason, Francis K. *Air Facts and Feats: A Record of Aerospace Achievement*. London: Guinness Superlatives, 1970.

Mason, Michael H. *In Pursuit of Big Fish*. London: Jenkins, 1968.

"Military Personnel Records." Accessed March 10, 2013. http://www.archives.gov/st-louis/military-personnel/.

Munn, Michael. *John Wayne: The Man Behind The Myth*. New York: New American Library, 2005.

National Personnel Records Center, Civilian Personnel Record Request, 1999. 111 Winnebago Street. St. Louis, MO 63118

Novosel, Michael J. *Dustoff:The Memoir of an Army Aviator*. Novato, CA: Presidio, 1999.

Olander, Doug. "Cabo Blanco, the Rise and Fall of the Greatest Blue Water Big Game Fishing the World has Ever Known." *Sport Fishing Magazine*, 2003.

Recknagel, Carl. *Just Off The Ground: Recollections Of An Early Aviator*. Santa Barbara: Narrative Press, 2001.

S. Kip Farrington, Jr. *Fishing with Hemingway and Glassell*. 1ST edition, 1971.

Saint-Exupéry, Antoine de. *Wind, Sand And Stars*. San Diego: Harcourt, 2002.

Schiaffino, Jose Antonio. *Cabo Blanco Fishing Club*. Imprenta Tipsal S.A, 2011. museokontiki@hotmail.com.

Scribner, Kimball J. *Adventures In Aviation An Autobiography Of Captain Kimball J. Scribner*. 1st ed. Scribner & Associates, 1990.

Simbeck, Rob. *Daughter Of The Air:The Brief Soaring Life Of Cornelia Fort*. New York: Atlantic Monthly Press, 1999.

St. Wendelin Yearbook. St. Wendelin Catholic School, Fostoria OH, 1930.

"The Black Marlin of Peru Is the Coveted Prize of Cabo - 03.19.56 - SI Vault." Accessed March 10, 2013. http://sportsillustrated.cnn.com/vault/article/magazine/MAG1130924/index.htm.

The Cabo Blanco Fishing Club. *Cabo Blanco Fishing Club Book, June 10,*

*1956.*The Cabo Blanco Fishing Club, 1956.

The Pegasus, "5 PT19s and 4 F-24s Fly from Hagerstown to Rio De Janeiro in Spring of 1942." September 1943.

"The Spirit of St. Louis (1957) - IMDb." Accessed March 10, 2013. http://www.imdb.com/title/tt0051003/.

Waitzkin, Fred. *The Last Marlin: The Story of a Family at Sea.* New York: Viking, 2000.

Weller, George, "Black Tails, Blue Ocean." *Sports Illustrated,* March, 1956.

About The Author

 Corinne Tippett grew up overseas and in the Southwestern USA, and saw her grandfather in every city that she and her family lived. She spent a childhood summer at Llangollen Farm. Later, when Colonel Tippett and Liz Whitney Tippett were hosting air attaché parties, Corinne was studying Industrial/Scientific Photography at Brooks Institute of Photography in Santa Barbara, California. An invitation to one of the parties gave her the unparalleled opportunity to raise a glass in the cockpit of the Spruce Goose.

 When No One Else Would Fly is Corinne's second book, and joins more than fifteen publication credits, along with her first book, *Just A Couple Of Chickens*, which tells most of Corinne's recent life story as she and her husband, Andrew Hunt, raised their children, and more, in rural New Mexico.

About The Westchester Press

 The Westchester Press was formed in Santa Fe, New Mexico in 2009, primarily to publish Corinne's books. The business (and family) moved to Portland, Oregon in 2010, where more titles are in production: www.TheWestchesterPress.com.

2682904R00217

Made in the USA
San Bernardino, CA
22 May 2013